IPSWICH TOWN
The 1978 FA Cup Story

IPSWICH TOWN
The 1978 FA Cup Story

Mel Henderson

First published in Great Britain in 2008 by
The Breedon Books Publishing Company Limited
Breedon House, 3 The Parker Centre,
Derby, DE21 4SZ.

This paperback edition published in Great Britain in 2013 by DB Publishing,
an imprint of JMD Media Ltd

ISBN: 978-1-78091-369-8

Printed and bound in the UK by Copytech (UK) Ltd Peterborough

Contents

INTRODUCTION

By Mel Henderson

It is not only boyish-looking policemen, or the fact that I consistently find myself sympathising with most of the views expressed on television's moan-in, namely *Grumpy Old Men*, that provide me with regular reminders of my advancing years. Another sure sign that I am growing old is provided courtesy of those supporters who are either too young to recall the occasion, or had not even been born, when Ipswich won the FA Cup for the first time. Indeed, it might prove to be the only time. The very fact that Town have triumphed once in their 70-year membership of the Football League suggests – big-money takeover or not – that a return visit to Wembley can never be taken for granted. All the more reason, therefore, to celebrate the anniversary of what could remain, for the foreseeable future at least, the most wonderful day in the club's history – an occasion that anyone present, and even those who had to settle for watching the game on television, will never, ever forget.

There have been a number of reunions for the 1978 heroes but as far as I am aware they never tire of meeting up. While their receding hairlines and expanding waistlines may suggest otherwise, it is as if they have been transported back in time and that the intervening years have simply evaporated.

On a personal note, I regard myself as immensely privileged to have been present at Wembley on that unforgettable day and I am sure the 30,000 or so members of the Blue and White Army feel likewise. For my part the memories are extra special, since I sat on the bench behind Bobby Robson and his backroom team. All in a day's work as the club's public relations officer, perhaps, but I felt as if my name had come out of the hat in a national newspaper's 'Win a VIP day out to end all VIP days out' competition. I was actually being paid to sit there and lap up the entertainment from one of the very best seats in the house. I had been in my job at Portman Road for less than four years, so no wonder I felt as if all my Christmases had come at once. I had expected to watch the game alongside my family in the stand but that all changed when the Football Association secretary, Ted Croker, paid us a visit at our pre-Wembley hotel, Sopwell House in St Albans. But more of that later.

Whenever I recall Town's glorious victory all those years ago, my brain is incapable of focusing only on the events of the big day itself. It demands that I go back even further in time, to the semi-final triumph over West Bromwich Albion, the unprecedented dressing-room celebrations and joining the players for an emotional return journey that, little did I realise at the time, was to put a question mark over every aspect of Ipswich's preparations for their biggest-ever game.

Bobby Robson had asked me to organise a coach to Highbury, in the main for players' wives, girlfriends and children, although a number of seats were also occupied by other club employees and members of their families. I remember feeling less than 100 per cent on the journey to Brentwood, where we stopped for lunch, and my condition worsened on the second leg of the journey to North London. But upon arriving at Highbury, and making sure everyone was headed in the right direction to take up their seats, I made my way to the press box to join Radio Orwell commentator Pete Barraclough, now Devon-based and a regular face on Sky Sports, to act as summariser for the station's live coverage of the match.

I remember Des Lynam, certainly not then the housewives' pin-up he was to become once he transferred his talents to television, sitting immediately in front of me. He worked for BBC Radio in those days and I realised that my parents in Scotland, where live TV coverage of the English semi-finals was outlawed at the time, would be wholly reliant on him to paint an accurate picture of events as they unfolded.

The semi-final was everything a semi-final should be – incident-packed, with goals, injury drama, a penalty and a sending-off. Most importantly of all, however, it resulted in an Ipswich win, meaning Wembley beckoned. Not surprisingly, scenes of great joy greeted me as I entered the dressing room. Players hugged and, in the case of defensive giants Allan Hunter and Kevin Beattie, puffed, while champagne corks popped and cameras flashed. Bobby Robson had thrown open the doors to the media and there was no way the photographers were going to miss out. It was mayhem, but of the very best sort. Brothers John and Patrick Cobbold, chairmen past and present, embraced the manager amid the surrounding chaos as the realisation sunk in that Ipswich, a club their father had done more than anyone else to convert to professionalism in 1936, were going to Wembley.

As I sipped some bubbly, it suddenly dawned on me: Ipswich were going to Wembley in four weeks. That was all the time I had in which to cram in all the many public relations and promotional events expected of Cup Final teams in those days. The FA Cup was the glamour tournament then, and was treated with the respect it deserved by the participating clubs, all of whom were genuinely disappointed – not relieved, as some appear to be today – when it was their turn to exit. Nevertheless, there was no time to spare and I headed back up the corridor, through the marbled hallway and up Highbury's spectacular stairway to track down Arsenal's managing director, Ken Friar – one of the game's leading administrators who was awarded the OBE in 2000 for his services to the game. Ken had asked me beforehand to visit his office if Ipswich won the game. He missed his own team's semi-final that day – they were playing across London at Stamford Bridge in an all-capital affair with Orient – because he was the man in charge at Highbury. I have to confess he had me puzzled as to why he wanted to see me in the event of an Ipswich victory.

The guessing was over when I met up with him and he handed over a document on behalf of the Milk Marketing Board. It was a contract guaranteeing the Ipswich Town Players' Pool a healthy sum if they would go along with the usual Wembley ritual of sipping the white stuff while facing the television cameras and being quizzed afterwards. That was merely the start. Ever since winning the quarter-final tie at Millwall, I had started to draw up provisional plans for a number of money-making ventures, among them a souvenir FA Cup brochure, and with time at a premium I decided to start work straight away.

Rather than board the same coach back to Ipswich I instead travelled back with the players and, throughout the journey along the A12, moved between them, filling my notebook as I interviewed each of them in turn – a far from easy task as they, and I, also enjoyed a few drinks in what became an increasingly raucous celebration.

I had every intention of commencing the job of writing the features the very next day at home, only for that plan, and many others in the weeks ahead, to be scuppered when I awoke to find myself covered in a nasty red rash. I called my doctor, explained the situation and he was quickly on the scene. After examining me, it did not take him long to deliver his verdict: I had measles. It turned out to be far more of a blow than I had imagined. 'Have you had any contact with the players?' the doctor asked, with an anxious look on his face. 'Yes,' I replied, 'I travelled back from London on the team bus last night.' The doctor's face dropped and he asked: 'Can I use your phone? I'd better ring Bobby (Robson).' I was in bed while the pair chatted and, from the way the doctor stressed the seriousness of the situation, it was clear all was far from well. 'It's the two-week incubation period that worries me,' I recall the doctor saying. 'Mel has been around the players and if any of them have not had measles we could have a real problem on our hands.' Bobby clearly asked if there was a risk of players missing out on the big day at Wembley and the doctor pulled no punches. 'Yes,' he said, 'because they could be struck down with measles before then.'

I started to feel very guilty after the doctor advised Bobby to speak to all the players and tell them, if they were in any way uncertain, to contact their parents and ascertain whether or not they had previously had measles. It was agreed that I would not set foot in the ground for a fortnight – I was effectively banned – which was a huge inconvenience given my workload and the limited time I had to complete it. After the doctor left I wracked my brain to come up with a tactical plan that would enable me to cope. Yes, I could work from home, but I was not feeling well enough – a piercing pain above my eyes was only relieved by resting in a darkened room.

Shortly after the diagnosis, I received a call from Jack Steggles, at that time a reporter on the *Daily Mirror* and a regular visitor to Portman Road. Little did he realise it, but he had stumbled across a decent story, a quirky follow-up to Ipswich's weekend win that had booked them a place in their first-ever FA Cup Final. I explained the situation and had to chuckle when I saw the next day's *Daily Mirror*. Right across the bottom of the front page, in capital letters and ticker-tape style, it read: 'FA CUP FINALISTS IN MEASLES SCARE'. And on the back page, in giant letters, screamed the headline: 'SPOTCHECK!'

Other newspapers also covered the story. The *Daily Mail*'s came complete with a cartoon – something about Town playing in a new spotted kit as I recall – but that did not detract from the seriousness of the problem confronting the club. Within a few days I was feeling well enough to leave my sickbed and start ploughing through a number of pressing commitments. The possibility of deferring my work to a colleague was not an option, as staffing levels at the club were rather different to what they are now – there are probably around 100 more employees on the current Portman Road payroll than there were in 1978. It was all 'hands to the pumps' 30 years ago. Even chairmen past and present, John and Patrick Cobbold, lent a hand in the ticket office where – and I swear this is true – a series of cardboard boxes were lined up to accommodate bank notes of varying denominations as they came flooding in from fans delighted to get their hands on the precious tickets.

With my 'ban' still effective, I had no alternative but to work from home, and it was there that a record company executive called to thrash out a deal for the players' Cup Final record. So if you are looking for someone to blame for *Ipswich, Ipswich, Get That Goal*, look no further, although I should add that it was not far from selling sufficient numbers to guarantee the players an appearance on *Top of the Pops*.

While recovering at home, I also agreed to appear in a phone-in on Radio Orwell – that's what SGR FM was called 30 years ago – to explain the club's FA Cup Final ticket allocation system. Dozens of callers rang the station in their frustration at not being able to lay their hands on a ticket, each with a different sob story, and my job was to defend what may have appeared to be a rather complicated formula but was, in fact, remarkably straightforward. Ipswich being Ipswich – I am certain other clubs would not have gone to such lengths – did their utmost to ensure that the tickets went to those most deserving of them. The idea was to reward those supporters who attended games on a regular basis. So the first move was to announce that all season-ticket holders would be able to purchase a Wembley ticket. Subsequently the voucher system kicked in, which was based on vouchers issued at a number of home games. The more you had, the greater your chances of obtaining a ticket. However, the radio station was bombarded with calls from irate fans, all of them claiming to be a special case and wanting to take out their frustration on yours truly. And not even the fact that I was responding from my sickbed was going to let me off the hook. It was difficult not to feel sorry for some fans but, short of the Football Association forwarding another few hundred tickets, which was never going to happen, there was no easy solution. However, I will let you into a secret: off the air, I asked the presenter to note the telephone numbers of the fans who appeared to have a genuine grouse and I contacted them later to let them know I had managed to lay my hands on some tickets.

(Photograph courtesy of Owen Hines)

Since I was confined to barracks, a number of other lucrative deals were also agreed via the telephone, while I also managed to complete the editorial for the players' brochure before eventually being given the all-clear to return to my office at the ground.

I was very relieved to learn that none of the players had been struck down by the illness, and I joined the official party on the team bus when it departed from Portman Road on the Wednesday of Cup Final week for our hotel base in St Albans. We stopped off at Colchester to collect the Wembley outfits of blazer and trousers to be worn by around 20 players and officials, another deal I had provisionally set up before we faced West Bromwich Albion in the semi-final. It was envisaged that this would only take a few minutes but we had not allowed for the fact that some of the female employees at the factory had decided to play a prank on the players, mixing up their clothes. Oh how they laughed as some lads struggled to do up the waistband on their trousers, while others were dwarfed by their jackets. The players saw the funny side, though, and when skipper Mick Mills was asked to look in one of the pockets of his blazer he found a good luck message from the women, together with an apology for the prank.

It was the following day, when Ted Croker visited the hotel, that I learned my Wembley vantage point would be the same bench on which hundreds of well-known stars had sat over the years. He stressed the need for a club official to be seated at ground level and I was nominated by Bobby Robson, meaning I was in the dressing room beforehand and walked up the tunnel and round to the mid-way point beneath the twin towers to find my seat. Squad members Russell Osman and Robin Turner, who I remember jumping on my back when Roger Osborne scored, were also there, along with chief scout Ron Gray, and coaches Bobby Ferguson and Charlie Woods, while Bobby

Robson, assistant Cyril Lea, substitute Mick Lambert and physio Tommy Eggleston were in the front row.

Like everyone in the stands and terraces, as well as those huddled round their television sets at home, I wondered if the goal would ever come. I saw John Wark, who had waited patiently for his first contact with the ball, twice come close to breaking the deadlock with near-identical shots that cannoned back off the same post. I winced as Paul Mariner, who starred in his demanding lone-striker role, came within inches of opening the scoring with an early effort that struck the crossbar. I shared George Burley's frustration as he steamed into the penalty box to get on the end of a cross by Clive Woods, only for Pat Jennings to make a breathtaking, world-class save from the future manager's net-bound header. I looked on as Arsenal were completely outplayed: Town's inspired tactical plan, the key to which was playing youngster David Geddis in an unfamiliar right-sided role, worked an absolute treat. Then finally, after fearing the Gunners would cruelly snatch victory against the run of play, I saw Geddis take on and go past Sammy Nelson. He crossed from the right, and big Willie Young could only direct his clearance straight to the feet of Roger Osborne. With a swing of his left foot and from a range of about 11 yards, Roger's shot zipped across the saturated surface, its pace and accuracy too much for Jennings, who made a vain attempt to keep the ball out. A goal, at last. Together with every other Ipswich fan in the capacity crowd, I was overjoyed and mightily relieved at the same time. Roger was also suffering from mixed emotions. He was elated yet exhausted, and he could not continue, so Mick Lambert was given the run his loyal service to the club deserved. As Roger sat just a couple of feet away, his head covered with a towel as he fought to regain his breath, the final 13 minutes or so seemed like an eternity. Finally, referee Derek Nippard, officiating at his last game, blew his whistle to signal the end of the game and the start of the celebrations.

The party kicked off at the side of the pitch and continued on a lap of honour, in the dressing room and at the evening banquet organised by the club at the Royal Garden Hotel – the same venue, incidentally, where ex-Ipswich boss Alf Ramsey and his England players had waved to the crowds before celebrating their wonderful World Cup victory 12 years earlier.

The mood was only slightly more subdued on the coach journey home the next day and then, as if they had gained their second wind, the players were again on top form for the open-top bus ride through Ipswich's crowded streets, on the Cornhill amid a sea of blue and white, and finally at the civic reception. It was a whirlwind 24 hours that none of those involved will ever forget, as their on-the-spot recollections and contributions to this commemorative publication prove. However, the FA Cup triumph was not just about the club, its players and officials, it was also about the supporters, who were given ample opportunity to play their part over the subsequent months when the club honoured its pledge to share its historic success with the people of Suffolk.

We were consequently inundated with requests for the trophy, which had its very own diary, to be on show at a variety of events around the county, even to the extent of being displayed at more than one location on the same day. Very few supporters who were around at the time could have missed the chance to be photographed alongside the famous silverware, the most famous Cup of them all. At the club's very own Fun Day, thousands queued patiently to have their souvenir pictures taken.

During the months before the trophy had to be returned to Football Association headquarters in London, to be polished and prepared for the 1979 Final, it was housed at the Ipswich police station in Civic Drive for security purposes – well, most of the time. I know of at least one night when it found itself in totally unfamiliar surroundings – when I took it home with me. I had been attending an evening function at the Copdock Hotel, as it was known back then, and had every intention of returning it to the police station. But the A12, the old one, was treacherous that evening, as I discovered when my car slid down the hill at Washbrook. Only the fact that there were no other vehicles on the road avoided a serious accident. So, having phoned the police to explain the situation, I instead managed to crawl back up the hill on the other side of the road and made my way to Capel St Mary, where I lived at the time. It would normally have taken five minutes but on this particular occasion, thanks to the icy, glass-like roads, it was closer to an hour. Not surprisingly, I hardly slept a wink that night as the trophy, which came with its own wooden cabinet, was perched beside my bed. But I must have fallen asleep at least once, as I recall waking in the morning to quite a commotion downstairs. To my horror, I discovered the Cup was gone, only to quickly realise it had been moved by one of my children to the breakfast bar (it was the 1970s, remember). Not only that, but a procession of their friends were snaking in through the front door, down the hall, through the kitchen and out of the back door. Most of the children, having been warned in advance while I was in the land of nod, were armed with cameras and paused long enough to take each other's souvenir snaps. Thirty years on, I guarantee their memory of that moment will be every bit as vivid as my own.

SIR BOBBY ROBSON

Sir Bobby Robson glows with pride – and rightly so – as he recalls the highlights of his career in management at home and abroad. He can reflect on a near miss with England, losing a penalty shoot-out to West Germany when a place in the 1990 World Cup Final beckoned, and he can reminisce about his eight trophy successes in three foreign countries – Holland, Portugal and Spain – as he took charge of PSV Eindhoven, Sporting Lisbon, Porto and Barcelona in his very own nine-year continental adventure. In addition, he can recall how close he came to winning the coveted League Championship on behalf of Ipswich Town, twice leading them to the

(Photograph courtesy of Owen Hines)

runners-up spot and on a further three occasions finishing third. Furthermore, he can regard himself as extremely unfortunate to have been sacked by Newcastle after five years in charge, the last three of which saw them finish third, fourth and fifth in the Premiership. But while all of these achievements confirm Sir Bobby's status as one of the leading football managers of all time, none of them come even remotely close to ousting Ipswich's FA Cup win of 1978 as the moment he cherishes more than any other from a lifetime in the game. He said:

> *There is really nothing quite like the FA Cup. It is the oldest and the best knockout competition in the world bar none – everybody knows it and they want to be a part of it. When we won the semi-final to book our Wembley place I was overcome with emotion and when I looked around the dressing room I wasn't the only one. I threw open the doors to the dressing room that day, that's how special it was. Patrick and John Cobbold were in there and the look on their*

faces made it all worthwhile. When their father had started the professional club in 1936 nobody had a clue what lay in store. Ipswich at Wembley, don't be daft – that's probably what they would have said. But now it was true. We were going to be in the FA Cup Final and I could see what it meant to Patrick and John, plus the players, the staff at the club and the fans. It was like we were living a dream. That semi-final was massive for us. Once it was over it was sheer joy as we looked ahead to Wembley. I remember I said we were going to enjoy the build-up because back then that was such a huge part of it.

Unlike the vast majority of his players, the Ipswich boss was no stranger to Wembley. His association with the national stadium went back more than a quarter of a century. He said:

I started going to Wembley when I played for Fulham. That's a long time ago – I signed for them in 1950 so you can imagine how many times I attended games at Wembley. I was a Wembley regular as manager of Ipswich, too, watching the big games and all the England internationals. I'd never miss one – all part of my education was how I saw it. I would go to FA Cup Finals and I'd be pretty envious, to be honest, just as I imagine any managers of clubs not involved would have been. It's the day all managers want to experience and I was no different. I used to tell myself: 'I want to be here with my team'. I could see myself leading them out. It was something I hoped for years would happen.

After a heartbreaking experience in 1975 that reduced many members of the Ipswich team to tears, the chance he feared had perhaps passed him by was again within touching distance just three years later. Unlike that miserable night when West Ham defeated his side in a semi-final replay at Stamford Bridge, it was glory all the way at Highbury against West Bromwich Albion, for whom the Town boss played between 1956 and 1962. He said:

An FA Cup semi-final is a huge occasion. Look at the prize for victory – Wembley and the Final. For the losers, nothing, as we knew only too well from our experience in 1975. That was a huge factor for a lot of the players, those who were around three years earlier. They didn't want to be losers again and that gave them a nice edge to their game. They deserved their success. They were the better team and apart from one blip, when Allan Hunter conceded a penalty to let Albion back in, we were pretty much in charge. Like I've said, the dressing room

(Photograph courtesy of Owen Hines)

Bobby Robson with his backroom team – Cyril Lea (first team coach), Charlie Woods (youth coach), Bobby Ferguson (reserve coach) and Ron Gray (chief scout).

(Photograph courtesy of Owen Hines)

Bobby Robson in his office at Portman Road with the FA Cup.

scene was amazing. And once we managed to get everyone on the bus I still don't know how we made it back to Ipswich. The coach was going along the A12 at 70 miles an hour and everybody was jumping up and down. The singing never stopped. It was one of the greatest days of my life.

Nevertheless, in the cold light of day, the professionalism kicked in and the manager set about the task of winning at Wembley – but not before he found the answer to the club's relegation dilemma. An unprecedented injury list, combined with a lack of depth to his squad, meant Town still had some work to do in the intervening weeks to preserve their First Division status, which was by far the priority for all concerned. Robson reported:

We couldn't afford to look as far ahead as Wembley when there was still a chance we might go down. There was no point in trying to hide from the fact that we had a relegation battle on our hands. We needed points. The response from the players was first class and they made sure we were safe in good time. It was a relief. We weren't a bad side but the injuries meant I was rarely able to field my strongest XI.

It was a brand new experience for Ipswich to be competing in the FA Cup Final and, as such, Robson wanted it to be an enjoyable one. However, mindful of the many distractions that presented themselves as the countdown began in earnest, the Town boss had to be careful to strike the right balance between on and off-field activity. He said:

We had to be professional and remember why we were going to Wembley. We would have a great time leading up to the Final and again on the day itself, but we did not want to be losers. To be honest the whole thing was bigger than I had anticipated – the telegrams congratulating us, the endless requests for interviews and, of course, the pleas for tickets. It was a balancing act. We were not blind to the commercial spin-offs. That was part and parcel of it, and the players were entitled to cash in if they could. The biggest prize, of course, was to go to Wembley and win. That's what made it perfect for everyone.

Since that unforgettable day 30 years ago, Sir Bobby has met up with his Wembley winners on a fairly regular basis at reunions and in the course of his work. His assessment of the men who won the FA Cup is as follows:

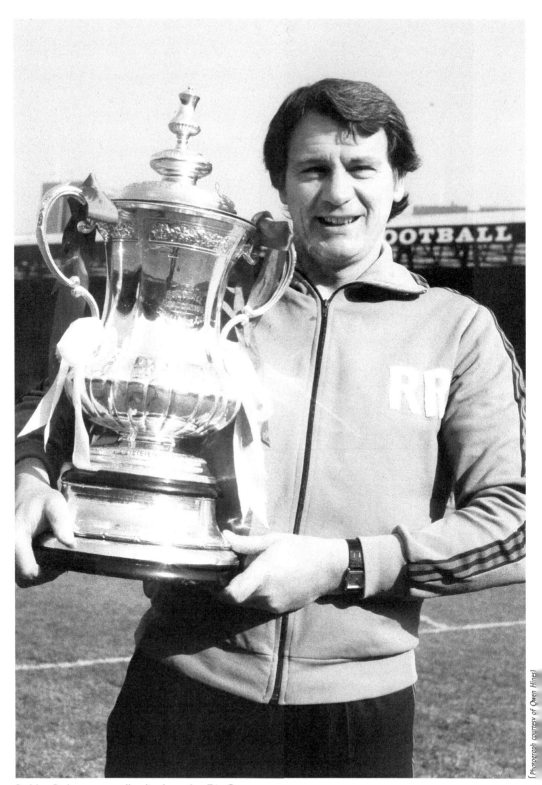

Bobby Robson proudly displays the FA Cup.

[Photograph courtesy of Owen Hines]

PAUL COOPER

Much better than the £23,000 I paid for him might suggest. He had powerful thighs that gave him wonderful agility. He jumped well on crosses and when he made up his mind to come for them he was always positive. He was never a coward and he kicked well, too. Paul was a decent footballer and it showed when he played outfield in training. He had a nice touch and it was never a problem when he had the ball at his feet. The back-pass rule wouldn't have been a problem for Paul. He was also incredibly quick, the only one in the squad who could give Beattie a race.

GEORGE BURLEY

George was so naturally fit that he looked as if he could run all day. As soon as I saw him in a trial game we arranged in Scotland I didn't want to let him out of my sight, just in case another club got hold of him. His timing in the tackle was crucial because he wasn't that strong, but his ability always overshadowed everything else. He made his debut against George Best and never looked back. He had a great career as a player – it would have been even better but for that cruciate ligament injury – and he has also done well as a manager.

MICK MILLS

Durable and tough, Millsy was the solid, dependable type, someone who was never afraid to take responsibility. Maybe he wasn't the biggest, but the other players still looked up to him, which is important for a captain. He could play in either full-back position and even in midfield, and his versatility was a huge plus for us. Millsy always had his own view and I didn't mind that. He thought about the game and Ron Greenwood made him England captain for all the same reasons I picked him to lead Ipswich. I doubt if his appearance record will ever be broken.

BRIAN TALBOT

Once Noddy got in he was there to stay. A real 100 per cent type and being local, he had a place in his heart for the club. He worked incredibly hard to make his mark in the game. He didn't have the passing ability to compare with Arnold Muhren, perhaps, but he had great stamina, enthusiasm and endurance. One of his strengths was that he knew his limitations. He kept it simple and his game improved as he listened and gained experience. He was the ideal team player, working his socks off, and he had that very useful knack of weighing in with some good goals.

ALLAN HUNTER

He was one half of a great double act with Kevin Beattie, and exactly what we wanted when I signed him – tall, commanding and with a thou-shalt-not-pass mentality. He could put the fear of God into some opponents with that snarl of his. A complex character? No, just an Irishman. I used to say he didn't know what he wanted and he would fight you tooth and nail to get it. Big Al was adored by the other players and the supporters. He was more than just a stopper because he could bring the ball out of defence, too, and had a few tricks. I liked him a lot.

KEVIN BEATTIE

I've never made any secret of what I thought of Beattie. This guy had the lot. He was a phenomenon. If you are talking about the best British players of all time, he's in there – and right near the top. What a tragedy it was that injuries meant he never fulfilled his full potential. He only won nine England caps and he should have beaten the record. A giant of a man, but he never resorted to anything underhand. He didn't need to because he was better than his opponents in every aspect of the game. When I first laid eyes on him I said we had uncovered a diamond. He was the best.

ROGER OSBORNE

You couldn't make up Roger's story. If you took it to Hollywood they would say it was too far-fetched. His route into the game was anything but orthodox but he was always determined to make the most of his chance. If you gave him a job – to mark Johann Cruyff when he was the best player in the world, for example – he was single-minded and did it. He would scrap to win the ball and was uncomplicated and dependable. He was popular with the others because he was good for the team. He gave balance on the right and had a great appetite for hard work.

JOHN WARK

Warky came to us as a central defender and became the country's highest-scoring midfielder. He was signed by Liverpool and that says an awful lot about him. He could win the ball at one end and stick it in the net at the other, because he had a tremendous knack of getting there at just the right time. He scored all sorts of goals – from close range, outside the area and headers. He was so good at penalties that when the referee pointed to the spot we would think 'goal' straight away. High, low or either side of the 'keeper, he very rarely missed. He was a goal machine for us.

[Photograph courtesy of Owen Hines]

Bobby Robson kisses the FA Cup on the Town Hall steps when it seemed the whole of Suffolk turned out to welcome the team home.

PAUL MARINER

It was such a relief that he joined us and not one of the other clubs in the race for his signature. He was just what we needed at the time – a top-class leader of the line. We were tipped off about him and every time we sent someone to watch him they came back praising him. He was a great signing and apart from all his attributes he also had a nasty streak and could look after himself. He had the lot and that's why he was the England centre-forward. When I look back at the many players I signed as a manager he was definitely one of the very best.

DAVID GEDDIS

It was Trevor Whymark's injury that presented David with his big chance and he really grabbed it. He was a big, raw striker, full of determination and aggression, but we gave him a different role at Wembley – to help break up Arsenal's left-sided triangle. It was quite a responsibility for the lad and he enjoyed himself out there. He didn't care for reputations and you could see some of the Arsenal lads thinking: 'Who's this bloody upstart?' His pace was a great asset, too, and the way he and others came through the ranks was a great advert for our youth system.

CLIVE WOODS

Woodsy loved Wembley and didn't it show? He was a wiry winger and a cheeky so-and-so with the ball at his feet. He was a defender's worst nightmare when he was on song. He would take the mickey and it didn't matter if he was on the right or the left because he had two good feet. He laid on a lot of goals but he scored some crackers as well, like the one at Leicester that decided our marathon quarter-final with Leeds in 1975. Woodsy applied himself well after joining us and benefited from listening and working at his game until he was very, very close to an England cap.

MICK LAMBERT

Another winger, but totally different. He was more direct and kept it simple, using his pace, and he carried more of a goalscoring threat. He didn't really look like a professional athlete. I thought he was a bit like Chris Waddle in that respect. He would work his way back, all hunched up and blowing so hard you thought one of his lungs had gone. He was uncomplicated both on and off the park, and never gave me any hassle. He was the perfect substitute because he always came on and did things. At other clubs, where he wouldn't have had Woodsy around, he'd have been an automatic choice.

KEVIN BEATTIE

FULL NAME: Thomas Kevin Beattie
DATE OF BIRTH: 18 December 1953
PLACE OF BIRTH: Carlisle, Cumbria
IPSWICH TOWN APPEARANCES: 307
IPSWICH TOWN GOALS: 32

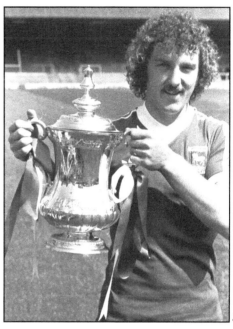

(Photograph courtesy of Owen Hines)

Without the FA Cup glory of 1978, Kevin Beattie's all-too-short football career would have been devoid of the success his enormous talent undoubtedly merited. The powerhouse defender, consistently voted Ipswich's best player of all time in a succession of supporter polls, might otherwise have had nothing to show for his outstanding contribution to the club's rise under Bobby Robson's shrewd management throughout the 70s and early 80s. Never mind Wembley – Beattie was fit to grace the best stadiums in the world and it was nothing short of a tragedy that a catalogue of knee injuries eventually led to him having to call it a day when he was only 28.

Sir Bobby devoted a large chunk of his autobiography to praising the player who first came to his attention when northern scout John Carruthers sent the youngster from a rough Carlisle council estate down south for a trial, after which chief scout Ron Gray was sufficiently enthralled that he begged the boss: 'You've got to sign him.' Robson paid Beattie a massive compliment when he wrote: 'George Best aside, I rate Kevin Beattie as the best player these islands produced in 25 years. George was special, as were Bobby Charlton and Denis Law from the same era. Duncan Edwards was colossal, strong and a destroyer, but Beattie had pace as well. He just had pure, natural ability.' Anyone who witnessed Beattie in action for Town will vouch for that, at the same time mourning the fact that a career spanning 307 games and nine England caps ended when he should still have had a great deal to offer both club and country.

In his commentary at the 1978 Final, BBC stalwart David Coleman stated that Beattie had not appeared since the semi-final victory over West Bromwich Albion. This is not strictly true, since he played the entire 90 minutes of the 0–0 draw at Birmingham City just three days after the Highbury win, which, in the circumstances, was no mean achievement. However, there was no Beattie as Ipswich played a further five League games in the build-up to Wembley. Manager Robson was aiming to hold him back for the big one, fitness permitting, of course, since a cartilage operation some months earlier and a subsequent return to action within the space of just over three weeks, to face Barcelona in a UEFA Cup-tie, which had left him with severe swelling to the knee after every respective outing. Talk of another operation was also put on hold as the player, who only managed to turn out with the aid of cortisone injections that left him in agony afterwards, was instead nursed along so he could face Arsenal before going under the knife all over again.

Just as defensive partner Allan Hunter had to contend with his own injury nightmare, Beattie was also rated doubtful and even after declaring himself fit on the day of the game he was by no means certain that he would survive for its entirety. He said:

> Basically, the boss left it up to me to decide whether I was fit enough or not. He often referred to me as his diamond and I remember him saying it again before adding: 'I want you out there.' That did help to perk me up even if I was in the background as the Final approached and became the main focus of our attention. I had to have three cortisone injections on the day of the FA Cup Final – one late morning at the hotel, another in the Wembley dressing room about half an hour before the kick-off and then a top-up at half-time just to make sure I could keep going right to the end.

While the hat-trick of jabs did their job in allowing Beattie to last the full 90 minutes, once the game and the celebrations that followed were over, he was back to square one and it was decided that the only answer was further surgery, which he duly underwent to have a second cartilage removed from his left knee. Beattie recuperated over the summer and wanted nothing more than to feature on a regular basis in the 1978–79 season, but instead he managed only 27 first-team appearances out of a possible 55, his progress hampered by a third operation to remedy a problem that flared up with his right knee.

The more he faded from the first-team scene as his injury problems mounted, the more grateful Beattie was that he had managed to not only appear but also star in the club's Wembley triumph over Arsenal, although his memory of the occasion is somewhat blurred. He said:

You go into the whole weekend, or several days as it was, since we left Ipswich on the Wednesday and still had sore heads on the following Monday, and you are determined to remember everything, right down to the tiniest detail. But as far as I was concerned it was all over in a flash. I know I loved every minute of it but, as for the game, I was concentrating so hard that the 90 minutes passed very quickly. Much as I was glad to hear the final whistle, I couldn't really believe it was that time. The sheer elation of winning is the thing I remember – that and scrounging a fag off a steward. It was Big Al, actually, who got two and lit them both before passing one to me. I was third behind Mick Mills and Clive Woods to go up the steps for my medal and when I got to the bottom again I was waiting for the big man. When he appeared he had these two lit cigarettes so we set off on our lap of honour puffing away like a steam train. I can't say for sure, but that might be a Wembley record. I'm sure I haven't seen any other players light up before the lap of honour.

Beattie played just three of Town's seven games en route to FA Cup glory – the fourth-round home clash with Hartlepool, the semi-final against West Bromwich Albion at Highbury and, of course, the Final itself. He said:

I was scared I was going to miss the semi. I needed a fitness test for that one and managed to come through, although my knee was probably three times its normal size by the time the game finished. I was just so relieved that I played because I must be the world's worst spectator, or at least I was back then. Playing was everything to me and I hated it when I had to watch from the stand. I was always a bag of nerves.

Beattie's presence at Highbury helped to curb the threat posed by Baggies striker Cyrille Regis, who was tipped as a potential match winner but restricted to a couple of harmless headers, which Paul Cooper had no trouble dealing with. Kevin said:

We played brilliantly to beat Albion and there was no lack of confidence about facing Arsenal in the Final. Right there and then, as we celebrated getting to Wembley, we really fancied our chances and that feeling never really went away. The semi-final was a lot harder than the Final, which suited me because

Kevin Beattie clashes with Arsenal striker Frank Stapleton at Wembley.

[Photograph courtesy Offside Sports Photography Ltd]

Defensive partners Kevin Beattie and Allan Hunter show off the FA Cup.

my fitness wasn't as good a few weeks later. It was really one-sided. We didn't have any scary moments and it was just a matter of time before we scored. It's funny what can happen in football. There was a time that season when I would have been happy to write it off and to concentrate on making a fresh start the following August, but Wembley changed all that. I'd rushed back to play against Barcelona the previous November and that probably wasn't sensible. I felt well enough but with about 10 minutes left I was beginning to feel it. My next appearance in the first team was against Hartlepool but after that I was sidelined for another few weeks and it really was touch and go as to whether or not I would play again that season. For the fact that I played in the semi and then the Final I will be eternally grateful. It enabled me to fulfil a boyhood ambition because I used to sit at home and watch the FA Cup Final every year, dreaming that I might one day play in it. Back then it was a million to one shot. I was no different to all the other kids up and down the country. But as soon as I was signed by Ipswich it was always something I hoped would happen. I also wanted to play for Ipswich against Carlisle and to play for my country, so I suppose I was lucky even if I did have to pack in early and, but for injury, I might have achieved a whole lot more.

It was Beattie's partnership with Hunter that led manager Robson to label them 'bacon and eggs', as if to suggest the pair were meant to be together, which most certainly appeared to be the case at the time, even if their relationship has cooled in recent years. The pair bonded very early in their time together at Ipswich and were as much a double act off the field as they were on it, as the thousands of fans who crammed into the Cornhill to witness the celebrations that followed the open-top bus ride round the town were able to testify. Beattie said:

We were dancing around on the steps of the Town Hall and we both had these silly hats on. To be honest we were still a bit drunk from the night before, plus we had stopped off at the Army and Navy pub in Chelmsford on our way back on the Sunday. We were having a right old laugh when I heard this bloke say: 'If we can get these two out of the way we can get on with it.' It was only the mayor waiting to make his speech!

Both Beattie and Hunter took great exception to suggestions that they were nowhere near as doubtful for the Final as had been made out in the build-up. Beattie insisted:

That was complete rubbish. Some people felt we were just putting it on as a bit of gamesmanship but when you think what happened to the pair of us after Wembley – we didn't play too many games

[Photograph courtesy Offside Sports Photography Ltd]

Ipswich defender Kevin Beattie challenges Arsenal striker Malcolm Macdonald in the FA Cup Final.

– it's clear we had genuine injuries. How injured did these people want us to be? The week after we played in the FA Cup Final we were both in hospital having knee operations. Do they think we went through with them just to keep up some ridiculous charade? I think the fact that we were both close to missing the game made the whole thing mean so much more to us. I remember I had to fight back the tears at the final whistle. I will treasure the memory for ever. I looked around and one half of the stadium was a sea of blue and white. It brought a lump to my throat – the sort of moment you dream about as a footballer and for so many players it doesn't come true. I was delighted for the big man. He had the happiest face I have ever seen at the end. We went through a lot together and that was the obvious highlight. Nothing could beat it.

Beattie was the centre of attention when Football Association secretary Ted Croker visited the Ipswich hotel two days before the game to discuss official protocol with manager Robson and his players. Beattie recalled:

CONFESSION TIME

One of Beattie's abiding memories and highlights of 1978 includes the time when he and substitute Mick Lambert shared a room at the pre-Wembley hotel in St Albans. He laughed:

Mick wasn't a giant by any means but when it came to eating he had an appetite that was very difficult to satisfy. Honestly, he could have eaten for England. It all came as a bit of a shock to me because I normally shared with Allan Hunter but I didn't play at the start of our FA Cup run at Cardiff when Big Al paired up with Mick Mills. They decided to stick together all the way through, so I ended up sharing with Mick [Lambert] and it was a real eye-opener. We would go down to the restaurant for dinner, and not long after we returned to our rooms Mick was on the phone to room service ordering sandwiches and tea. Our room started to look like the kitchen, we had so many trays, plates, cups and saucers lying around. We decided one night it was time for a major tidy-up. But rather than place all the stuff outside our own room, which would have given the game away, we went along the corridor leaving some stuff outside every one of the other rooms. That way, nobody was any the wiser, although I half expected the boss to say something when he examined all the room bills. Maybe it's just as well we won the FA Cup. Had we lost the Final, Mick would have probably had to face the music.

Ted was going through a few things and when he mentioned HRH Princess Alexandra he looked straight at me and said: 'You should not shake her hand too firmly'. I knew what he meant. I told John Motson about it and when we were interviewed live by him on the morning of the match for the BBC he made a big thing of it. I just looked into the camera and for a laugh I said: 'Don't worry, love, I'll be gentle with you,' or something similar. After that I never thought any more about it. When we were all being presented to her before the game, Paul Cooper and I were looking at the crowd and seeing if we could spot any famous faces. We picked out Rod Stewart and Justin Hayward of the Moody Blues before the princess got to us. Millsy introduced me and she completely floored me when she smiled and said: 'Mr Beattie, I saw you on television earlier.' I said I hoped I hadn't offended her, but I could feel myself going as red as a beetroot.

Beattie does not deny that he was accident prone and still cannot believe what he did on the morning of the match as he looked to kill time until joining his colleagues for their pre-match meal. Smiling, he said:

I was having a wander around the hotel and there were some kids at the main door looking for autographs, so I went out and was busy signing away when I noticed a copper there. He was one of the outriders who had been assigned to providing the team bus with a police escort all the way to Wembley and we got chatting. I was impressed with his motorbike, which was a big BMW 850cc job. I went and had a closer look, then I said to him: 'Any chance of taking it for a spin?' I was amazed when he said: 'Yes, but not too far.' I hopped on and I was away in a flash. I think I did two circuits of the hotel grounds and came back. Thankfully, I was still in one piece and the boss knew nothing about it. Looking back, I must have been mad. I had ridden motorbikes back in Carlisle – even if I didn't have a licence – but nothing as powerful as that. Can you imagine what would have happened if I'd come off it at speed and suffered an injury that kept me out of the game at Wembley? The boss would have gone mental and, even worse, I might have cost Ipswich the FA Cup.

Beattie hardly needs reminding of how his career turned sour because injuries forced his premature retirement, and the FA Cup semi-final against Manchester City at Villa Park in 1981 was to prove his very last game. Typically, some would say, he was injured, suffering a broken arm in what seemed an innocuous challenge, and by the time he returned with it in plaster from a Birmingham hospital, he learned that a Paul Power free-kick had condemned Town to defeat. They were the first victims of the decision to play extra-time at the end of semi-final stalemates. Cruelly, Beattie suffered the fracture just two minutes from the end of the regulation 90. With a pained expression he recalled:

Ironically, that was one of my very best games for Ipswich, definitely in the top ten of more than 300 I played. The boss had faith in me because I had missed about half a dozen games and my attitude was always the same – there was absolutely no way that I was going to let him down. I had a great game that day, even if I say so myself. I nearly scored on at least a couple of occasions. As the end of the game was approaching I had no doubt that we would win it in extra-time and to this day I believe we would have done had I not been forced to come off. When the accident happened it was a real fluke. It was probably 60:40 in David Bennett's favour but I couldn't stand back and let him have a free header, so I went in determined to win the ball. I made contact with the ball but as I swung my arm round it hit David on the head. I was in full flight, and when I landed on the ground the arm felt a bit dead. When our physio, Tommy Eggleston, came on I told him I would be okay in a minute. Tommy took one look at it and said: 'You're joking, son, it's broken.' No doubt about it – my worst moment in football.

The broken arm would heal, of course, but Beattie's knees were not responding to treatment and he had to accept the inevitable, that his career was over. Cambridge-based surgeon David Dandy delivered the news that all players dread. He told Beattie there were signs of arthritis in his right knee and warned that if he continued playing he would risk becoming a cripple by the time he was 40. But it was a risk worth taking, Beattie thought, only to discover the truth as attempts at reviving his career were short-lived at both Colchester and Middlesbrough, where he appeared alongside future Portman Road favourite Tony Mowbray.

The money he made from a testimonial that included a game against Dynamo Moscow at Portman Road in March 1982 has long since disappeared, and the subsequent years have been anything but easy. By his own admission, he turned to drink but it amazed the medical experts when he enjoyed a return to health after it seemed a bout of pancreatitis, brought on by years of alcohol abuse, would end his life in 1991. Fearing he was not going to make it through the night, doctors called his wife and she sat with him until his eyes opened and he asked what she was doing there. Rather than confront him with the horrible truth, Maggie lied and said she had brought some clean pyjamas to the hospital. Beattie is still going strong 17 years later, much to the amazement of the doctors who told him not to drink but whose advice, he would have to concede, he has hardly taken to heart.

There have been some other very grim times, and in his autobiography, published in 2006, he admitted an attempt to take his own life, which only failed when a friend knocked on his door and immediately called an ambulance that took him to hospital in the nick of time. Despite his brush with death on more than one occasion, Beattie remains a larger-than-life character and cherishes the many special memories afforded him by his special talent as a professional sportsman, none of which come remotely close to topping Wembley 1978. However, it is interesting to hear that he very nearly axed himself from the starting line-up. He explained:

Of course, I badly wanted to play in the Final but about a fortnight beforehand I actually went to Bobby Robson and said I didn't think it would be fair if I did. I was genuinely concerned that

Hat's the way to do it! Kevin Beattie celebrates at Wembley along with skipper Mick Mills.

Russell Osman was playing in all the League games that I was missing and I tried to imagine how he must have been feeling. He was only young at the time but he was doing a very good job for the club. If you remember, we were poor in the League that season compared to previous years and Russell did his bit to win the points that meant we were safe from relegation. The boss was brilliant when I went to see him. He heard what I was saying but he made it clear he wanted to wait for me to show I was fit enough. Deep down, I'm sure he knew I wouldn't be 100 per cent but that didn't seem to matter. He wanted me to play just as much as I wanted it myself. To tell the truth, I felt a bit guilty the way I was hanging back just waiting for the Final to come around while the rest of the guys were out there battling for important League points. All I was doing was training and playing in practice games – nothing very strenuous by comparison. Come the big day I was probably only about 80 per cent fit. After the semi-final my knee was about three times its normal size and at that point I really began to fear the worst, so to actually be a part of the FA Cup Final was a big, big thing for me.

Hearing the Wembley loudspeaker announcement that first choice defenders Allan Hunter and Beattie were both to play lifted the Ipswich fans and deflated opponents Arsenal, striker Malcolm Macdonald in particular. 'You should have seen Malcolm's face when he heard Big Al had passed his fitness test,' laughed Beattie. He added:

He went as white as a sheet when I told him during the walkabout on the pitch and I added: 'You better watch yourself.' I liked Malcolm and had played for England alongside him but he could be a bit flash and arrogant at times. It brought him down to earth when I told him the big man was fit. They had many a tussle over the years and Malcolm knew what to expect. Big Al caught him with a solid early tackle and we didn't see too much of him after that.

Another abiding memory of 1978 is from the eve of the big game when Beattie and Hunter were in the hotel bar having an orange juice, and Town's first-team coach Cyril Lea came in. Beattie said:

Cyril was a bit of a taskmaster, I suppose, but it was all done with the best interests of the team at heart,' said Beattie. 'He completely floored the pair of us that night. He came in and asked if we fancied a pint. We thought he was winding us up and just laughed. 'Go on,' he said, 'it will calm your nerves,' so we each had a Guinness and it went down very well.

Beattie was a star virtually from day one for Ipswich, winning the fans' Player of the Year trophy in each of his first two seasons as a regular in the senior side, and in 1974 he became the first-ever winner of the PFA Young Player of the Year accolade. The latter award earned him subsequent invitations to the annual dinner and he was twice a special guest of the Football Association: firstly to attend the first FA Cup Final to be staged at the new Wembley, when he took part in a parade of legends representing previous winners of the trophy; and secondly when he and ex-Arsenal star Sammy Nelson conducted the FA Cup third-round draw in December 2007. He reflected:

I didn't do too badly for a kid from the rough part of Carlisle. I've got four brothers and four sisters, and believe me it was a real struggle for my parents. I had loads of jobs before I got into football. I worked in a slaughterhouse, I helped to deliver furniture, I was a coalman and

I worked in two different laundries. When I arrived in Ipswich I had nothing, just the clothes I was wearing and my old boots wrapped in brown paper. I remember both the boss and Cyril giving me shirts to wear.

It wasn't long before Beattie was earning the sort of money that enabled him to dress in style, although his generosity, particularly when it came to buying drinks for so-called friends who turned out to be nothing more than freeloaders, contributed to his financial downfall. Life did not deal Beattie a particularly good hand. He may have been blessed with extraordinary ability but, as Bobby Robson observed more than once: 'Talent isn't always easy to handle.'

Beattie had a lot in common with the likes of George Best and Paul Gascoigne – flawed geniuses in that none of them seemed capable of leading a normal life in tandem with their sporting stardom. However, it is best to remember him for what he was: a phenomenal defender who was never second best and could run faster, leap higher and tackle more strongly than the next guy. The way he coasted through the 1978 Final was so typical of Beattie, making it look so straightforward and simple, just as he did throughout his career for Ipswich and England.

For a time he enjoyed reporting on Town's fortunes, both home and away, for BBC Radio Suffolk. But nowadays, while he remains a Portman Road regular, the majority of his time is taken up with caring for his wife, who has multiple sclerosis and is confined to a wheelchair.

GEORGE BURLEY

FULL NAME: George Elder Burley
DATE OF BIRTH: 3 June 1956
PLACE OF BIRTH: Cumnock, Ayrshire
IPSWICH TOWN APPEARANCES: 500
IPSWICH TOWN GOALS: 11

(Photograph courtesy of Owen Hines)

Wembley hero George Burley holds a unique place in Ipswich Town's history as the only person to both play for and manage the club at the national stadium, as well as representing his country there. Not a bad record for someone who packed his bags soon after leaving school in his native Scotland and headed south in 1971 with little idea of what the future held in store. He also came within a whisker of deciding the FA Cup Final, which would have been some achievement for a right-back hardly renowned as a goalscorer, as his record of netting a mere 11 times in his 500 games for the club confirms. Three minutes before Roger Osborne finally broke Arsenal's stubborn resistance to decide what everyone agreed was a one-sided Final, Burley was denied his moment of glory by the giant right hand of one of the world's finest goalkeepers of all time. He could hardly have been closer to marking his first Wembley appearance with a goal and he recalled:

I didn't get that many throughout my career but I really did think that one was going in. It was a header, too. Clive Woods was out on the left and I just read what was going to happen. Woodsy sent over a deep cross with his right foot and I saw my chance. I liked to get forward whenever I could but being a full-back it was more a case of overlapping and I didn't often get headers in. I got in between Willie Young and another player, and Woodsy's cross was just right for me to make contact with the ball. I connected with it well but Pat Jennings was one of the top 'keepers around and he had huge hands. It was as if his right arm just kept on stretching until it made contact with the ball to push it away for a corner. I've watched re-runs of the game many times over the years and it has never ceased to amaze me that he managed to get his right hand to the ball. Pushing it away for a corner was also a vital part of the save because Paul Mariner was ready to pounce on the rebound. When I got my head on the ball I really thought I'd scored.

Instead Burley was frustrated, just as fellow countryman John Wark had been with two almost-identical shots that struck the same upright, and again when Mariner saw an 11th minute left-foot shot crash back off the crossbar. When Jennings' fabulous, full-length save denied Burley, it was feared that Ipswich would never find a way past the Northern Ireland custodian, although all that changed soon afterwards when another unlikely hero, Roger Osborne, came up trumps.

Burley's first appearance in the shadow of the famous twin towers was something he had eagerly anticipated since playing his part in Town's semi-final triumph over favourites West Bromwich Albion at Highbury. The realisation that he was going to Wembley with Ipswich put him on an incredible high, as it did all the players, but especially those who had suffered defeat at the very same stage three years earlier, when West Ham edged to victory in a Stamford Bridge replay in somewhat controversial circumstances. The experience was torture for the Suffolk contingent of players and fans, and Burley said:

I loved that semi-final at Highbury. The feeling at the end was every bit as good as it was when I heard the final whistle at Wembley. Going back to 1975, it was the worst feeling in the world. You are so close and then it is snatched away from you. Plus, we knew we didn't deserve to lose that game. We scored perfectly good goals but Clive Thomas thought differently. Maybe one of them was debatable but no one will ever convince me that the other one was anything other than a perfectly good goal. We felt it was an injustice, but it was just the losing that hit us hard. I was just 18 at the time with my career in front of me, and I remember thinking to myself: 'This could be my last chance'. You hope it will not be, but you have no way of knowing if the same opportunity will ever come along again. The older players took it worse, for obvious reasons, and there were a lot of tears shed that night. The other lads were also thinking: 'Will we ever get this close again?' That's why Highbury meant as much as it did to so many of the players, because they had the memory of what had happened three years earlier at the back of

---

Home-grown heroes

George Burley was one of nine home-grown stars in Ipswich Town's FA Cup-winning side, which is probably a Wembley record. Only Paul Cooper, Allan Hunter and Paul Mariner cost the club a fee, with the others all products of the prolific Portman Road youth scheme, the forerunner of today's academy set-up.

Bobby Robson took tremendous pride in the fact that Ipswich reared so much talent, and Burley, who helped the club win the FA Youth Cup in 1973, was one of the early successes. Robson later said:

I suppose George was lightweight as full-backs go and in the beginning I had some doubts about his physical presence, although I needn't have worried. His ability was never in doubt from when we saw him in a trial. After that we didn't want to let him out of our sight in case we lost him. I used to say his delivery of the ball was so accurate because that right foot of his was like a golf club that could play every shot in the book. No matter the range, he always found the perfect weight. It was educated, that right foot of his.

---

their minds. We couldn't believe it when we heard Clive Thomas was to be the referee again, but fortunately there were no problems. At the end of the semi-final I think every one of us was thinking the same thing – we're going to Wembley and nobody can take it away from us.

Burley, a model of consistency throughout his time as a player, had come a long way in a comparatively short space of time, departing for Ipswich in July 1971 within a few weeks of leaving school, little realising how quickly his career would take off or the heights he would reach. Despite going on to enjoy a long and successful career, he was actually rejected by Leeds at the age of 14 but their loss proved to be Ipswich's gain, and the fact he still had a trial at Portman Road softened the blow for the youngster. He remembered:

Don Revie was the Leeds manager at the time and he watched the trial game, but I never expected to be hearing from them again because I knew I had not played well enough on the day. I was very disappointed with the Leeds episode. They were such a big club. At that time it must have been almost every kid's ambition to play for Leeds but I knew I wasn't going to make it.

A few months later he travelled down to Ipswich to receive a very different response after being assessed along with several other young hopefuls in a series of trial games. Baby-faced Burley was called up for his Town debut in December 1973, lining up against Manchester United legend George Best – in what proved to be the Northern Ireland star's very last game at Old Trafford. Three days earlier, Burley and his landlord had travelled up the A140 to Carrow Road for the Boxing Day clash with the Canaries, and he had thought little of the possible consequences as Town right-back Geoff Hammond was carried off and later declared unfit for the trip north. Burley recalled:

When Geoff was carried off at Norwich my only thought was to feel sorry for him. I didn't really bother to think about who would replace him. I just assumed it would be Bruce Twamley. Even the following day, I wasn't thinking I had any chance of making my debut. I just trained as usual and it was on the Friday that Bobby Robson called me over for a chat. Right out of the blue he said I would be playing against Manchester United the next day and I was just stunned. I really couldn't believe it was true.

A quick phone call to his parents had them packing their bags and they were joined by other relatives to form Burley's very own fan club at Old Trafford. He found himself much in demand as reporters from a number of national newspapers rang the team's hotel in Cheshire. Burley said:

They really built it up into a big story because I was going to be facing the great George Best in my very first game, but I wasn't too bothered and just wanted to get a decent night's sleep. The next day I was a bit keyed up beforehand but once I was out there I felt just fine. I thought I played quite well, nothing brilliant but fairly steady, and the boss seemed quite happy with my performance. George Best had lost a bit of pace by then but he showed some brilliant touches. I still take a lot of pride in the fact that I played against him on my debut, even if he was getting towards the end of his career at the top.

Suddenly from cleaning the boots of the senior stars, Burley was lining up alongside them. Although he retained the number two shirt for the remainder of that season, and for years to come, he had not dared to think such rapid progress would be possible when he left Scotland to take his chance at Portman Road. He admitted:

(*Photograph courtesy Offside Sports Photography Ltd*)

George Burley in action at Wembley with Arsenal's David Price in close attention.

Back then, if you had told me that I would be playing in the FA Cup Final at Wembley, I'd probably have just laughed. I was a boy in a man's world then and didn't even dream I would go on to achieve so much in football. When I first arrived at Ipswich all the talk was about hopefully keeping the club in the First Division. At that point, obviously, I wasn't in the first team but everyone at the club got a great boost from what the senior players achieved. It felt good to be with a club that was clearly going places. As a youngster, I was chuffed that the future looked promising. It was the same for all the youth team players. Things happened pretty quickly, I suppose. Within a couple of years we were qualifying for Europe. After that we didn't look back and it just got better and better. It wasn't just that the players were doing so well on the pitch. Things were coming together off it as well, as Bobby Robson and the directors set about turning Portman Road into a stadium more in keeping with the club's First Division status. The ground has changed a great deal over the years but it was in the early part of my time with the club that the transformation began. It looked far more professional as the improvements kept on coming.

Burley, who gave his usual assured display in the 1978 Final, was relieved just to be there as he had missed a chunk of the campaign through injury, including the third round trip to Cardiff. He was in his usual place for all the other ties en route to Wembley and even weighed in with a goal – the one that opened the floodgates at Millwall at the quarter-final stage and which, come the end of his career, he had no hesitation in nominating as his best-ever. Despite being an FA Cup winner, Burley had to wait until May the following year before winning his first Scottish senior cap, coincidentally in the same game that marked club colleague John Wark's full debut – a 3–0 defeat by Wales at Ninian Park, Cardiff.

There were few classier full-backs around at the time, although Celtic's Danny McGrain was undoubtedly a top performer and it was he who was often preferred in the number two shirt, keeping Burley on the sidelines. Given that Burley established himself in the Ipswich side at such an early age, recognition was a long time in coming, although he appeared for his country's Youth, Under-23 and Under-21 sides along the way. By the time he faced Arsenal at Wembley the young Scot was a seasoned campaigner with more than 200 appearances to his credit, turning in polished performances in the vast majority of them. This was certainly the case in the Final, which rounded off a memorable few weeks following the semi-final battle. He recalled:

The build-up in those days started when the referee blew his whistle to signal the end of the semi. It was an incredible feeling. We celebrated in the dressing room and the trip home to Ipswich was fantastic. There were people in the streets waiting to greet us and in the weeks after that it was as if every shop had a dedicated window display. It might have been old hat for some clubs that had been to Wembley a few times but it was all new for Ipswich so you could understand the reaction. People talked about little else but the Final. It was like one long party. Then there were the ticket requests from far and wide. Suddenly, we all heard from long-lost friends. We'd been warned what to expect but of course we'd never experienced anything like that before. I didn't realise I had so many aunts and uncles but I just made sure my immediate family were fixed up. My parents and my big brother, Tommy, were there and so was Jill. She was my fiancée at the time and we got married in the summer of 1978 – a very good year. The thing I remember most about the day itself, apart from the sheer joy of seeing Roger's goal go in and the relief that I felt when the referee blew his whistle, was going up to receive my medal. In those days the crowd were much closer to the steps where the players climbed up to the Royal Box. I was being grabbed, then hugged and even kissed by complete strangers. My mother had made her way into that area and got hold of me. I didn't think she was ever going to let me go.

Thanks to a morning downpour, which came on top of heavy rainfall the previous day, there were puddles on the pitch, although the Wembley ground staff deserved the praise that came their way for ensuring the game went ahead. Burley said:

The pitch was stamina-sapping for both sets of players and the fact that the sun was also beating down meant the conditions were difficult. We had dominated the game and come close to scoring on a number of occasions. In fact, we did everything but score and when that happens you do begin to wonder what you are going to have to do to get a goal – or if you are ever going to actually get one. Even worse, you fear the opposition will have just one decent attack and score. That sort of thing often does happen. The conditions really took their toll on us. Not only was the pitch very heavy but it was a hot and sticky day once the sun came out and some of the players reckoned they lost six or seven pounds during the 90 minutes. You only had to look at the state Roger was in after he scored. It was all too much for him and he was absolutely shattered. That tended to set the mood for the celebrations as well. The club had arranged a banquet at the Royal Garden Hotel in Kensington, which was a super gesture. But to be honest we were all a bit numb. I think we were all drained and it was difficult to lift ourselves. We had been to Wembley and we had won. We had given everything. We had done it. That was such a different feeling to winning the semi-final, because then we had everything to look forward to.

Burley was in the side hammered 6–1 at Aston Villa just seven days before the Final but after that he felt everything went according to plan, as the team made one final push for the big prize. He said:

Maybe it didn't look like the ideal preparation but we managed to put it behind us and it might even have made us more determined not to slip up on the day. Roger didn't play at Villa Park that day and he was missed. He was such a popular lad. We were all keen for him to play in the Final but we also felt sorry for young Paul Overton in goal. It should have been a big day for him but instead it turned out to be his one and only appearance for the club, and he'd let in six goals. But we had to put that result behind us and look forward. We were all relaxed in the week leading up to Wembley – don't forget, it was a team full of international players. In the previous three or four years we had done well in the League and in Europe. We had won a few battles. But although we had a very strong squad, the 1977–78 season was actually our poorest in the League for a number of years, mainly because of the injuries we suffered. We were always confident, however, that in a one-off game against Arsenal we could beat them. We had a very good spirit in the squad. The atmosphere was so positive and we didn't feel any pressure. It was everyone's aim to go out and enjoy themselves. We weren't uptight but quite relaxed considering the occasion. There were the usual pre-match nerves – butterflies in the stomach, that sort of thing – but you expect that before any game. The fact that it was Wembley held no fears for us. We had been to have a look round a few weeks earlier and we also trained there a couple of days beforehand. That gave us a feel for it. Far from being apprehensive, we were looking forward to getting out there and getting on with it. When I look back on my playing career it's an obvious highlight. Not bad for a wee lad from a village in Ayrshire, and I had my family there to share my big moment. These are the things you cherish and remember for the rest of your life. It tends to stand out from the rest because of the occasion. Deep down, when they start their careers, I think every player probably wants to play at Wembley in the FA Cup Final. When you do it, the feeling is incredible.

Of course, Burley was to experience the Wembley winning feeling all over again 22 years later when, as Ipswich manager, he led them out to face Barnsley in the First Division Play-off Final, with a place in the Premiership worth millions up for grabs. Again, it was a memorable day and again Burley emerged triumphant after seeing his team cast aside three years of heartache. After being eliminated at the semi-final stage by Sheffield United, Charlton and Bolton, Ipswich finally returned to the top flight after a five-year absence.

Burley, who had served his apprenticeship as a manager with Ayr United and Colchester United, returned to Portman Road as manager in December 1994 following the resignation of John Lyall, with Ipswich already firm favourites to be relegated. He was unable to prevent the inevitable and instead set about rebuilding the club in tandem with new chairman David Sheepshanks. They succeeded in restoring the feel-good factor and when promotion was finally clinched after three near misses it appeared to be the start of something big.

When Burley led his team to fifth place in the Premiership in the 2001–02 season, he deservedly carried off the Manager of the Year accolade and at the time looked capable of following in the footsteps of his mentor, Bobby Robson. Burley was quick to acknowledge Robson's influence in helping to mould him as a manager but, unfortunately, he found it difficult to sustain the success of that first season in the Premiership and relegation followed 12 months later.

Burley was surprisingly sacked in October 2002, following a 3–0 defeat at Grimsby, and we will never know how subsequent seasons might have worked out. But he showed his credentials when he bounced back at next club Derby, joining them late in the 2002–03 season, at a time when the very real prospect of relegation to what is now League One had the alarm bells ringing at Pride Park. Burley steered them clear of trouble, kept them up again the following season and, in the 2004–05 campaign, exceeded Derby's wildest expectations by booking a place in the play-offs, only for Billy Davies' Preston, whom Derby had defeated 3–1 in the last game of the League programme, to get the better of them over the two semi-final clashes.

Burley resigned the following month and did not have to wait long for his next job, back in Scotland with Hearts. Edinburgh derby games promised to be even more interesting than usual, with Burley's former Ipswich coach Tony Mowbray in charge at Hibernian. Hearts soared to the top of the Scottish Premier League under Burley's guidance, winning their first eight games of the season and losing just one of his opening 12. However, he was treated shabbily when temperamental majority shareholder Vladimir Romanov, who subsequently gained full control at Tynecastle in October 2005, mysteriously decided on a parting of the ways – news that both stunned and disappointed supporters. No satisfactory explanation has been forthcoming for one of the strangest managerial sackings of all time, and we may have to wait for Burley's own autobiography before we are fully acquainted with the facts.

Within a couple of months, and just two days before Christmas, Burley was unveiled as the new manager of Southampton, a family club with a number of similarities to Ipswich, one being their struggle to regain Premiership status. Burley was forced to sell a number of star players as the club counted the high cost of relegation, while a change of ownership at St Mary's provided another major talking point. Burley revealed early in the 2006–07 season that the reason for further departures from the squad had been the club's precarious financial state, along with the need to stave off the threat of administration. It may even have been with a sense of relief that he departed in January 2008 to become the new manager of Scotland in succession to Alex McLeish, with qualification for the World Cup Finals in South Africa in 2010 his immediate goal.

If Burley has not always had it easy as a manager, the same could certainly be said of a playing career, which was laced with success but not without its frustrations. The biggest mishap, by far, occurred in January 1981 when he suffered a serious injury in a goalless FA

Cup fourth-round tie at Shrewsbury, landing awkwardly and tearing the cruciate ligaments in his right knee. It was a major blow, although he was fortunate that Cambridge-based surgeon David Dandy's pioneering surgery repaired the problem, and Burley became the first player to have his career saved in that way. He said:

It was thanks to the surgeon that I was able to recover sufficiently to play again. He told me that had it happened a few years earlier I could well have been forced to retire. I was fortunate that I was able to have probably the country's number one specialist perform what was a very delicate operation because the whole knee joint had to be virtually rebuilt. His reassurance was another bonus because I was obviously very concerned. But he told me that being young and fit – until the injury occurred – would help and he was confident I would fully recover. For five months afterwards it was important that I received the proper supervision and I used to go over to Cambridge every day. It was virtually 10 months after the game at Shrewsbury that I was finally able to return to the first team.

It was a bad time to be injured because Ipswich were chasing success on three fronts in the 1980–81 campaign and Burley missed out on a UEFA Cup-winner's medal, although his contribution in playing five games to help book a quarter-final place did not go unnoticed.

I'd have loved to have played in the UEFA Cup Final but at the time I was more concerned with getting fit again,' he adds. 'I didn't go over to Amsterdam for the second leg because I wasn't going to be involved. I wasn't one for hanging around when I was injured. I preferred to watch the game and go home, rather than go into the dressing room at the end. I think that would have made me feel worse.

Burley graced the big stage for most of his playing career, but his love of the game saw him step down a few levels as he later represented Sunderland, Gillingham, Motherwell (twice), Ayr, Falkirk and Colchester before concentrating on management. He won 11 caps for Scotland, the last of them in 1982 when he was included in the squad for the World Cup Finals in Spain but did not play.

Paul Cooper

FULL NAME: Paul David Cooper
DATE OF BIRTH: 21 December 1953
PLACE OF BIRTH: Cannock, Staffs
IPSWICH TOWN APPEARANCES: 575

(Photograph courtesy of Owen Hines)

When Bobby Robson handed over £23,000 to sign Paul Cooper from Birmingham City in July 1974, even he could not have anticipated what a tremendous, value-for-money deal it would prove to be. Robson was renowned for his shrewdness in the transfer market and simple arithmetic tells us that the sturdy goalkeeper with a penchant for penalty saves, who went on to help Town win the UEFA Cup three years after their Wembley success, only cost the club a paltry £40 per game. Okay, he earned a decent salary on top, not to mention a host of win bonuses, but it was still a bargain. He proved his worth over and over again, maturing into the role of first-team regular and making the goalkeeper's shirt his own. But for the likes of Ray Clemence and Peter Shilton, who virtually shared the England number one shirt for a while, he might have been able to rid himself of the label 'the only non-international in the Ipswich team', as was the case for a fairly lengthy period of his predominantly successful Portman Road career.

Cooper made an inauspicious start with Ipswich, joining on loan and conceding three goals in a 3–2 defeat away to Leeds United, in the penultimate game of the 1973–74 season. With Laurie Sivell restored for the final fixture one week later, he might have been forgiven for thinking it was merely a one-off cameo role rather than the start of something big. But manager Robson had seen enough in that one outing – against the season's League champions – to want to make the move permanent and he was pleasantly surprised when Birmingham boss Freddie Goodwin, having knocked back Ipswich's initial £20,000 offer, relented when it was increased by a further 15 per cent. Robson, who made very few transfer market excursions in comparison to his contemporaries, recalled:

When I paid £23,000 for Paul I suppose everyone was thinking we had got ourselves a £23,000 goalkeeper – in other words nothing special, a routine 'keeper who might offer a bit of competition to Laurie for his first-team place. But I could hardly conceal my delight at snatching him for such a reasonable fee. I remember trying hard not to let Freddie know how highly I rated Paul when we were negotiating the price. In the end I could hardly believe my luck in managing to persuade him to accept so little for a 'keeper I was convinced was much, much better than his price tag might have suggested. To be fair to Freddie, he put me on to Paul in the first place. He said he could no longer guarantee him a first-team place and was willing to let him go. I was in no position to go out and spend the kind of money that other First Division clubs would have wanted for their first-choice goalkeepers. Paul came to us, took his chance when it came along and matured into one of the most consistent 'keepers in the country. I had considered a lot of goalkeepers all over the country before I finally decided on Paul – definitely one of my best decisions as a manager.

Cooper was the only arrival at Portman Road prior to the start of the 1974–75 season, as Robson sought to build on the considerable achievement of having steered his side to consecutive top-four finishes in the First Division. With the deal done and dusted, the shrewd Robson, safe in the knowledge that a rich crop of young talent was forcing its way through, banked more than seven times his outlay by allowing a quartet of fringe players to move on. Both Peter Morris and Johnny Miller joined neighbours Norwich, while Geoff Hammond was signed by Manchester City and Glenn Keeley was transferred to Newcastle.

Cooper had to be patient before establishing himself in the side, registering a mere two first-team appearances, both in the League, in his first full season – a drop in the ocean compared to first-choice Sivell, who clocked up 40 League outings, plus nine in the FA Cup, five in the League Cup and two in the UEFA Cup, for a grand total of 56. However, it was a different story in the 1975–76 season. Sivell was in his usual place for the opening game at home to Newcastle, which resulted in a 3–0 defeat for Ipswich, in which England striker Malcolm Macdonald, who was to draw a blank with Arsenal at Wembley in 1978, scored twice. But the tables were turned very quickly and it was the man from Lowestoft's turn to play second fiddle, eventually emulating Cooper's two-game tally from the previous year.

Incidentally, the Newcastle game was played in front of the biggest opening-day attendance in the club's history – 27,680 – although that record lasted just 12 months, until 28,490 fans witnessed a 3–1 win over Tottenham. In 1977 it was shattered again as Ipswich started with a 1–0 win over Arsenal – a scoreline repeated at Wembley – in front of a 30,154 crowd.

Back in 1975 Cooper took his chance with a commanding performance as Town went to Tottenham just four days after the embarrassing 3–0 home defeat inflicted by Newcastle and earned a respectable 1–1 draw, which led Robson to remark: 'Paul took his opportunity well and turned in a faultless display and made many excellent saves. His handling of crosses was extremely good and his kicking was a feature of the game.'

The new man enjoyed an uninterrupted run of 37 games before giving way, for one game only, to Sivell. Sivell had the misfortune to suffer a horrible injury and lose several teeth as a result of a clash with Andy Gray in a goalless draw at Aston Villa, thus ensuring that Cooper would return for the club's remaining fixtures. No Ipswich player featured more regularly in the club's FA Cup-winning campaign than Cooper, and the fact that Town conceded a total of 11 goals in the only two games he missed – five at Chelsea and six at Aston Villa a week before Wembley – underlined the goalkeeper's immense value to the side.

Soon after celebrating his 24th birthday at the beginning of 1978, Cooper completed a century of League appearances for the club in advance of the FA Cup trip to Cardiff. At that point he regarded himself as fortunate to still be at the club, never mind holding down the first-team spot, after beginning to wonder if his days were numbered when pre-season reports suggested Ipswich were in the market for a new number one. Little realising he was less than one fifth of the way through his Town career, he said:

Every time I picked up a newspaper there was a story about Ipswich looking for a new 'keeper. Pat Jennings was the big favourite and if he'd joined the club it would not have been to play in the reserves. So I began to think I might be on the move. A new club might have been a fresh challenge but also staying with Ipswich presented me with a similar challenge because I had to prove I was good enough. To think I have played 100 League games is tremendous. I hope I can keep going for a long time to come because I feel I'm getting better all the time.

Manager Robson clearly agreed because he decided not to take the opportunity to sign Jennings when he left Tottenham in the summer of 1977. The Northern Ireland international's wage demands, together with his request to not only remain living in Hertfordshire but also train less frequently at Portman Road than the other players, might have influenced Robson's decision, but in the end it was his confidence in Cooper that prevailed.

Robson's faith was to be repaid several times over, starting with Cooper's part in the club's FA Cup success when he was ever present in the seven-game run and joined that elite group of goalkeepers to keep a clean sheet in a Wembley Final – not bad for a player who had often been referred to as his team's weakest link. Countless critics had blamed Town's failure to win a major honour under Robson on the fact that the team did not possess a goalkeeper of sufficient quality, but that slur proved to be a spur to Cooper. He set about proving people wrong in spectacular style, collecting both FA Cup and UEFA Cup-winner's medals and making 575 senior appearances for the club, the vast majority of them in the top division. In addition he collected the fans' Player of the Year accolade in the 1980–81 campaign, which most people privileged to be around at the time agree was the finest in the club's history. Looking back on his time with the club, Cooper said:

I suppose I just got used to the criticism and got on with things. Even the night before the FA Cup Final, when I was nice and relaxed and just looking forward to my big day, it came back to haunt me. I switched on the television in my hotel room and there was a preview show on – the usual sort of format with plenty of people saying what they thought was going to happen on the day. I remember Dickie Davies and Jack Charlton were among those involved. I couldn't believe what I was watching. They absolutely slaughtered me. All they kept going on about was how many goals Arsenal would be knocking past me. It didn't bother me much because I'd been putting up with it for years. The next day some of the lads came up to me and said: 'Did you see that rubbish?' but I didn't care. I had the last laugh, I suppose. I had very little to do on the day and I've got my winner's medal to show for it. Not bad for the weakest link, eh? I played all those games for Ipswich so I suppose I couldn't have been that bad or they would have done something about it. If you've got a car that keeps breaking down you change it, don't you?

Nonetheless, Cooper was not confused by Arsenal being billed as red-hot favourites – after all, they were fifth in the First Division that season and Town had to settle for 18th place, 17 points worse off at a time when League wins were rewarded with just two points rather than three. Furthermore, they had scored 13 goals fewer than the Gunners and conceded a whopping 24 more. As someone who liked a bet, he confessed: 'If I'd been a neutral and they had asked me to pick a winner I would have probably picked Arsenal. I wouldn't have had the

(Photograph courtesy Offside Sports Photography Ltd)

Paul Cooper with the Basil Brush soft toy made by a supporter and adopted as the players' FA Cup mascot.

inside knowledge that made me know things were going to turn out very differently to the way most people expected.'

On the day itself, along with 30,000 disbelieving Ipswich supporters, Cooper's main worry was that his outfield colleagues, despite their total dominance, might never find a way past the formidable Jennings, the man who had come so close to succeeding him less than a year before. He added:

I thought it was going to be a 0–0 slaughter. I'd seen PM [Paul Mariner] hit the bar, Warky hit the post twice and Pat pull off a great save from George Burley's header. We were so much on top and I was starting to convince myself that it was going to be one of those games and that we'd never actually score. So as soon as Roger [Osborne] hit the back of the net I was looking for the final whistle. The final 13 minutes or so seemed to take forever. I remember spotting Owen Hines, the local paper photographer, and I asked him how long we had left. It was as if time was standing still and I just wanted it over with. If I remember rightly, we only had one anxious moment, when Alan Sunderland got through and I had to come rushing out to save at his feet. Almost six years later Alan came to Ipswich and it was quite funny when we had a chat about the 1978 Final. He recalled that very incident when he was close to getting a goal and he said: 'I'd heard you were quick but I didn't know you were that bloody quick.'

Only Kevin Beattie prevented Cooper being the fastest player at Portman Road, and the 'keeper's scorching pace proved to be a huge asset in confronting opposition attackers in those one-to-one situations that can often decide games, in which, more often than not, he came out on top. His ability on the ball was another extremely useful part of his armoury. As he confidently swept up at the back, exiting the penalty area and showing the talent that had seen him score goals for Shrewsbury's second team long before he decided to apply himself as a goalkeeper, Cooper constantly caught the eye.

In many ways he was years ahead of his time, since the rule change that prohibited a goalkeeper from touching the ball from a back-pass, and which reduced and even ruined a number of careers, would have suited him down to the ground, so comfortable was he with the ball at his feet. But the mere mention of Cooper's name to those fans who remember how well he performed in those halcyon days under Robson's astute management is bound to revive memories of how he carved out a reputation as a penalty expert. Unbelievably, he managed to save eight of the 10 spot-kicks he faced in the 1979–80 season, which led former

Arsenal and Scotland goalkeeper Bob Wilson, who by then was a leading light with the BBC, to dub him the 'penalty king'. He even saved two in one game in front of the *Match of the Day* cameras, denying both Barry Powell and ex-Manchester United midfielder Gerry Daly to help earn Ipswich a 1–1 draw with Derby County at Portman Road on 29 March 1980. Just a few weeks earlier he came to his side's rescue by keeping out a Terry McDermott spot-kick at a packed Anfield, to ensure Town returned from Liverpool with a point courtesy of a 1–1 draw.

After the Liverpool game the home side's goalkeeper, Ray Clemence, recorded an interview with Cooper to be used on a midweek Merseyside radio show which he co-hosted with Everton skipper Mike Lyons. However, Cooper remained tight-lipped when quizzed about the secret of his success and he later said: 'Ray was interested from a professional point of view but there was no way I was going to give anything away.'

Cooper tended to put the taker in two minds by not standing exactly in the middle of his goal and it was amazing the number of times the ploy succeeded. Among his confused victims was Liam Brady of Arsenal, and an interesting battle of wits would surely have ensued had the Gunners been awarded a penalty at Wembley. Cooper added: 'There was a certain routine that I followed but to be honest every save was a bonus because 'keepers were not really expected to save penalties. The real pressure was on the player taking the kick. It was the opposite with them – they were expected to score.'

Cooper, whose penalty heroics earned him a place in the *Guinness Book of Records*, made sure a nagging groin strain was not going to prevent him playing at Wembley by sitting out the previous week's League visit to Aston Villa, when Ipswich's shock 6–1 defeat did nothing to alter the bookmakers' verdict that it would be a one-sided Final.

Teenager Paul Overton came into the side for what proved his only senior appearance and Cooper recalled:

I sat in the stand with PM, who was also injured, and I just thought to myself: 'What the hell is going on?' But we were able to quickly forget about that game and concentrate on the Final. Let's face it, for Ipswich it was a step into the unknown. Our attitude was just right. We were going to win – you had to be there to believe the confidence we had in ourselves – but we were just like our fans in that we were determined to have a good day out. All the pressure was on Arsenal because they were expected to win and we weren't. Maybe that was what fired us up, I don't really know, but we were a confident team that day. There was no sign of nerves. Personally, the bigger the game, the more I was up for it.

SURPRISE TELEGRAM

After helping Ipswich win the FA Cup in 1978, Paul Cooper received a surprise telegram from his former boss at a steel-rolling mill in the Midlands. Cooper remembered: 'It took a lot for him to send that telegram because although he may have been pleased for me, I know he would have been gutted inside. He was a West Bromwich Albion fan, you see, and we beat his team in the semi-final – another occasion when few people fancied us to win.'

In common with the other players, Cooper felt for Trevor Whymark, who missed what proved to be a once-in-a-lifetime opportunity because he was unable to prove his fitness in time. He says:

Trevor was a good player, a good servant, and he was unlucky. The lads tried to cheer him up by telling him he might have another chance, but it was no consolation. If you think about it, not playing is even worse than finishing on the losing side – and that must be awful. Thank goodness it wasn't us. You have to hang around at the end to go up and get your runners-up medal, but you would probably prefer to get straight off the pitch and into the dressing room. It's true what they say about Wembley being for winners.

However, despite the joy of being an FA Cup winner – something that has eluded many of the game's biggest stars over the years – Cooper believes that Ipswich's feat three years later was worthy of far greater recognition. He said:

From a professional point of view I would have to say that winning the UEFA Cup was a far greater achievement than winning the FA Cup. We played seven games to win it in 1978, but we had a replay against Bristol Rovers and it is possible to do it with six, whereas we had to play 12 to win the UEFA Cup and we also had to handle some pretty hostile situations. Another thing – you don't have Second, Third and Fourth Division teams in the European competition. When I think back to 1978, I can't escape the fact that we should probably have gone out in the fifth round at Bristol Rovers. They scored what was probably a perfectly good goal and the referee disallowed it, but that's typical of Cup football. You get the breaks and you start to think it really might be your year. There's the luck of the draw, too, which is a huge factor. But I agree the FA Cup is the glamour tournament, or at least it was then, and the 1978 Final will always be my most memorable game. It's all about that one big day at Wembley. Back then it was far more important to players than it seems now. You felt special, as if you'd really arrived in the game, and you knew the whole world was watching.

Cooper, who was one of several players based in Capel St Mary during his time with Ipswich, had a far more successful career than he might have imagined when he left Kingsmead County Secondary School. He started work as a storeman for a plastics firm in Sutton Coldfield, then six months later became a £16-a-week despatch clerk at a steel-rolling mill, although his earnings were boosted by an additional £30 a month from non-League club Sutton Town. He decided to join Sutton in preference to the offer of an apprenticeship from Shrewsbury, managed at the time by Manchester United legend Harry Gregg, who fancied him on the strength of outfield displays in midfield and up front for their youth and reserve sides.

It was the two-hour coach journey to and from Gay Meadow that helped him to make up his mind and he had no regrets when his goalkeeping displays with Sutton attracted the attention of Birmingham City. He did not take long to make an impact at St Andrew's, playing in the semi-final of the FA Cup at the age of 18, six years before he was to become a Wembley winner with Ipswich. The club's third-choice 'keeper when an injury crisis ruled out both Dave Latchford and Mike Kelly, he was thrust into the first-team picture and made his debut on 8 January 1972, when he conceded two goals in the opening 20 minutes but recovered well to help the Blues thump Portsmouth 6–3.

Cooper also kept a clean sheet as the Blues defeated Ipswich in a fourth-round tie that year – Latchford's brother Bob scored the only goal in the second minute. Latchford was recalled for eight games before Birmingham again turned to Cooper, and his performance in a crucial home League win over promotion rivals Millwall, watched by a 43,000 crowd, prompted Brian Glanville to write in the *Sunday Times*: 'City, so famous for their goalkeepers – Hibbs, Merrick – have discovered a gifted 18-year-old in Paul Cooper.' However, the youngster's hopes of appearing in the FA Cup Final were cruelly dashed at the semi-final stage, when he was unable to prevent Leeds winning 3–0 at Hillsborough, although Birmingham's promotion from the Second Division, finishing one point behind champions Norwich, meant the campaign still ended on a comparative high.

Ipswich rewarded Cooper with a testimonial in 1986 and the following year he moved to Leicester City, who were managed at the time by his former Town teammate Bryan Hamilton. He would have been content to stay put at Portman Road on the same wages but the club

---

NEAR MISS

Paul Cooper was fortunate that he was still around to collect an FA Cup-winner's medal with Ipswich. Just 12 months after buying him in 1974, Town boss Bobby Robson considered trading him to Millwall, along with £40,000, for Lions' goalkeeper Bryan King. Robson admitted:

Every manager looks around for ways of making his team better. You're never really satisfied with what you've got and you're always looking for ways of improving it. I've got to be honest and say that Paul had the odd flaw here and there, and I really fancied Bryan King as a 'keeper. But when it was time to take stock of the situation I decided against doing a deal and that decision didn't hurt us one bit.

---

wanted him to take a pay cut and that led to a parting of ways. He later joined Manchester City before moving to Stockport, where he finished his career.

Cooper's achievements as a rising star at St Andrew's paled into insignificance when compared to his roll of honour at Portman Road, where he was rarely out of the First Division's top six, in addition to the UEFA Cup-winning season, and played in Europe on a regular basis. Only by winning the title, or by representing his country, could his career have been any better, although he has no regrets as he looks back, not even at the absence of any Scottish, Irish or Welsh blood in his family, which might have enabled him to realise his international dream. There were times when he virtually had the home dressing room to himself, but he laughed: 'I got used to it – and my golf came on a bundle during those weeks because there was time for a game here and there.'

Golf figures prominently in Cooper's life now as he and second wife Sue have been based in Tenerife for more than 10 years, and their company, which helps remove the hassle from arranging golf facilities on the island, continues to go from strength to strength. He enjoys the leisurely pace of life out there and, apart from a number of corporate clients, he occasionally comes across Ipswich fans who are keen to reminisce about the part of his 22-year career that was spent in Suffolk. To them, he remains a hero. After all, there is no doubt he spent his best years with Ipswich, to the extent that he would almost certainly top a supporters' poll to name the best goalkeeper in the history of the club.

DAVID GEDDIS

FULL NAME: David Geddis
DATE OF BIRTH: 12 March 1958
PLACE OF BIRTH: Carlisle, Cumbria
IPSWICH TOWN APPEARANCES: 56
IPSWICH TOWN GOALS: 6

The records show that David Geddis made just two FA Cup starts for Ipswich – and one of them was at Wembley when he collected a winner's medal. Quite an achievement, especially when one considers the huge number of professionals who spend an entire career trying to scale such heights only to fall short, and the youngest participant in the 1978 Final knows how fortunate he was.

Geddis featured three times altogether in the competition during his time at Portman Road – he also came off the bench to score in a 6–1 fifth-round defeat of Bristol Rovers in February 1979. It should have been four because he was all set to line up against West Bromwich Albion in the semi-final, but he picked up a groin strain in training and failed a fitness test on the morning of the match. Geddis' only complete 90-minute appearance in 1978 was in the Final against Arsenal – he had been replaced by debut-making Tommy Parkin seven minutes from the end of the third-round win at Cardiff, so it was a remarkable feat to pick up a winner's medal after playing such a minor part in the tournament. Geddis earned his much-prized souvenir, though, and not just because it was his low centre from the right that led to Roger Osborne breaking the deadlock in a one-sided Final, just when the Town players and supporters were beginning to wonder if their dominance would be rewarded with a goal.

Geddis was absolutely essential to Ipswich's success because the team's innovative tactical ploy centred on him carrying out an unfamiliar right-flank role designed to nullify the attacking instincts of Arsenal left-back Sammy Nelson, identified by Town's spies as the player who instigated the majority of Arsenal's attacks. The fact that Bobby Robson entrusted the role to a youngster who had turned 20 just a few weeks earlier and who had limited first-team experience – just 19 senior starts prior to the Final – said a great deal about the faith the Ipswich manager had in him. Geddis' debut had been against Arsenal on the opening day of the season, when he had scored the only goal in front of a 30,000-plus crowd and the *Match of the Day* cameras, at a time when only two top-flight games were covered. Oddly enough, a torrential downpour during that match led to Leicester referee Roger Kirkpatrick taking the teams off for several minutes until he felt the game could continue, which was a tribute to the new drainage system the club had installed that close season. Fast-forward to Wembley on FA Cup Final day and it was equally soggy, whistler Derek Nippard later admitting that he had come far closer than anyone realised to calling it off. Maybe it was something about saturated surfaces that brought the best out in Geddis, who could never be accused of giving less than 100 per cent, as many seasoned defenders who found him difficult to contain would willingly testify. His raw aggression and willingness to take the bumps and bruises marked him as a difficult customer, around whom opponents found it difficult to relax.

It was around 48 hours before the Wembley kick-off that Robson pulled Geddis to one side and explained he had decided on his starting line up and confirmed he would wear the number 10 shirt that would have gone to Trevor Whymark had he been fully fit. Whymark, who was celebrating his 28th birthday as Robson delivered the news Geddis had been waiting to hear, had suffered torn knee ligaments in the Boxing Day derby with Norwich less than five months earlier and the medical experts warned he would probably be out for the rest of the season. The big striker, undoubtedly one of the best headers of a ball ever to play for the club, proved them wrong when he returned to action and scored in his comeback game, a reserve fixture against Reading, before Robson gave him an opportunity to show what he could do one week prior to the Final, in the 6–1 League defeat at Aston Villa. Although he scored his side's consolation goal, he was unable to convince himself, never mind the manager and his staff, that he should earn a Wembley place.

Geddis deputised for Whymark on a number of occasions that season – and was also chosen ahead of him on merit – so doing so at Wembley was nothing new, and it was typical of him that rather than fret about his new role in the side he actually relished it. He admitted:

The big thing was to hear from the boss that I was definitely playing. That helped to settle my nerves and when I heard the game plan I felt even better. I really liked the sound of it and I couldn't wait for the game to come round. Missing the semi-final was a massive blow: it would have been the biggest game of my career, yet here I was just a couple of days from playing in the FA Cup Final and as far as I was concerned back then it didn't get any bigger and better than that. It didn't take long for me to get over the groin strain and I was keeping my fingers crossed that I would get the nod for Wembley. But I couldn't take it for granted with Trevor trying to prove he was fully fit and Robin [Turner] had done his bit at Highbury, and in other games, so he clearly had a claim too. I was thinking to myself that I had time on my side so as to cushion the blow a bit if I wasn't picked for the Final. I tried to convince myself that if I didn't play this time there would be another chance but there was also a voice at the back of my mind saying 'That isn't necessarily the case.' Deep down inside, I knew that if I didn't play against Arsenal it didn't follow that I would have another opportunity later in my career. I also recalled how I had scored past Pat Jennings at Portman Road on the opening day of the season and how fantastic it would be to have a chance of doing it all over again at Wembley. In the end, of course, it was all about winning the game, and to play a part in setting up the winner for Roger was a great feeling in itself.

The tactics drawn up by Robson, with input from coach Bobby Ferguson, who had seen Arsenal on several occasions in a fairly short space of time, required Paul Mariner to operate as a lone striker through the middle with Geddis wide on the right and Clive Woods in his preferred slot on the left. Far from finding the task too daunting, Geddis' initial reaction was 'bring it on' or it would have been had that phrase been in vogue at the time. He said:

When the manager outlined his intentions I was thinking: 'Great, I really fancy this. It's right up my street.' I felt it took the pressure away. I would be facing the game most of the time and I felt confident I would be able to put my pace to good use out there. To be honest, I think I contributed more there than I would have done through the middle. Also, my toughest opponent in all my years in football, starting when we were up against each other in youth games, was Arsenal defender David O'Leary. He maybe didn't enjoy playing against me, either, but he always seemed to have the upper hand. So the change of tactics suited me fine. I might have struggled through the middle.

Geddis was not short of support, with an 11-strong family group cheering him on, which included his then girlfriend Christine – now his wife and mother to their two sons, Lorne and Ryan, and daughter Megan – not to mention almost 30,000 Ipswich fans shouting themselves hoarse to be heard above the sound of a similar number of red and white clad Arsenal followers. With his film-star looks – a tremendous physique and long, blond hair – he was a big favourite with the female fans, many of whom bombarded him with requests for pictures and autographs, and after Wembley he noticed a marked increase in the amount of fan mail that was waiting for him when he reported to the club for training each morning.

As he joined his colleagues in standing shoulder to shoulder with the Arsenal team to begin the march up the tunnel, Geddis had real purpose in his every stride. The words of skipper Mick Mills were also ringing in his ears, ensuring he was in exactly the right frame of mind for the challenge that lay ahead. He recalled:

Mick had told me to savour the moment; not just the game, but the build-up as well. He warned it would pass so quickly and he stressed the importance of being positive and not nervous. He said if I was overtaken by nerves my game would suffer and I would not enjoy it. I could hear his words echoing as I walked on to the pitch. I was determined to make the most of it. I thought to myself as the noise and the atmosphere hit me: 'If you can't do it here, you can't do it anywhere.' It was all so frenetic in the hour or so before the kick-off. I was one of the last out of the dressing room and we were in the tunnel, waiting for the signal to move, when I realised I had no shin pads or tie-ups with me. I raced back in to collect them with just seconds to spare. It was time for the business to start.

One week earlier, along with the other Town players, Geddis had been caught up in the mayhem of Villa Park when both he and Whymark were named in the starting line up. Manager Robson had thrown down the same challenge in a fairly forthright fashion to the pair of them. Geddis said:

They were trying to get Trevor fit after a lengthy absence and the atmosphere on the day wasn't right. It was tense and nervous. Paul Mariner was out with an injury but we all knew he would be okay for Wembley. The manager held up a shirt, looked at Trevor and I, and announced: 'There it is, now go out and fight for it.' I found that a strange management tactic, to be honest.

I knew he had a major dilemma, but they were strong words to a lad of my age and I felt they increased the pressure on me. I worked really hard in that game and felt I had done enough to warrant a place at Wembley. But Trevor, although short of fitness, had managed to score our goal in a 6–1 defeat. I convinced myself that his goal would deny me my reward, what I felt was justifiably mine. But I was delighted to be proved wrong five days later when the manager came and delivered the news I feared I might not be hearing.

It was the sale of Keith Bertschin to Birmingham City less than a year earlier that led to Geddis moving into the first team firing line as stand-by striker to both Mariner and Whymark, and it did not take him long to make his mark. Remembering his part in the all-important winning goal at Wembley he said: 'I just tried to create a crossing opportunity. I went on the outside, did a bit of a step-over and Sammy Nelson was wrong-footed. I hit the ball firmly and the greasy surface helped it on its way. Willie Young couldn't get his clearance away and the rest is history.'

Although Geddis went on to join Aston Villa a year later, winning a League Championship medal as his new club pipped Ipswich to the title in 1981, he does not have to dwell too long on the question of his number one career highlight. He said:

It would have to be the FA Cup Final. That was the single most memorable moment of my time as a player. I was on such a high after that. I couldn't sleep for two or three days. It was a truly amazing experience – the build-up, the game, the celebrations and then the journey back to Ipswich for the civic reception on the Sunday. I remember our reserve coach, Bobby Ferguson, drumming it into us beforehand. He said we would be famous if we won, our achievement would be featured in magazines and shown on television all round the world. He also reminded us: 'It will keep coming back.' He was right. You never forget something like that.

Part of the maturing process in football these days is for players to go out on loan from the top flight and play in the Championship, League One or League Two. First team football elsewhere is regarded as being more beneficial than playing for their own club's reserve side and even future England captain David Beckham did it in his youth, leaving Manchester United for a stint with Preston North End. It is regarded as a vital part of a player's education in the game but it is not a new concept and Geddis himself did it, enjoying a lengthy loan spell with Luton Town that brought him into contact with their number one fan, Eric Morecambe – one

> **CARLISLE CONNECTION**
>
> Nine of the 12 Ipswich players on duty at Wembley in 1978 were home-grown and two of them, David Geddis and Kevin Beattie, not only hailed from Carlisle but attended the very same school there. The third, Robin Turner, only narrowly missed out on a place in the side to face Arsenal but made five out of a possible seven appearances in the competition that season, including the semi-final against West Bromwich Albion at Highbury. All three were sent to Portman Road by full-time scout John Carruthers, who lived in Carlisle and was responsible for unearthing several other northern-based youngsters. Their involvement in winning the FA Cup for Ipswich led to Geddis, Beattie and Turner returning to Carlisle for a glittering ceremony that saw them granted the Freedom of the City.

half of the cherished comedy duo Morecambe and Wise. One of Geddis' most prized possessions is a letter he received from the showbiz star following the FA Cup Final. He said:

I had three months at Luton the previous season and Eric was a director there. Most of the time you wouldn't have known he was a comedian. The letter was dated Berlin 1941 and said: 'Great to see you on the box, old son. Many congratulations.' It was a lovely touch and I'll never part with the letter.

Geddis was one of many successful graduates of the Portman Road academy, although it was not called that in those days. He rejected an offer from Liverpool and instead went to Portman Road straight from school, helping Wembley colleague John Wark lift the FA Youth Cup after a two-leg Final against West Ham United in 1975. He said:

I have very fond memories of my apprenticeship there but I was right to leave when I did. I didn't have the quality to stay in the first team. I wasn't a technically gifted player but I was determined and I had pace. It was hustle and bustle, really, and I scored typical striker's goals rather than ones that stick in the memory. The time was right for me to leave. I could see the writing on the wall. I had made the England B team and didn't want to slide backwards. Alan Brazil had pushed his way through to challenge for a place, so it was the right decision from a professional point of view. I had six months as a first team regular at Villa, then they bought Peter Withe and I became the stand-in striker, but I still managed to score goals when I got the chance. In the 1980–81 season I scored four winning goals and that was worth eight points. It was ironic that we pipped Ipswich that year. They were one of the most entertaining teams around at that time.

Despite the fact that he opted to move on early in his senior career, there is no way Geddis will ever be forgotten at Ipswich after his leading role in the FA Cup triumph – a great example, surely, of someone being in exactly the right place at the right time. He said: 'I once heard Paul Daniels talking about that. He said you're not lucky, that you work hard for the opportunity. That's how I prefer to see it. I'd grafted before Wembley and when my chance came I made sure I grabbed it.'

Soon after the hullabaloo surrounding Town's success died down, Geddis was genuinely taken aback to be included in the England B squad to tour Singapore, Malaysia, Australia and New Zealand, completing a trio of FA Cup heroes alongside Brian Talbot, who was appointed skipper, and Paul Mariner. Current Norwich boss Glenn Roeder was also a member of the touring party. Club boss Bobby Robson was in charge of the soccer safari – even then, four years before he succeeded Ron Greenwood, the Football Association was grooming him for his future role as England manager. Geddis said: 'I was really amazed when I heard I had been selected because although I had won Youth international honours I hadn't won a single Under-21 cap and I'd have expected to play a couple of games at that level before being picked for the B squad.' The tour was scheduled to last almost four weeks and take in seven games, but Geddis developed back trouble after the first couple of fixtures and the injury was deemed serious enough for him to be packed off home to receive specialist treatment immediately.

Villa later paid £300,000 to sign him and he was with the Midlands giants long enough to add a European Cup-winner's medal to his impressive collection. Next stop was Barnsley, where one of his heroes, ex-Leeds and England hard man Norman Hunter, was in charge. After delivering just short of a goal every two games on behalf of the Tykes. Geddis moved on to Birmingham City, where his former Villa boss Ron Saunders was in charge, and he netted 13 goals in 22 games to help them win promotion back to the First Division. Spells at Shrewsbury, Swindon and finally Darlington followed before he called time on his playing career, and in June 1991 he was appointed as Middlesbrough's very first Football in the Community Officer, later also taking on responsibility for running the club's Centre of Excellence and grooming a number of future first team stars. He also worked as reserve coach at Newcastle when former Ipswich manager Bobby Robson was in charge and, after that, was part of Sven-Goran Eriksson's backroom team with England, clocking up lots of air miles in a role that required him to compile detailed reports on the national team's future opponents. That job ended when Eriksson stepped down after the World Cup in Germany in 2006, but Geddis did not have to wait too long for another opportunity at club level. He joined Leeds as their reserve coach and in October 2006, following Kevin Blackwell's departure from Elland Road, he became caretaker manager for one game only before new boss Dennis Wise assumed control. Two months later, just before Christmas, Geddis left the club.

In May 2006 millions of television viewers saw him assist ex-national boss Terry Venables in coaching an England celebrity team captained by singer Robbie Williams and also featuring television presenters Angus Deayton and Jamie Theakston, singer David Gray and actor Bradley Walsh. The showbiz stars, with football legends such as David Seaman, John Barnes, Tony Adams and Bryan Robson also onboard, defeated a World XI that included celebrity chef Gordon Ramsay and ex-Argentina star Diego Maradona 2–1 in front of a sell-out 72,000

David Geddis (right) and George Burley hold the FA Cup aloft during a lap of honour at Portman Road.

crowd at Old Trafford. The game was also screened live on television and helped raise £3 million for children's charity UNICEF, and during the build-up both squads went to 10 Downing Street to meet the Prime Minister, Tony Blair.

Another Prime Minister, Margaret Thatcher, who was actually Leader of the Opposition when she was a guest at the 1978 Final, was very impressed with Geddis' performance at Wembley. Delighted that the Blues had beaten the Reds, she was asked afterwards by Radio 2 to nominate her own Man of the Match. She replied: 'The Ipswich number 10, Trevor Whymark.' Poor Mrs Thatcher had not realised the change to the team printed in the match programme and it was, in fact, Geddis who had caught her eye. It was during a break in Ipswich's official banquet at the Royal Garden Hotel in London, that Geddis was finally given the seal of approval that meant a great deal to him. He explained:

I bumped into the reserve coach, Bobby Ferguson, in the gents' toilet of all places. Ever since I'd arrived at the club we hadn't hit it off. We both had fiery tempers and I had a number of run-ins with him. On one occasion I scored two goals for the reserves and the next morning he had a real go at me. One of the goals was a speculative shot, the type that if Ryan Giggs was to score it would look great. But Fergie obviously felt he had to bring me down a peg or two. He said it was a fluke and the more he went on about it, the more I bit back. He didn't like it and challenged me to a fight, complete with boxing gloves, behind the gym. There was always a flashpoint or two when he took a training session, but I still had the utmost respect for him as a coach. When I bumped into him in the gents I wondered what was going to happen, but I needn't have worried. He just said: 'Well done, son, you can call yourself a player now.' After what we had been through they were sweet words.

ALLAN HUNTER

FULL NAME: Allan Hunter

DATE OF BIRTH: 30 June 1946

PLACE OF BIRTH: Sion Mills, Northern Ireland

IPSWICH TOWN APPEARANCES: 355

IPSWICH TOWN GOALS: 10

(Photograph courtesy of Owen Hines)

Allan Hunter was up with the lark on 6 May 1978. He was scheduled to have a fitness test at 11am but there was no way the experienced central defender was going to delay it that long. At 7am he was wide awake, having been unable to sleep properly because of the fear of missing out, and within an hour he was downstairs in the restaurant of the team's St Albans hotel tucking into breakfast. With his patience approaching breaking point, he bumped into coach Bobby Ferguson and told him he was so desperate to learn his fate that he was going to change into his tracksuit and head for the hotel lawn to try out his suspect knee.

Manager Bobby Robson and his assistant, Cyril Lea, were summoned from their rooms, but most of Hunter's teammates were still asleep as the drama unfolded, although those who had stirred wasted little time in leaning out of their windows to shout encouragement at their inspirational colleague. Hunter remembered: 'I really did fear the worst, so much so that the previous evening I had even rung my wife to tell her I didn't think I would be playing. I wanted it over and done with. If I wasn't going to play, I at least wanted time to get drunk!'

As manager, coaches and a group of concerned colleagues looked on anxiously, the big defender did a few sprints then twisted and turned with the ball at his feet in as rigorous a workout as the limited facilities would allow. To his surprise he coped far better than he had dared to hope and smiled as he announced: 'I don't feel anything.' Robson calmly replied: 'Okay, you're playing' and the question mark against his availability was instantly removed. Hunter added:

The uncertainty that week had taken the edge off the build-up, which is such a big part of the occasion. But to finally know that I was definitely going to be playing made up for that. I was miserable all week leading up to Wembley because I genuinely didn't know whether I would be playing or watching from the bench or the stand. I didn't train at all because I was scared my right knee would puff up and that would be the end of me. On the Monday and Tuesday of Wembley week I didn't think I was going to make it but after the club doctor drained about a pint of fluid from my knee I gradually started to improve. I was nearly 32 at the time and knew it could be my last chance. If I'd been 22 my attitude might have been different and if I hadn't had the knee problem I'd have been confident about being the Ipswich centre-half for another two or three years.

Hunter boarded the bus three days before the Final and headed for the team's pre-Wembley base, not knowing how things would work out. He added:

We all agreed that I would have a test on the Saturday morning but I was so worried at the thought of failing it that I hardly got any sleep at all the night before. I was sharing a room with the captain, Mick Mills, because we had made a pact after the third-round win at Cardiff that we would continue to share all the way, hopefully, to Wembley. My usual room-mate at the time was Kevin Beattie but he was injured for the Cardiff game and once he was fit again I explained the situation to him. On the Friday night before Wembley I sat chatting with Millsy for a while and then he went to bed. But it was hours later before I turned in myself. I just sat there thinking about the next day and what it meant to me. My mind was in turmoil and it could have been Christmas Eve for all I knew. I must have smoked about 40 cigarettes to try to calm my nerves and I remember thinking: 'If I do play I'm not going to have any wind left.' I would say the FA Cup Final is the most wonderful occasion in a footballer's career and to think I almost missed out...I can't imagine what I would have been like if I'd failed that fitness test.

The memory of 1978 will live with every one of the Ipswich heroes until the day they die, but it could not have meant more to any player than the one they called Big Al. He added:

The FA Cup Final was a big, big thing in my life. When I was a kid at primary school I wrote an essay about what I was going to do when I grew up. I said that I was going to be a footballer, I would play for an Irish club, I would then move to England, I would go on to play for my country and I would play in an FA Cup Final.

To achieve this full house was no mean feat. Hunter quickly established a special place in the hearts of Ipswich supporters, becoming a cult favourite not only because of his 100 per cent commitment but also his extraordinary sense of fun. Whereas so many of today's 'pop star' footballers are distant heroes to their adoring public, Hunter was unaffected by success and stardom, regularly brushing shoulders with those who idolised him at a series of supporters' functions throughout his time at Portman Road.

Those who lament the fact that there are no longer any characters in the game may do so with Hunter firmly in mind. He enjoyed a special rapport with Town fans, who loved him for his eccentricity and were grateful that one of the most accomplished centre-halves in the game was playing for their club. If you were around at the time you will recall how the big defender would often try to clear what is now called the Cobbold Stand with at least one hefty clearance per match, or how the deftest piece of skill, perhaps unexpected from someone of his physique, would flummox an opponent and thrill the fans. Hunter, who completed an apprenticeship as a joiner before becoming a full-time footballer, said:

I never classed myself as any different to the guys on the terraces. I was an ordinary lad who just happened to be on the other side of the fence. I played darts at my local with a lot of them – doctors and dockers, even a vicar – and they were good to me. I hope I gave them something back on the pitch. In my view, football was to be enjoyed. When I went over to the crowd to collect the ball for a throw-in, I couldn't believe the hatred on opposing fans' faces. I didn't like that.

Hunter was voted Player of the Year by the Ipswich supporters in 1976 and two years later those same fans were in an apprehensive mood as they headed for Wembley and pondered whether he would be declared fit. No wonder they were thrilled when they eventually heard he had been given the all-clear to play – they knew his presence would count for a great deal. When they saw him make a full-blooded tackle on Arsenal striker Malcolm Macdonald in the early stages of the game, which earned him a ticking-off from referee Derek Nippard, the Ipswich faithful were in no doubt that he was up for the challenge.

A mere five minutes into the 6–1 League defeat at Aston Villa the week before, Hunter's pride would not allow him to quit after his knee appeared to give way. He said: 'In my mind I felt people would think I was just saving myself for the Final if I came off early, so

I stuck it out for the entire 90 minutes.' He dismissed the suggestion that so-called player power forced manager Robson into a drastic rethink of his Wembley plans and insisted:

It was nothing of the sort. I'll tell you why we were so awful at Villa – we were all in a state of shock. It was about an hour and a quarter before the game and we were in the dressing room when the boss named his team. Colin Viljoen was in and Roger Osborne was out. Roger was sitting on my left and I could see he was stunned. We all were. 'What's he [Robson] playing at?' we were thinking. One player said he wasn't going to give Viljoen the ball, but I won't hear the argument about player power. I can't explain it, but it wasn't player power. No way. I can vividly recall sitting in the Villa dressing room. We were knocked for six and I think we were still in a state of shock when we went out. We certainly didn't go out trying to prove a point to the manager or teach him a lesson. I felt sorry for young Paul Overton, our 17-year-old 'keeper. That was his one and only game for us and we let him down in a big way. That was the tragedy of it. I couldn't do myself justice because my knee went but I'm not using that as an excuse. I'll admit my mind wasn't on the game. I was thinking ahead seven days and wondering if I would be fit.

Hunter is of the opinion that Robson mishandled the situation, although he is quick to point out it was the only time he found fault with his management. He added: 'We had a good team spirit at the time and Roger was very much part of it. In my view the manager should have taken Roger to one side and had a word with him – but look how it turned out, with Roger getting the winner at Wembley. It couldn't have worked out any better and it couldn't have happened to a nicer lad.'

Town's tactic of playing David Geddis in a right-sided role worked a treat, not just because he created the chance from which the winning goal was scored. The youngster also curbed the attacking threat posed by Arsenal left-back Sammy Nelson, who had been identified by Town scouts as not only a key defender but the player who tended to get the Gunners moving upon receiving the ball short from goalkeeper Pat Jennings. Hunter was an international colleague of Nelson and remembers how he tried to console him after the final whistle at Wembley. He said:

I went over to him and I think I said sorry. He was actually crying like a baby – that's how badly it affected him – and I was thinking: 'That could have been me.' I like to think I wouldn't have done the same but I don't know. Afterwards, when we were on international trips together, I used to wind Sammy up. On one occasion we were in a hotel before a big game, and the other players had all gone out to the pictures. Sammy and I sat down to have a game of Scrabble. He was winning when I said: 'David Geddis sends his regards,' and it was all too much for Sammy. He kicked the whole lot up in the air. But Arsenal beat Manchester United the following year and both Sammy and Pat got their winner's medals, so things didn't work out too badly. After the 1978 Final, Pat told me in that deep voice of his: 'If I wasn't going to win it myself, I can't think of anyone better.' That was nice of him but also typical of the man.

Hunter can recall just about every kick of the Final and how he helped to calm the nerves of young teammate John Wark in the dressing room beforehand. He said: 'Warky was the type who would visit the toilet just before going out. He was a bit nervous and I just told him "If you weren't good enough for this you wouldn't be here".'

Hunter also remembers that after attending the official banquet, he went on to party until the early hours of Sunday morning, but was perfectly sober as he boarded the bus for the journey back to Ipswich just a few hours later. He added:

We were on our way up the A12 and I thought it would be a good idea if we stopped for a drink. I just felt it would be a bit embarrassing on the open-top bus parade if we weren't a bit merry. It would kill the atmosphere. I asked Millsy if he would have a word with the manager but he wasn't keen, so I went down to the front of the bus and asked him myself. He agreed that we would stop but insisted that everyone should have no more than two pints each. So we pulled into the Army and Navy at Chelmsford, where we regularly stopped on the way back from games in London, and we took the FA Cup in with us. I had my two pints and the boss paid for the whole round. But I also bought a bottle of vodka that I smuggled on to the bus. I sat on the back seat of the bus and shared it with a reporter from a national newspaper who had been invited to join us. If you look at the pictures that were taken at the time you can see I was under the influence. It was as if the whole of Suffolk had come to Ipswich for the day and it brought a lump to my throat. When Carol and I eventually got home we found the neighbours had decorated our house from top to bottom in blue and white. That was a nice touch.

Although his memory of the Final and all that surrounded it will never be extinguished Hunter believes he played his best-ever game for the club in the semi-final victory over West Bromwich Albion. He said:

A CHANGE OF HEART

Allan Hunter was relieved for two reasons – first that he passed that fitness test, and second that he was still an Ipswich Town player. In 1974 it seemed he was about to leave Portman Road when Leicester City's bid of £200,000 was accepted. Hunter travelled to the East Midlands to meet Leicester boss Jimmy Bloomfield to finalise the deal. The pair completed their discussion, so all that remained to conclude business was to complete the necessary paperwork. Suddenly, with the pen in his hand and the contract in front of him, the player had a change of heart, apologised to the Leicester officials and said his farewells. He later said: 'I just couldn't do it. As I went to sign the contract I began to realise how much I would miss Ipswich. It wasn't just the club but the town as well. It's a nice part of the country and we enjoy living here, which is something that not all First Division footballers can say.'

Hunter also decided against moving after the FA Cup Final when Chelsea, by then managed by his former Northern Ireland boss Danny Blanchflower, wanted him.

Beforehand I was a bit apprehensive. Not nervous, but just a bit tense because it was such an important game and there was such a lot at stake. Cyrille Regis had just hit the headlines about then and Albion were really fancied to beat us. I was happy with my game and we were 2–0 up when I made a hell of a mistake. The ball came over from the left and I knew I wasn't going to get my head to it. I thought Regis was right beside me and I thought he was going to get a free header. But I misjudged the distance. I thought I was about six yards out and he was bound to score. So I stuck my hand up and took a chance. Of course it was a penalty and they scored. For a while we were under pressure but then Warky scored our third goal and we were safe. I'll tell you how well I played that day – Clive Thomas was the referee and he congratulated me on my performance.

Hunter had a hunch that the 1977–78 season, while mediocre by Ipswich's high standards as consistent Championship challengers, would prove extra special for him, his colleagues and the club's supporters. Five months earlier, while dismantling the Christmas tree and packing up the decorations, the superstitious defender removed everything but a bell that was hanging from the ceiling. He said: 'My wife wondered what I was doing and I told her I would leave the bell there until we got to Wembley. Visitors to the house couldn't help but notice it and we had a few odd looks. But there was no way that bell was coming down until we'd played Arsenal.' Furthermore, throughout his playing career he adhered to a rather strange dressing room ritual that saw him don his kit in the same order, before half-tying the laces on his left boot. Next he would always tie the laces on his right boot before returning to the left to complete the job. There was no way he was going to risk deviating from the same old routine for the Final, which also included being last out of the tunnel behind manager Robson and the other players.

Hunter insisted that playing for Ipswich at the national stadium meant more to him than representing Northern Ireland there. He added:

> To play for your club at Wembley must be the aim of every professional and I was no exception. I didn't take our run too seriously in 1978 until we were drawn against Millwall in the quarter-finals and I realised we had a great chance. We all knew we couldn't expect an easy draw in the semis but I think we all had Wembley in the back of our minds and no one was going to stop us getting there. I wasn't just pleased for myself but also delighted for everyone connected with the club. There was such togetherness about the place that you felt like a member of a big family, from the directors all the way down.

More than 20 years had elapsed since he had watched his first Wembley showdown on television – Aston Villa's 2–1 defeat of Manchester United in 1957, when Peter McParland, a native of Northern Ireland, was the two-goal hero. Hunter said of the game: 'I remember thinking, as I sat and watched it, how great it would be to play in a game like that. It looked such a glamorous occasion and I couldn't believe my luck when my turn finally arrived.' Unlike most of his Ipswich teammates, he was no stranger to Wembley. In his very first appearance there in 1972, Northern Ireland defeated England 1–0 thanks to a goal from Terry Neill, who was in charge of Arsenal six years on.

Hunter remembers how Danny Blanchflower, his international manager and a boyhood idol, visited the Town hotel to interview him on behalf of an American television station. He said: 'I told Danny about my dilemma. I didn't believe in having injections, but he talked me into it. He said I could forget it if I was seven or eight years younger but he reminded me I was nearly 32 and wondered if I would ever get another chance.' The gamble paid off, even though Hunter's knee was twice its normal size after Wembley and he was ruled out of that year's home international series. He said:

At least that proved I was really injured. There was a lot of talk after the FA Cup Final that we had made up a lot of injuries but the facts speak for themselves. I managed to patch myself up to play against Arsenal but I couldn't play for Northern Ireland against England, Scotland and Wales, which I'd loved to have done. I also needed an operation in the close season and was absent from Ipswich's first 12 games of the 1978-79 season.

Hunter faded from the first-team scene after Wembley, making just 28 senior appearances in the four seasons that followed, but if his injuries took their toll his sense of humour never deserted him. He joked that he would know when it was time to call it a day – because Malcolm Macdonald would be able to get past him. He added: 'I'm only joking about Supermac really. It's just that over the years he always talked about what he was going to do but against Ipswich it never really worked out for him.'

Hunter bowed out in the 1981–82 season, being forced into action twice in the space of four days as several younger players were ruled out through injury. Having answered the club's SOS to play in the second leg of a League Cup semi-final against Liverpool, he retained his place for an FA Cup fifth-round tie at Shrewsbury that Town lost 2–1. He recalled: 'The game at Liverpool was amazing because the squad had gone up there the previous day and on the morning of the game I was out on the practice pitch when Charlie Woods came running out and said we had to leave for Anfield straight away.'

Town, who trailed 2–0 from the first game at Portman Road, were already without injured pair Russell Osman and Terry Butcher, while Kevin Steggles was also declared unfit for duty with a bout of conjunctivitis, drastically reducing the options available to manager Robson. Hence the late call to Hunter, who added with a grin: 'I was at least a stone overweight at the time and I'd had a few brandies the night before. Charlie and I only got up there about an hour and a half before the kick-off, which was hardly ideal preparation for facing Ian Rush and Kenny Dalglish. But we managed to draw 2–2 and, even though I say so myself, I played well.'

It was in 1971, after he had starred in the Home International Championship for Northern Ireland, that Hunter moved from Blackburn to Ipswich, disappointing First Division rivals Leeds United and Everton, both of whom had been keen to sign him. Interestingly, to this day, he and wife Carol still live in the same house they bought after first having to consult a road map to pinpoint the exact location of his new club.

The manager who signed him, Bobby Robson, nominated Hunter as his best-ever pound for pound purchase, adding:

I would have no hesitation in naming him as the pick of what I consider a very good bunch. He came at a vital time. I was trying to build the club. I wanted a top side playing in a top stadium – and I needed strong foundations. Allan, with his very presence, supplied them. He was an inspiration to others with his never-say-die attitude and he became the rock around which we built the side. It was Allan's fellow countryman, George Best, who had a lot to do with us buying him. George really turned it on at Portman Road one night as Manchester United beat us 3–1 and some supporters wanted me out. There was a board meeting the next day and I genuinely felt I might be sacked. But instead the chairman apologised for the behaviour of the fans and readily agreed to my suggestion that we should sign Allan. We needed to add a bit of steel to reinforce what we already had. Allan was always at his best when things weren't going well. He would roll up his sleeves, grit his teeth and tackle as if his life depended upon it. He loved a challenge and never backed off. And apart from his own performances, he deserves a great deal of credit for the way he helped other players. It all started with Kevin Beattie joining him in the side to form a wonderful partnership and towards the end of his time with us he was a father figure to the likes of Osman, Butcher and Steggles, all of whom benefited from playing alongside him.

Hunter treasures his many mementos from a glorious career with club and country, none more so than the FA Cup-winner's medal, which occupies pride of place among his souvenirs. He even feels a little hard done by the fact that he did not collect two winner's medals, because he believes Ipswich should have won the trophy three years earlier when they went out to eventual winners West Ham in a Stamford Bridge replay he missed because of injury. Eventually, all the wear and tear on his knees took its toll and he had no option but to take the advice of the specialist, who told him his time had come. Hunter recalled:

It was obvious something had to be done and I remember being very drowsy as the anaesthetic was wearing off and the surgeon told me he had removed 300 pieces of bone from the joint. When Carol came to visit me I told her what he had said. She thought I'd heard him wrongly and it was probably 30 pieces. But when she'd gone and I was feeling more awake I double-checked. The surgeon confirmed it was 300 pieces and even showed me a jar with some of them in it. They were just like flakes. After that, every game was a bonus.

MICK LAMBERT

FULL NAME: Michael Arnold Lambert
DATE OF BIRTH: 20 May 1950
PLACE OF BIRTH: Balsham, Cambridgeshire
IPSWICH TOWN APPEARANCES: 263
IPSWICH TOWN GOALS: 45

(Photograph courtesy of Owen Hines)

The place, Wembley Stadium; the precise location, towards the top end of the famous old tunnel behind the goal, leading from the dressing room area to the pitch. Several days prior to the FA Cup Final, Ipswich manager Bobby Robson was leading his players on the same route they would take before the head-on clash with Arsenal in English football's eagerly-awaited showpiece.

Robson had decided to take his squad on a recce of the national stadium and for several members it was a memorable first. The idea was to help familiarise them with the venue and hopefully to dispel any fears and inhibitions they might be harbouring ahead of the big day. The group was heading for daylight at the end of the tunnel when one player broke ranks and jogged ahead of the pack. Mick Lambert appeared to be displaying admirable enthusiasm, something which manager Robson was not slow to recognise. He beamed: 'Look at that, he can't wait to get out there. He wants to see the famous Wembley playing surface and who can blame him?' Lambert, by now sprinting as if trying to outpace an opposing full-back, closed in on the hallowed turf. But what happened next reduced each and every member of the party to uncontrollable laughter. Stopping short of the pitch, Lambert instead bent down to inspect an important piece of apparatus crucial to another sport hosted by Wembley – the artificial hare, without which there would be no greyhound racing.

Unknown to his manager and most, if not all, of his playing colleagues, Lambert was no stranger to Wembley, having visited the venue more than 100 times to indulge in one of his favourite pastimes. Therefore, the opportunity to have a close-up look at the hare was too good to miss.

As befits someone who enjoyed a day at the races – he was born and raised not far from Newmarket – Lambert loved to gamble, and on the day of the FA Cup Final, while enjoying breakfast with other members of the squad, he glanced at the morning newspapers and saw, alongside the various preview articles and pictures focusing on the players from both teams, the leading bookmakers' advertisements. They were meant to entice customers and it worked. Lambert remembered:

We were just looking through the papers and chatting when I spotted that we were being quoted at 5–2 to win the game. Basically, the bookies weren't giving us a chance. As far as they were concerned, we were wasting our time even bothering to turn up. We were underdogs by a mile. Well, we saw things quite a bit differently to that. We really did think it was our destiny to win the FA Cup that year. I wasn't the only gambler in the team and when the others saw the odds it was pretty much a case of 'Let's have some of that.' It doesn't sound much these days when players are earning a fortune but we all – pretty much all of us – decided to have at least £20 to win £50. We had no doubts about collecting our winnings. It seemed like too good a chance to miss, easy money if you like. I collected the cash in and then went off to phone the bet. The way I saw it, we were all on to a good thing. The manager, who wasn't a gambler, was in on it too. He was probably trying to demonstrate his confidence in us but I think the prospect of making an easy profit also appealed to him. It was as near to a certainty as you could get. That was the feeling within the squad. People might find it strange and wonder why we fancied ourselves so strongly, but we knew we were in a false position in the League and we were convinced we would beat Arsenal. When I went to the bookies on the Monday to collect our winnings it was a nice little bonus, but in all honesty I had been sure of the outcome all along and so were virtually all the players. There was absolutely no way we were going to lose that game.

Lambert had more reason than most to toast the club's Wembley success. Within little more than 48 hours of the trophy being presented to skipper Mick Mills, it was being paraded at Portman Road as the winger celebrated 10 years on the payroll with a testimonial game. The opposition was provided by a London all-star team skippered by his former teammate Bryan Hamilton, who captained a Millwall side trounced 6–1 at The Den by a rampant Town in an eventful quarter-final tie a couple of months earlier. Had Arsenal triumphed at the national stadium, the gamble of choosing that date for his benefit game might have backfired quite spectacularly and hit the player where it hurts most – in the pocket. However, he insisted: 'The main reason I wanted to win at Wembley was to pick up a winner's medal. I'm not saying I didn't appreciate the fact that winning the FA Cup put a few thousand on the gate for my game, but getting my hands on that medal really did mean more to me than the money. How do you put a price on something like that?'

Their FA Cup success apart, the 1977–78 season was one of Town's least memorable campaigns under Bobby Robson's management, as injuries impacted on their League form and saw them finish a lowly 18th in the table, a far cry from the top four finishes that had been the norm. Oddly enough, it was also a season in which Lambert failed to start a single First Division fixture, which was down to a combination of two things – his own injury problems and, when he was fully fit, the tip-top form displayed by his rival for the left-wing slot, Clive Woods, who peaked that season with a Man of the Match display at Wembley.

In the club's epic FA Cup campaign he started just one game, the fourth-round home victory over lowly Hartlepool, when a tactical switch by manager Robson saw Town operating with two wide men. His performance that day, allied to his solid contribution from the bench in other games, earned him the nod ahead of other contenders for the number 12 shirt in the Final. Robson might have gone for Russell Osman, handy to have in reserve as Allan Hunter or Kevin Beattie, both doubtful beforehand, were at risk of not being able to complete the 90 minutes. Or he might have opted for the attacking option provided by Robin Turner, who had done well in the semi-final and, in particular, at Bristol Rovers in the fifth round. But in the end the role of substitute went to Lambert, and it was probably the significant part he played in Ipswich's 3–1 semi-final defeat of West Bromwich Albion at Highbury, when he was thrown into the fray with just 18 minutes on the clock, that tipped the scales in his favour. With Brian Talbot, the scorer of the early first goal, unable to continue after suffering a nasty head wound, Lambert came on to patrol the right side of the field. He was given strict orders to stop the forward sorties of Albion left-back Derek Statham, who was earning a reputation as a future England star thanks not only to his defensive capabilities but also his marauding runs into enemy territory. Just as David Geddis performed a similar role in the Final, stifling the threat of Sammy Nelson going forward, Lambert did a tremendous job in preventing Statham overlapping and linking up with one of Albion's key players, Scotland left-winger Willie Johnston. Lambert said:

I was really pleased with the way I played in the semi-final after I went on. I think the fact that I had been used as a substitute so many times enabled me to get into games fairly soon after coming off the bench. You often hear players saying it takes time in that situation but I felt I had adjusted so well to the role that I was generally able to get straight into the game. I was made well aware of what I had to do defensively at Highbury that day. We were leading 1–0 when I went on and pretty soon after that Millsy scored a second goal. It would have been easy to think 'job done' but that could have been suicidal. We had to stay firmly focused and try not to let Albion back into the game. Statham was as much of a winger as a full-back in many ways so it was just a case of sticking with him as much as I could.

Albion got back into the game thanks to Tony Brown's penalty but John Wark's late goal made it 3–1 and there was no way back for Ron Atkinson's team as Ipswich booked their place at Wembley, the substitute helping to kill valuable time with some late, lengthy runs that stretched an already over-committed opposition defence. Once the final whistle had sounded, Lambert found himself recalling the events of three years earlier, when he and a number of Highbury colleagues had been on the wrong side of a semi-final result across London at Stamford Bridge. At the time he said:

Ever since the disappointment of losing to West Ham in 1975 I have believed in fate. We were easily the better side but we were just meant to lose – that's how I looked at it. I even think the result of the Final against Arsenal has already been decided. But I don't know the score and if I did, as a betting man, I would go off and earn a few bob.

Thirty years ago, before that infamous game, Lambert was in a bit of a sweat as to whether he would be involved at Wembley. He said:

I didn't really know what to think because a week beforehand, when the manager changed a few things and we lost 6–1 at Aston Villa, I was playing for the reserves. The boss had hinted I would be substitute in the Final but when I heard the score from Villa I wondered if it might change his thinking. For all I knew it might have been a case of back to the drawing board. The day before the Final, the boss mentioned it again but in all honesty it wasn't until the morning of the match that I knew for sure I was definitely going to be substitute. The BBC cameras were at our hotel and all the players were to be interviewed live. They had a room set aside for it and

12 seats with everybody's names on them. My name was on the one at the end of the line and that's how I found out for sure.

It looked as if sitting on the bench might be the sum total of his involvement at Wembley a few hours later – but Roger Osborne's unexpected reaction to finally breaking the deadlock changed all that. He recalled:

As far as the game itself is concerned, the events of 1978 are a bit of a blur. In fact it's almost as if it didn't happen. As the substitute you don't feel totally involved when you are sitting on the bench. It's only when you get the chance to go on that you begin to feel a part of what's happening. When we got to the stadium and went up the tunnel to have a look at the pitch, I found all that a bit nerve-racking. My legs turned to jelly, I remember, but other than that I was fine and I was soon feeling normal. I got settled in and it felt like we were on a day out. I remember getting changed into my kit and as we were leaving the dressing room to line up in the tunnel I said to someone: 'What's all the fuss about?' I was joking, of course, but I suppose it showed how relaxed we were. The mood was really upbeat with no real sign of nerves. At least, if anyone was nervous they were doing a good job of not showing it. Once we were out there and the game got going I think it showed that the Ipswich players were in a very positive frame of mind. As I sat on the bench and we dominated the game, I was just like everybody else in wondering when we were going to make our superiority really count with a goal. When it happened I had no idea it would affect me the way it did. I'd be lying if I said I wasn't hoping to get on – of course I was. Like I said, that is when you really feel involved, when you get the chance to go on and do your bit. We were so much on top that I would have had no argument if I hadn't been called upon. But Roger being Roger, I got my chance. He's such an honest bloke and it was typical of him to admit he was struggling. Other players would have been reluctant to come off in such a big game but not him. He knew it made sense for some fresh legs to be brought on because he was just about running on empty by then and some of the others were feeling the pace. I suppose I had about 15 minutes or so with injury time, not long but long enough to feel involved. I was quite lucky in that I saw a fair bit of the ball. I had no specific instructions but I remember John Wark dropped a bit deeper and I was like an old fashioned right-half, a position completely new to me. I ran around a bit, and although it was only 15 minutes I would have to say it was the highlight of my career. I played a lot of games for the club – a lot of big games, too, like Real Madrid in the Bernabeu Stadium, when we outplayed them, got a 0–0 draw and marched on in Europe. But it's true what people say – nothing can beat the FA Cup Final as

Substitute Mick Lambert enjoys his appearance in the FA Cup Final as he gets the better of Arsenal opponent David Price.

an occasion. It was a fabulous feeling to win, so different to how we had felt when we lost the semi three years earlier. It wasn't just the game, either. There was the banquet that night, the journey home, the amazing scenes in the town when we went to the civic reception in the open-top bus and so much more besides. I also had my testimonial, so it was absolutely perfect. It was an unbelievable way to end a season that had looked like being instantly forgettable.

I was struggling with a pelvic injury and missed about three months of it. It's typical of football – you are about as low as you can get for a while and then everything comes right and you are on an incredible high. You appreciate the good times all the more if you have had a few down periods and, to be honest, I'd had more than my fair share of being injured. The 1976–77 season was a bit of a wash-out because as soon as I got over an injury and regained my place in the side I would get injured again. In the summer of 1977 I was told to do absolutely nothing in the hope that things would settle down. It seemed to work and I definitely felt better for it. A week before we reported back for pre-season training I did some road-running and everything was looking good. The way I was feeling then I was confident of putting up a fight for the number 11 shirt. But I picked up a groin strain during our pre-season trip to Holland and although I played in a friendly at Millwall I started the season in the reserves. That was frustrating enough but then things got even worse when I was training one day. I was suffering from severe pains at the bottom of my stomach and it made me double up in agony. Being out for those three months with the pelvic injury meant it was anything but easy forcing my way

WEMBLEY REGULAR

Although his love of greyhound racing took Mick Lambert to Wembley on numerous occasions, he was one of the few members of the 1978 Ipswich squad to have previous FA Cup Final experience of the national stadium. He recalled:

I went there in 1971 to see Arsenal play Liverpool, when it went to extra-time and Charlie George scored the winning goal. I know it sounds corny but I was a professional footballer myself by then and I remember thinking: 'Wouldn't it be great if I could play in a Final one day?' In 1978 it was such a relief to hear I would be on the bench. I would have been the most disappointed person in the world if I had not been selected because I genuinely believed I had earned my place. These days you have five substitutes and if it had been like that 30 years ago I wouldn't have had any cause for concern. We'd have been hard-pushed to fill the bench but when there was only one you couldn't take anything for granted.

Lambert also went to Wembley to see several England international games, including the World Cup semi-final win over Portugal in 1966, little realising that he would one day retrace the steps of Alf Ramsey's heroes on the very same pitch.

back into the team. In fact, the nearest I got to a run was when I became a sort of permanent substitute towards the end and the boss kept me there for the Final.

Lambert hoped to leave his injury problems behind when he and his family headed off to Canada in the summer of 1978. With Ipswich's blessing, he was to play for Vancouver Whitecaps in the North American Soccer League then return to England having made up for lost time and reap the benefit of a full campaign with the side where Bobby Robson had cut his managerial teeth more than a decade earlier. Alas, a torn hamstring put paid to that idea and he flew back well ahead of schedule with strict orders to rest ahead of his 12th season as an Ipswich player. But the 1978–79 campaign, in which he started just one game and appeared as a substitute on a further four occasions, turned out to be his last and he was sold to Peterborough for a fee of £40,000.

Lambert certainly had no regrets about deciding to put football ahead of his other sporting love, cricket. Having played for Cambridge City and Newmarket Town, where Ipswich were first attracted to him, he was signed on amateur forms at a time when he was also on the ground staff at Lord's, and his first professional football contract was actually addressed to him at the home of cricket. Lambert has the unique distinction of being 12th man in both an FA Cup Final and a Test match, when England met the West Indies at Lord's, a feat so rare that it is unlikely ever to be equalled. He added:

> They said I was the best fielder on the ground staff and made me substitute while the others went back to their counties. I would have been involved had someone picked up an injury, although I was never going to bat or bowl. But no such luck. I was only called into action once, when I took the drinks out. I remember Ray Illingworth was the England captain but I've forgotten who won the match. I do recall meeting Muhammad Ali, though, or plain Cassius Clay as he was then, in the West Indies' dressing room.

Lambert was a natural at just about every sport, representing his native Cambridgeshire at tennis and playing for both the Middlesex and Essex second XIs before turning to football for a living. A tad ungainly on the pitch, owing to an unusual running action, there was no questioning Lambert's effectiveness when he was in full flight and it was a real luxury for Ipswich that they had two such effective left-wingers from which to choose. As a bonus, both Lambert and Clive Woods could also operate through the middle. While Woods possessed numerous tricks and could send a full-back the wrong way with a sway of his hips, Lambert was more direct and preferred a pass inside the defender, at which point he would more often than not show him a clean pair of heels and get close to the by-line before delivering a cross into the middle. That is not to say he did not have dribbling skills of his own, and he was also a key figure in a well rehearsed throw-in routine that, despite being repeated on a regular basis year after year, never ceased to be effective and paved the way for a remarkable number of goals.

There is a new in-phrase 'impact player' that refers to those who consistently change the course of a game when they are introduced from the bench. In Lambert's time, they were plain old-fashioned substitutes, but he was similarly a useful weapon to be able to call upon.

Always unassuming throughout his sporting career, Lambert remains the same down-to-earth individual now, grateful for what his sporting prowess earned him. Rather than measure his success in financial terms, he would far rather point to the FA Cup-winner's medal he cherishes and which consistently prompts a host of happy memories.

Paul MarineR

FULL NAME: Paul Mariner
DATE OF BIRTH: 22 May 1953
PLACE OF BIRTH: Bolton, Lancashire
IPSWICH TOWN APPEARANCES: 339
IPSWICH TOWN GOALS: 135

(Photograph courtesy of Owen Hines)

It would be hard to imagine a more complete centre-forward – or striker, if you prefer – than Paul Mariner, which makes it all the more puzzling that it took him so long to make his mark in the game. He was in good company, mind. England aces Ian Wright, Malcolm Macdonald, Les Ferdinand, Stuart Pearce and Garry Birtles all had something in common with him as products of non-League football who graduated with honours, of the international kind, that is.

Mariner quickly compensated for the 'wasted' years playing non-League for Chorley and, to a lesser extent, Plymouth in both the Third and Second Divisions, the stage at which Bobby Robson and a host of other managers were alerted to the fact that the time had come to give him a top-flight chance.

Within five months of signing for Ipswich he was called up by England, a Wembley full house virtually demanding his introduction off the bench in a World Cup qualifier against Luxembourg, which resulted in a comfortable 5–0 home win. Next time out, in a home international against Northern Ireland in Belfast and with Portman Road colleague Allan Hunter in direct opposition, Mariner was in from the start. He went on to win a total of 35 senior caps, only two of them coming after he joined Arsenal in February 1984, and scored 13 goals. It is just as well the squad numbering system was not in operation at the time because no shirt other than number nine would have suited him.

PANIC BUTTON

It was the eve of the FA Cup Final when Paul Mariner pressed the panic button – but it had nothing to do with the game against Arsenal the following day. The reason for the star striker's anxiety concerned the fact that he might have to stand out from the rest of his teammates on the biggest day of his career. Mariner was having a 'dress rehearsal' when he discovered that the zip on his trousers was broken and it seemed too late to do anything about it. Luckily, the receptionist at the team's hotel came to the rescue. She heard of Paul's plight when a club official asked if she might know anyone who could help. 'I can,' she replied. 'I can take the trousers home with me tonight. My mother's a seamstress and will sort it out, and I'll bring them back here before breakfast in the morning.' The receptionist was true to her word, sparing Paul's blushes so that he was able to wear the same blazer-and-trousers outfit as the other members of Town's official party.

Mariner's best years were undoubtedly at Ipswich, and the Town supporters took to him straight away, although given his initial impact it was probably more a case of him instantly winning them over.

Crucial to the club's FA Cup win at Wembley in 1978 was an innovative tactical system designed to frustrate Arsenal and prevent influential midfielder Liam Brady dictating play. Brady was a player Ipswich's chief scout, Ron Gray, tried but failed to sign as a schoolboy in his native Dublin. While David Geddis was cast in a right-sided role to counter left-back Sammy Nelson, a launching pad for many of Arsenal's attacks, and Roger Osborne was charged with the task of man-marking Brady, the plan would have been at risk of falling apart had Mariner not possessed all the attributes necessary to operate through the middle as a lone striker.

Under normal circumstances Bobby Robson would have unleashed the strike partnership of Mariner and Trevor Whymark on Arsenal, but a long-term injury to the latter and his subsequent failure to regain full fitness in time prompted the rethink. In the games they did play together, the double act was as prolific as any around at the time, and who could possibly forget the first time they teamed up at Portman Road against West Bromwich Albion? Mariner's debut had come seven days earlier in a 1–0 win at Manchester United, when he played a part in Clive Woods' goal, but no one could have anticipated the outcome against the Baggies. Ironically, they were one of the sides keen to prise Mariner away from Plymouth and their failure to do so bitterly disappointed manager Johnny Giles. The former Leeds midfielder was even more down in the dumps after seeing Mariner make a dream home debut, helping to destroy his team in a 7–0 humiliation and linking with Whymark as if the pair had been buddies for years rather than just a matter of days. While Trevor helped himself to four goals, his new sidekick had to be satisfied with one.

Mariner's transfer fee was £220,000, a record for Ipswich, comprising a £100,000 cheque and two players, defender John Peddelty and striker Terry Austin, who were valued at £120,000. Plymouth also received a further £20,000 after he clocked up three full international appearances, and Town were only too delighted to hand over the extra cash. Mariner was a tad uneasy about the attention that accompanied his arrival in the big-time and he admitted: 'Yes, I was a little bit embarrassed to be transferred for that amount of money. I had come from a background where I had to work very hard for a living and I knew what it was like for the lads going into the factories.' His former life, working shifts as a fitter at a tin can factory, had evidently instilled in Mariner the attitude that helped fire him to international stardom as a footballer. Without the application to supplement his skill he could have fallen short and drifted backwards, but instead he rocketed right to the very top as one of the leading members of a star-studded Ipswich side.

Mariner's capture plugged the gap caused by David Johnson's sale to Liverpool in the summer of 1976 and, despite reservations about the size of the fee, he seemed at home from day one in his new surroundings. He was utterly unpretentious in those days – when he first arrived he drove a Mini that had seen far better days – and he quickly settled in rural Suffolk, never happier in his spare time than when attending auctions throughout the county or organising bus trips to the Chelsea Flower Show in his role as president of the village gardening club. However, he had a fascinating mix of interests and also loved heavy metal music, later striking up a friendship with former Deep Purple front man Ian Gillan that saw the pair team up on stage, not just in Ipswich but at the Hammersmith Odeon in London. People in the audience could hardly believe their eyes at seeing Mariner in the background on the bongos.

By his own admission, Mariner changed – or allowed stardom to change him. Years later he reflected:

I got a little bit carried away with myself early on because I was going so well it was unbelievable. I started to believe my own press, which is one of the worst things you can do. They build you up to knock you down in England and I was in the process of being built up and built up. When I was 25 I was at my worst. I didn't like myself back then. You know, you're young and you have an opinion. You think you know everything about the game and you don't. It came down to one or two sensible teammates, senior players, who had a word with me. They just said: 'You've got to give and take a little bit.'

Mariner's 25th birthday was just 16 days after Ipswich won the FA Cup, a game in which he almost opened the scoring after just 11 minutes but instead saw his effort strike the crossbar, setting a somewhat worrying trend that continued until Roger Osborne provided the precious winner. It frustrated him that he did not find the net and he recalled: 'It came very early and I still kick myself for not putting it away. Clive Woods squared the ball, Roger got a touch and it spun into my path. I had to act quickly and as I stretched to make contact I was leaning back to keep my balance. I just knocked it a bit too high, only by an inch or two, and it came back off the bar.'

Mariner can remember a great deal about the big day, starting when the two teams were called from their dressing rooms by referee Derek Nippard and stood shoulder to shoulder in the tunnel, in readiness for the short walk into the arena in full view of their fans and millions of television viewers around the globe. He said:

*I was at the back with Allan Hunter and Malcolm Macdonald, who was an amiable sort of guy, was right next to us. Malcolm leaned over and said to Allan in a really nice voice: 'good luck this afternoon,' and I thought to myself 'what a nice gesture'. But the big man just looked back and sort of growled as he replied: 'I'm going to break your f*****g leg.' Now Big Al wasn't really that nasty – he's a great bloke – but there was no way he was going to lose that game! There's another funny story about Willie Young. By the time I joined Arsenal, Big Willie had moved on. But he was still close to the club and he was at Highbury one day. I'd never bumped into him since the Final and he popped his head into the dressing room. He saw me and said: 'Bloody hell, not only does he take the piss at Wembley but he comes here and takes my bloody peg as well.'*

Mariner has little doubt that the tactical ploy devised by Town had a lot to do with the result at Wembley, adding:

GREAT GOALSCORERS

Had Paul Mariner's 11th minute shot in the FA Cup Final not struck the bar and instead hit the back of the net he would now be alongside Tom Garneys as the club's joint highest scorer in the competition. Garneys, unfortunate to have his career interrupted by World War Two, was at Portman Road for eight years after signing from Brentford in 1951. He went on to make 273 appearances and scored 143 goals, 20 of them in the FA Cup – one more than Wembley hero Mariner.

Garneys never scored more than twice in an FA Cup tie, while Mariner claimed a hat-trick in the 6–1 quarter-final win at Millwall at the quarter-final en route to his 19-goal total. The pair had something else in common – they both scored on their FA Cup debuts for Ipswich. Garneys netted once in a first-round tie at Merthyr Tydfil in November 1951 and Mariner struck at the double in a third-round home clash with Bristol City in January 1977. The best FA Cup scoring performance in a game was by Fred Chadwick in November 1938, when he scored four times in Town's 7–0 first-round home win over Street.

You have to give credit to Bobby Robson and his coaches, Cyril Lea and Bobby Ferguson, for devising the master plan. And the players did really well, not only in the way they carried out the instructions on the day but for the way they took it all onboard in just a few days leading up to the game. We had never played that system before but it was just perfect, with everything going according to plan – eventually.

The FA Cup victory came just 18 months after Mariner convinced himself that of the three clubs leading the race for his signature, Ipswich would be the best bet, with Robson painting a perfect picture of how he wanted his career to develop away from the bright lights. Mariner said:

At the time I joined I firmly believe Ipswich were the best-run club in the country. I could have gone to West Brom or West Ham but Ipswich were really flying at first-team level and they had a fabulous youth system churning out good players. To begin with I was a bit in awe of the place. I looked around me and saw all the top internationals, people like Mick Mills and Kevin Beattie, and it was difficult to grasp that they were teammates of mine. I was driving my battered old Mini and I suppose I was a bit embarrassed about it. But then I saw Kevin drive in one morning in an old Jeep-style vehicle that had the back end hanging off. He jumped out, said hello and asked if I fancied joining him in the groundsman's hut under the stand for a cup of tea. That's when I knew I had nothing to worry about. I hit it off with Trevor Whymark big time and it was unbelievable how well things went for me right from the word go. I knew I'd made the right choice and it turned out to be the perfect move. I got into the England team, scored the only goal against Hungary that got us to the World Cup Finals in Spain in 1982, and I also scored over there. Winning the UEFA Cup was fantastic – we turned in some great performances along the way, especially over in St Etienne – but you can't really beat going to Wembley for the FA Cup Final and picking up a winner's medal. You're aware of it being special at the time but later in life it dawns on you just how big an occasion it was. When I think back to us in the tunnel before the kick-off the memories come flooding back. There was the incident with Big Al and Supermac, then we came out at the end where our fans were packed in. As we came up the tunnel, all we could see was the Arsenal crowd but as we actually emerged from the tunnel and we looked

Paul Mariner on the attack in the FA Cup Final.

behind us it was just blue and white everywhere – and what a noise. You know that saying about the hairs on the back of your neck standing up? It's absolutely true. That's exactly how it was. This wall of sound hit us. It reached a crescendo as we came out and it seemed to hit us in the back of the head. We all felt about 10 feet tall and with the Arsenal supporters being at the other end, about 150 yards away, I think that gave us a little jab to take it to them, which we did.

With the FA Cup in the bag, Mariner became the subject of extensive speculation suggesting he would make a big-money move away from Portman Road. But that all ended when Robson and the Ipswich board of directors got their heads together and drew up a more lucrative deal to run over the next six years, to which the player was quick to add his signature. Apart from ensuring Mariner stayed put, it was also a statement of intent on the club's part that they envisaged further success over the period of his new contract. Mariner added:

I was reading the papers just like everyone else and I saw the stories linking me with just about every top club in the country. But what they seemed to forget was that I was already with a top club. I believed the FA Cup win was just the start and that Ipswich would be in the forefront of football for the next few years, so I had no problem signing the contract. I achieved a great deal in the game, especially in my time with Ipswich – more than a lot of top pros at so-called bigger clubs. Back in 1978 I had a hunch it would be our year. We got through against Cardiff and Hartlepool then we had a difficult time down at Bristol. We equalised late on and I was thinking: 'Somebody up there likes us.' From then on we never looked back – everything pointed to us winning the FA Cup. We had to work for it and no more so than at Wembley. We were all close to collapsing – and that was just at half-time. It was so humid out there with the sun beating down on us. The turf was wet after a lot of rain and it was sapping all our energy. It wasn't really surprising that Roger Osborne was overcome by the conditions because he had done a lot of running about that day. I couldn't quite believe it at the end. A few years earlier I'd have been sitting watching the FA Cup Final at home with my parents and I'd joke: 'Wait until I'm out there,' because it was just about the last thing I expected would happen to me.

At that time Mariner was playing part-time football for Chorley in the Cheshire league and working full-time on about £35 a week in a factory manufacturing tin cans, predominantly for Heinz and leading soft drinks companies. He wore a navy blue boiler suit and perfected a lot of his skills during lunchtime kickabouts with workmates, little realising how his life would change when Plymouth gave him his big chance at the age of 20. Even then, however, he never dared to think too far ahead. Mariner added:

I suppose I had what is commonly known in the business as a meteoric rise to fame. I had some great times at Plymouth, where I played up front with a lad called Billy Rafferty and we scored a few goals together. But Ipswich was a different world and it gave me access to another world with England. In my first season at Ipswich we were close to winning the title. We were third on the same points as Manchester City and one behind Liverpool. When we got to Wembley in 1978 it reminded me of a hat-trick of ambitions I'd had for a few years. In my Chorley days I wanted to get into the Football League, then after that I set my heart on playing in a Cup Final at Wembley and playing for my country. The first time I ever went to Wembley was as a member of the England squad for that qualifier against Luxembourg. I played the whole of the second half and the place was everything I expected it to be – very, very special.

Earlier in the 1977–78 season he had mentioned his ambition to play at Wembley through the popular *Paul's Postbag* column he wrote in the matchday magazine. Seven-year-old fan Jason Fulcher of Shamrock Avenue, Ipswich, had asked Mariner to name his dream come true, and he replied: 'My dream come true would be to line up with Ipswich at Wembley in a Cup Final, either FA or League.' Within eight months the dream was realised.

Mariner took hardly any time to emerge from his shell once he became an Ipswich player. He soon ditched the softly-softly approach to display his true colours as an infectious personality with a wicked sense of humour, as his new teammates were quickly able to testify after falling victim to his dressing room pranks and jokes. His brashness also helped to while away the hours on the many wearisome coach trips they had to undertake in those days. More than anything, the Ipswich management, playing staff and supporters warmed to Mariner the footballer, someone who grafted non-stop, not just in games but also behind the scenes as he worked endlessly on honing his skills to become the country's best all-round striker. He said:

In my first season at Ipswich I realised I still had a fair way to go. The pace of the game was what I noticed most when I moved into the First Division. I had always been one of the faster players at Plymouth but when I arrived at Portman Road I was really astounded at the speed of some of the lads, especially Kevin Beattie and Paul Cooper. I used to put in extra hours of sprint training and I soon felt the difference. I was always trying to improve my time over 100 yards and I used to team up with Roger Osborne to help improve my finishing. He would send crosses into me at different heights and I tried to get shots or headers on target. I think we both benefitted from these sessions because Roger had a good run that season and the next one, of course, was even better for him.

Mariner regards his first goal, in the 7–0 battering of West Bromwich Albion, as the best of the 13 he scored in 31 League and Cup games in the 1976–77 campaign. Just as Albion's boss Johnny Giles was made to rue his failure to sign the player, the West Ham management duo of Ron Greenwood and John Lyall must have felt the same when their team was hammered 4–1 and Mariner helped himself to his first Ipswich hat-trick. He also scored the only goal in the home win over eventual champions Liverpool, rising above visiting captain Phil Neal to power in an unstoppable header, which confirmed his outstanding aerial ability, but he proceeded to tell reporters afterwards that when he started as a professional with Plymouth he was warned that to be a successful striker he would have to learn to head the ball from scratch. He explained: 'At first I would keep my eyes closed and not get any power behind it, but constant practice helped me to improve.'

[Photograph courtesy Offside Sports Photography Ltd]

Paul Mariner points the way to FA Cup success over favourites Arsenal.

> ### BOOTS IN THE CUPBOARD
>
> As he climbed the steps at Wembley to collect his winners' medal, Paul Mariner could not help but cast his mind back more than a decade. He remembered how his local club Bolton Wanderers had taken an interest in him at the age of 14. Since he was a terrace regular at Burnden Park – the Reebok Stadium was still a long way off in those days – he was keen to sign. He recalled: 'My school teacher advised me against it. According to him I would get a better offer from a bigger club.' But the opposite happened. The scrawny youngster seemed to stop growing and his prospects of being taken on by a top professional club nosedived as a result. He recalled:
>
> *I was being brushed aside in school games. Word soon got round that I wasn't going to be big enough for the senior game. I began to believe it and actually packed in football. For a whole year my boots stayed in the cupboard and I got more into cricket. Then a local youth side asked me to play because they were short of players.*
>
> The team included Micky Walsh, who went on to play for Blackpool, Everton and QPR, and they made a clean sweep of local honours. That was when Chorley came in for Paul, then later moves to Plymouth and Ipswich catapulted him into the England team. 'Thankfully, when I quit playing I didn't throw my boots away,' he laughed, 'or my career might never have happened.'

So to the 1977–78 season, when Town toiled in the League as they struggled to cope with a crippling injury list. Thankfully, Mariner was absent far less than several other key players and claimed the crown of top marksman with 22 goals, seven of them coming in the FA Cup as he was one of five stars who were ever present in the club's successful, seven-game campaign. His haul included a hat-trick in the 6–1 demolition of Millwall at the quarter-final stage, but his failure to find the net in the semi-final at Highbury, the ground that was to become his home, meant Mariner could not become a member of the rather exclusive 'scored in every round of the competition' club. Unselfishly, he was more interested in what he achieved as a team member rather than as an individual. He said:

Of course it would have been nice to have got goals in every round and I wouldn't be normal if I said I hadn't thought of scoring in the Final, and I nearly did. When I didn't get one in the semi I said I was saving it for Wembley. But it didn't matter who scored, as long as we won the Cup. I actually believed we might have the edge against Arsenal because I felt we had more players capable of scoring than they did. It was great how it turned out because Roger was not a prolific scorer – the goal that won the game was only his second that season – but there wasn't a more popular lad in the dressing room.

Of the 12 players on duty on that unforgettable day in 1978, Mariner was one of the very last to leave the club, moving to Arsenal for £150,000 in February 1984, his last game coinciding with the appearance of 16-year-old Jason Dozzell from the bench, who was still a pupil at the town's Chantry High School. Mariner had been on the transfer list for four months and only the club's financial plight at the time prompted them to sanction the deal. Mariner later claimed he was looking for an extra £10,000 a year and that leaving the club saddened him as he would have preferred to finish his career there, but at least the Ipswich fans had seen the best of him. After scoring 17 goals in 70 games for Arsenal, he moved on to Portsmouth where he helped them to win promotion back to the First Division after a 30-year absence. He then played in Malta and in 1988 was lured to the US, first with Albany Capitals in New York and most recently as assistant to ex-Liverpool and Scotland star Steve Nicol, head coach of Major League Soccer team New England Revolution, based in Foxborough, Massachusetts.

Remarried in 1996, bespectacled and close to his 55th birthday, his hair longer than when he first arrived at Ipswich almost 32 years ago, Mariner helped the Revs to victory over Dallas in the 2007 US Open Cup, but also suffered the disappointment of losing the MLS Championship – or MLS Cup as it is known Stateside – to Houston for the second year in a row.

Only Ray Crawford, whose goals helped Ipswich win the Second Division title in 1961 and then, to the amazement of the football world at large, the First Division crown just 12 months later, can come close to being compared to Mariner as the club's all-time best striker. Crawford won two England caps to Mariner's 35, but he did collect that League Championship medal while Mariner can only claim to have come close helping Town to runners-up finishes in both 1981 and 1982, and third place in 1977 and 1980.

It would be no exaggeration, nor would it provoke too much in the way of argument, to say that of the England strikers to have emerged since Mariner was first choice, only Alan Shearer compares, and while the ex-Newcastle man's scoring record speaks for itself, there were aspects of his game in which he was second best to the former Ipswich star.

Mariner also has the proud distinction of having matched the great Jimmy Greaves' record of goals in six successive England games, an achievement he clinched on the very highest stage – the 1982 World Cup Finals in Spain, in the 3–1 win over France. The side, skippered by his Ipswich captain Mick Mills, returned unbeaten in five games but still failed to make it into the semi-finals.

The previous year, of course, Mariner helped Ipswich to success in the UEFA Cup, scoring six of his 26 goals for the season in that competition. He was also third behind John Wark and Frans Thijssen in the PFA Player of the Year poll. Add his achievements with the Three Lions on his chest and it was quite a career, although he is adamant that nothing even comes close to the feeling of being an FA Cup winner at Wembley.

MICK MILLS

FULL NAME: Michael Dennis Mills
DATE OF BIRTH: 4 January 1949
PLACE OF BIRTH: Godalming, Surrey
IPSWICH TOWN APPEARANCES: 741
IPSWICH TOWN GOALS: 30

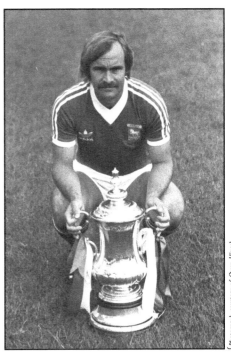

(Photograph courtesy of Owen Hines)

Mick Mills would not have been alone in reacting incredulously to the comments attributed to Dave Kitson on the subject of the FA Cup as third-round day approached. When the Reading striker insisted he didn't care' about a competition that will always be close to the heart of the former Ipswich captain, his dismissive and disrespectful views must also have made the blood of many an ex-professional soar to boiling point. Sadly, Kitson's opinion is probably shared by the majority of modern-day footballers, while a growing number of leading managers are also responsible for helping to remove the gloss from the most famous old trophy of them all. Kitson's views, expressed during the build-up to the Royals' third-round trip to Tottenham, angered Mills – a member of the select and distinguished group of Cup-winning skippers and a leading ambassador for both club and country, who was awarded the MBE for services to football. He commented:

I was absolutely amazed when I read what Kitson had to say. For a footballer to turn round and virtually say the FA Cup is a waste of time really hurt me and I hate it every time someone says something along similar lines. I think Kitson's comments could have been down to cowardice. They were at least partly prompted by the fact that his team had been drawn away to Tottenham. It was as if he wanted to say these things beforehand just in case they were knocked out. Yes, it was a tough draw, especially at the third-round stage. But for me that is part of the appeal of the competition. Is it the right attitude to say you don't care if you lose? Not for me it isn't. As far as I am concerned you get on with it and the last thing you should be saying is that the result doesn't bother you. I know times have changed but I will always regard the FA Cup as a terrific competition. It's pretty unique these days, too. I don't think there is enough of a sudden-death feel to the modern game. If anything, that aspect is disappearing. Look at the Champions League and all the meaningless group games in the early stages. The UEFA Cup is the same – three teams qualifying from a group of five. What's all that about? We all know the extra games have been created for television and to bump up revenue. Thankfully, the FA Cup has stayed the same and is still all about what happens on the day. It's do or die and I think that's a concept that any sportsman should love. It's head to head, two teams going together in a genuine knockout tournament. One goes through, the other disappears. I hear today's pros putting it down and I can scarcely believe it. What better competition could you hope to be involved in?

Mills speaks from the heart and his beliefs are in no way inspired by his status as a winning Wembley captain. Nor is his a voice in the wilderness; there are plenty who will sympathise with his point of view and lament the way attitudes have changed. His face lights up at the memory of 1978, when the incredible high of FA Cup success was the perfect antidote to a League campaign in which Ipswich, who had emerged as genuine title challengers some years earlier, were always off the pace. Mills, the fans' choice as Player of the Year, recalled:

It was an awful season in many ways – we had too many injuries to have a settled side. We never really got going in the League and we had another major disappointment in going out of the UEFA Cup to Barcelona in a penalty shoot-out at the Nou Camp. Come January that season we only had the FA Cup to grab at. There was also a slight threat of relegation, although I have to say the self-belief in the camp was such that we didn't worry about that too much. But you get the picture – it wasn't what we had come to regard as a typical season. The third round of the FA Cup was a big thing in those days. There was a real atmosphere about it and everybody loved it. First, there was the draw, and then you wanted to make sure you got through. We didn't have our strongest side out at Cardiff but we coped quite comfortably. The fourth-round day was possibly the poorest of the lot. The big hoo-hah of the third round has gone and it doesn't do much for anyone. You know there is still a mile to go. But if you were in the fifth round you got a slight tingle. It had a lot to do with the caption on the television screen – all on one page and just eight names down each side. It made you realise you were getting close, plus the TV companies were able to give each game a proper preview and that gave it more impetus. When you got to the quarter-finals you were in no doubt that it was serious stuff and you didn't want to fail. You wanted to be in the last four and once we were there we reminded ourselves of 1975 and how we failed. Quite a lot of the lads were still around and they didn't want a repeat.

Ipswich cruised smoothly past Cardiff and Hartlepool before travelling back down the M4 to take on Bristol Rovers, the recollection of which still has Mills bristling with frustration and anger at referee Brian Daniels' insistence that the show must go on, despite near-farcical conditions. Mills added:

Today's football fans, those who weren't around in the 70s, would never believe the sort of pitches we had to play on – even when there wasn't snow and ice about. The one at Eastville that day was an absolute joke. It was dangerous and I have never been able to understand the referee even contemplating that the game should go ahead. It was a difficult situation for us. We got to the hotel on the Friday night and because it was snowing quite heavily we all thought it would be postponed. Because of that you tend to switch off mentally and you are thinking about jumping on the bus the next morning to travel home again. Come the Saturday, though, we were told it was definitely on and because we thought it was the wrong decision it created a bit of a problem with us. You have to fight your mind in that situation and not allow your anger to spill over, which might mean you are not giving it your best shot once the game gets under way. I worked on my own mind first but as captain I was always aware of my other duties. I felt that if I was going to do my job properly I should also monitor everyone else and make sure they were firmly focused on what we had to do, however unfair we felt it was. There's no question that the pitch was a leveller. Bad players could appear good and vice versa. We coped with all sorts of pitches, as I've said, but very few players liked having to play on a frozen surface. I hated it because my game was about doing things quickly. It took a lot of the sting out of the game, playing on something close to an ice rink. Yes, we rode our luck, but I think we deserved to ride our luck. I still blame the ref because I don't think he did his job properly. While his decision nearly cost us, Bristol almost cashed in. It was unfair to play that game and it was only right that we had a second chance. We made the most of it to go through and I can remember exactly where I was when the sixth-round draw was made. I was with the England squad at a hotel near Heathrow. We were getting ready to fly out to Munich for a friendly against West Germany and a lot of the players in the squad were eagerly awaiting the line-up for the quarter-finals. I was sharing with Paul Mariner and when we heard we were going to Millwall we were absolutely delighted. We went out in the corridor and were really celebrating. Then other doors opened and some of the lads came out. I remember Kevin Keegan trying to wind us up, warning us it wouldn't be easy, but we were having none of it. We knew it was a good draw for us and our attitude was very much one of: 'Bring it on.'

The other quarter-final ties – Wrexham v Arsenal, Middlesbrough v Orient and West Bromwich Albion v Nottingham Forest – confirmed Mills was right in thinking Ipswich could have been handed a much tougher assignment. He said:

On the day of the game against Millwall there were plenty of mixed emotions. We knew what to expect. We always got unmerciful stick from the fans there but we were in no way intimidated by the venue. We had plenty of experience of it, including in Europe against teams from the Eastern bloc. The crowd trouble was awful but in the '70s, sadly, you almost expected it. Millwall had a reputation and were notorious. It was horrible to see supporters being led away for treatment and it took the edge off our win. I've often wondered if the fact that we were so much better than them on the day was one of the reasons the fans reacted the way they did. I have very few regrets when I look back on my career and there isn't much I would change, but the one thing I wish had never happened was the hooliganism. It almost ruined football as attendances suffered and the fences went up. Not a good time for the game.

So to the last four, when Town had a one in three chance of meeting lower-level opposition in the shape of Orient, who were then fighting a battle to avoid being relegated from the Second Division. But instead they were paired with West Bromwich Albion. Mills insisted:

I really didn't worry who we were drawn against. Okay, it might have been nice to get Orient, but even with Albion being one of the teams others feared back then, I just accepted it. They were an exciting team with good individual players and a flamboyant manager in Ron Atkinson, and they had all the ingredients you might associate with a good Cup team – power, pace and flair. Once the draw was made I was anxious to know the venue and when I heard it was to be Highbury I was very happy. We had a good record there and enjoyed playing there, plus it was just down the road for our supporters and that was a big thing as far as I was concerned.

Mills was 29 back then and admits he had begun to wonder how many other FA Cup-winning opportunities would arise in his career. He said:

When you start out in football you can probably say you have about 15 chances, say from the age of 19 to 34 or from 20 to 35 to do it. It meant that a lot of my chances had gone, and when you are as close as being in the semi-finals you quickly realise it is a great chance to go all the way – maybe your one and only chance. Allan Hunter was nearly 32 and I guess he was only too aware that he might not be in that position again. Allan and I, plus several others, had been losers in 1975 and that was another important factor. We didn't want that experience all over again. Three years isn't really long enough to remove the hurt and we were still feeling it. A chance to make amends was very welcome.

[Photograph courtesy of Owen Hines]

The sweatshirt message says it all as Ipswich skipper Mick Mills prepares for the big day.

Ipswich still had to attend to the important business of accumulating sufficient points to secure their First Division status but it was before one of those League games, while they were sitting in a hotel watching the lunchtime television preview shows, that they were presented with an unexpected boost to their semi-final victory hopes. Mills explained:

I can't remember if it was Football Focus on BBC or the ITV one, On the Ball, but they had managed to persuade Big Ron to go to Wembley and do the whole bit. The FA Cup was there and he climbed up the steps as if it was a rehearsal. He was full of it. We were all in a conference room watching the TV and we couldn't quite believe he had done it. I was sitting there thinking: 'If I was a manager I wouldn't have gone along with that,' and we all thought it was a bit arrogant, or maybe naïve, because he had only been in charge of Albion for a few weeks after moving from Cambridge. We took that onboard and I am convinced it made us that bit more determined to be winners on the day. Come the game at Highbury we naturally wanted

Skipper Mick Mills leads the way for Ipswich at Wembley.

to get as strong a team as we could muster out on the pitch. In the end we were only without Trevor [Whymark] and it was a great shame for him. He was a terrific player, and because he was injured for the semi and then the Final he doesn't feature as prominently in the history of the club as he deserves to. One of the things I remember in the build-up to the game at Highbury is an interview that Brian Talbot did. He mentioned that he thought the respective left-backs – yours truly and Derek Statham, who was a bit of a rising star at the time – could have a real influence on the game. The atmosphere in the ground that day was unbelievable. Before the game I can remember doing something that I now think was a bit naff. We were warming up in front of our own fans at the Clock End and I ran down to the North Bank, where the Albion fans were packed in. Of course I knew what sort of reception I would get but players love that sort of thing. It was a bit of a wind-up, harmless fun, on my part, and I suppose it showed how confident we were going into the game. We made a good start, too, and it was a reflection of how positive we were. I remember taking a free-kick near the halfway line and I played it up to Paul Mariner, to his feet. With that I was gone. I could have stayed put but I was thinking: 'I'll go and support this.' As I'm bombing forward PM knocked it back to Clive Woods and he's spotted my run down the left and laid me in. I knocked it over towards the near post and there's Brian Talbot diving in to head the ball into the net. We showed such a positive attitude so early in the game – me, a defender, getting forward to cross the ball and Brian, a midfielder, also having a little dabble to get forward and threaten. Of course, Brian was injured and we all felt for him having to go off. But it was from our first corner, taken by his replacement, Mick Lambert, that we scored our second goal. Just 20 minutes on the clock and we were already 2–0 up. It couldn't have been any better.

Earlier that season Mills had chatted to Bobby Robson about taking up a specific position at corners that might give Ipswich a set-piece advantage – and this was not the first time it had paid off. Mills said:

The manager was very receptive to the idea. I just mentioned that I thought it would help us if I took the run of the 'keeper – in other words make him run round me if he wants to come and take the ball. On that occasion Mick Lambert sent the ball in low with pace and it came off the shins of Cyrille Regis. It was there, right at my feet, and I was nice and central, not even six yards out. I had to spin round as I connected with the ball and it flew low past several players into the net. It might even have gone through Derek Statham's legs.

Ipswich were comfortably in command as the clock ticked down but no one had bargained for the controversial intervention of Hunter, who climbed above Regis and fisted the ball away. There could be no argument – it was a blatant penalty and Tony Brown, the only survivor from Albion's FA Cup win 10 years earlier, converted from the spot. Mills said:

I can't repeat what I said to Allan. I couldn't believe what he had done and I really gave him quite a mouthful. I'm not sure he even heard what I said because right then I think he was on a different planet. He deliberately handled the ball – it was no accident – because he didn't want Regis to get in a header, but in reality Regis was going to have to produce one hell of a header to hurt us. We were so comfortable until then; we felt we had it won. But the penalty gave them a lift and it knocked us down. We still had about 14 minutes left and that was long enough for them to come back at us again. We still had a bit of work to do and it was an anxious last few minutes. I remember going down with cramp in both calf muscles and there was a lot of tension in the air.

Not even the dismissal of midfielder Mick Martin, six minutes from the end, could knock Albion off course. Booked for an earlier challenge on Woods, he picked up another caution when he tackled Mariner from behind and had to go, but the 10 men were in no mood to surrender and did all they could to force an equaliser. Into the 89th minute Town forced a corner. From Woods' kick, a completely unmarked John Wark headed past Tony Godden and immediately disappeared under a mass of bodies as his teammates rushed to congratulate him, no doubt feeling a mixture of joy and relief that there was no way back for their opponents. Mills said:

If the penalty had put us on a low, Warky's goal put us on an incredible high. We knew the game was as good as over and victory was ours. From that moment on we knew we were going to Wembley and there was nothing that anyone could do to stop us. The feeling then was as good as it was when we won the FA Cup at Wembley. There is something special about winning a semi-final. We'd lost our previous one so we didn't know until then, but it was everything we wanted it to be and more. The feeling of relief that ran through my body when Warky's header went in was unbelievable. The party started straight away in the dressing room and we couldn't wait to get back to Ipswich and find a pub to carry on celebrating.

TOP ATTENDANCE

Skipper Mick Mills is one of a handful of Ipswich stars who might have appeared in three FA Cup Finals rather than just one. He made more appearances in the competition than any of the other 198 players to have represented the club in their 303 Cup ties dating back to 1936, the year Town turned professional. He was there in 1975 when West Ham inflicted a semi-final replay defeat on Bobby Robson's team and appeared again when Manchester City edged to an extra-time victory in 1981 as Ipswich chased an unprecedented treble of major honours. Mills played in both games against the Hammers – the first at Villa Park and the replay at Stamford Bridge – to make it four semi-final outings out of four, a record he shares with only one player, Kevin Beattie, who had the misfortune to break his arm in the game against City, in what proved to be his last Town appearance.

Their semi-final success launched the Town squad into a hectic but extremely enjoyable four weeks of promotional work. Although this was accepted as part and parcel of an FA Cup Final team's normal routine, it had to be done alongside a series of League games of far greater importance. If that was not demanding enough, Ipswich also had to contend with the fallout from their 6–1 defeat at Aston Villa just seven days before they were due to face Arsenal at Wembley, an experience that manager Bobby Robson and his players could have done without. Even in the week of the Final, according to Mills, things did not always go according to plan. He said:

To be honest, our preparations were hopeless – not through anyone's fault. For example, we went down to Wembley on the Tuesday for a training session and it was a sensible thing to do. I'd seen a fair bit of Wembley when I was there with England and I was comfortable with it, but for some of the players it was a whole new experience. Unfortunately, it was waterlogged and therefore a complete waste of time. It had been raining non-stop and there were puddles all over the pitch. It was impossible. Then on the Friday, for our very last session before the game, we went to a pitch near our hotel in St Albans and they had only just cut the grass. The trouble was, they had left all the cuttings and it was obvious that it must have been a foot long before they took the mower to it. Again, a waste of time, but we didn't let any of that put us off. We were in the swing of things and we knew what we had to do. On the morning of the match, once Allan [Hunter] had passed his fitness test, we could hardly wait to get going. We were all delighted for Allan: we saw him as a crucial member of the team and it also solved a problem for the management team. I roomed with Allan throughout the FA Cup campaign that season – it was a pact we made down at Cardiff. He would normally be with Kevin (Beattie) but Beat was injured. The night before the game, not knowing whether he would be fit or not, was doing the big man's head in. He didn't sleep too well. He was nervous, in a world of his own, and puffed his way through quite a few cigarettes. We had to do a sort of 'who's who' feature for the BBC on the Saturday morning – it was live and John Motson was doing it. We were all so relaxed and John even mentioned it. Everybody was up for it and determined to enjoy it. There was no sign of nerves and that continued right the way through to the game itself, which was great because an occasion of that size and importance could easily get to you. If anything, it was Arsenal who seemed to be most affected. None of the Ipswich players looked to be struggling in any way. They certainly weren't unnerved by it but the Arsenal players seemed to be in their shell. They were definitely caught up in it – you know, a bit like the rabbit in the headlights. The game passed quite quickly but I thoroughly enjoyed it. They had to put a real effort into getting the game on and I doubt if many playing surfaces at that time could have coped with all the rain that fell, not just on the day but for most of the week. There was a little bit of surface water here and there, but the pitch played really well in difficult circumstances. We took the game to Arsenal and our tactic of playing David Geddis wide on the right worked a treat. We were firmly in charge but we had all lived through these sort of games and we knew what could happen, even if Arsenal weren't really causing us any problems. There's no doubt that when you don't score during the good spells you do start fearing the worst – that the other team will sneak one against the run of play.

Fortunately, the worst did not happen and instead Ipswich were rewarded for their total dominance by Roger Osborne's goal. Around 20 minutes later, Mills was climbing the 39 steps to receive the trophy from HRH Princess Alexandra. He proudly held it aloft, fulfilling a boyhood dream and at the same time realising an ambition shared with every single footballer in the land. Just in case the measure of his achievement had not sunk in, Mills received a letter a few days later from his former headmaster, mapping out in statistics what he had done. Mills said:

It was a lovely letter and he emphasised how big an honour it was to be a winning captain in an FA Cup Final. It was the 50th Final at Wembley and, allowing for the fact that some people had

Mick Mills demonstrates the all-action style that was his trademark.

(Photograph courtesy Offside Sports Photography Ltd)

done it twice, he pointed out that I was in a group of less than 50 people who had captained a team and picked up the trophy at the national stadium. Based on the fact that just about every male born in this country wants to be a professional footballer and be a Wembley winner, he made me realise I was one of a very fortunate group. Funnily enough, I had a couple of run-ins with him at school but towards the end of my time there he was very helpful and even drove me up to Chelsea for a trial he'd arranged for me. I hadn't seen him in 14 years and it was nice of him to write. From the tone of the letter it was clear he was very pleased for me and it also demonstrated how special the FA Cup is, or should I say was, to people. As an occasion, the FA Cup Final beat everything else: it was about more than just the game. It was a remarkable day that involved everyone close to me – my family, my friends and my work colleagues. It was totally different to anything else I experienced as a footballer. Going off to play international football for your country is tremendous but it tends to be more of an individual thing, whereas with the FA Cup it seemed to be about sharing the occasion with others. The whole day was amazing and it is something that stays with you. We are still talking, writing and reminiscing about it 30 years on and it will always be a major topic of conversation. For everyone who talks to me about our UEFA Cup win in 1981 or the 1982 World Cup, when I captained England, there are dozens or hundreds more who talk about the FA Cup win. From a professional point of view the UEFA Cup was a far bigger achievement. You are taking on Europe and it is tough from the word go. In those days all the teams that came second in the various Leagues, who now qualify for the Champions League, were in the UEFA Cup. But for sheer glamour, excitement and, I suppose, romance there was nothing to beat the FA Cup. Knowing what I know now, if I had never gone to Wembley with Ipswich and won the trophy there would be a massive void in my career. We might have played better games and we might have won a tougher tournament, but it was extra, extra special. Without doubt, the experience of a lifetime.

ROGER OSBORNE

FULL NAME: Roger Charles Osborne
DATE OF BIRTH: 9 March 1950
PLACE OF BIRTH: Otley, Suffolk
IPSWICH TOWN APPEARANCES: 149
IPSWICH TOWN GOALS: 10

(Photograph courtesy of Owen Hines)

His Wembley winner gave Roger Osborne membership of a very elite club – so exclusive, in fact, that it can only open its doors to a maximum of one new member per year. Some years the doors stay firmly shut, and since our hero was welcomed aboard in 1978 a mere 10 new members have been recruited. We are talking FA Cup Final goalscorers, of course, but the club to which Osborne earned lifelong membership is so exclusive that only those who score the only goal to decide the destination of football's most famous trophy need apply.

It is a feat that has not been lost on Osborne – perhaps the unlikeliest Wembley match-winner of them all since he was axed from the starting line-up for Ipswich's League visit to Aston Villa a mere seven days earlier. That bizarre episode had convinced him he would be absent from the greatest day in the club's history, but by full-time at Villa Park he realised his place had become more secure. Even so, the Suffolk-born midfielder seemed destined to be one of the most anonymous finalists of all time until he scored his goal. Too harsh? Not according to the man himself, who agrees wholeheartedly. He said:

If I hadn't scored the goal that won us the FA Cup and someone was asked years later to name the victorious Ipswich side I am pretty sure the one player they would struggle to identify would be me. As it is, though, they tend to remember the scorers, especially if they scored the winning goal – and particularly if it was the only goal. That's what made it even more special for me. I'd have been chuffed to say I played in an FA Cup-winning team and even more delighted to say I scored a goal in the Final. But, believe me, for it to have been the only goal was even better than a dream coming true. I was living my dream just playing at Wembley. There was nothing in my dream about scoring. Maybe Paul Mariner, as a centre-forward, dreamt he would score the winner but definitely not me. I really can't emphasise the point any stronger. I remember a League game against Middlesbrough and I scored – it looked as if it might be the only goal and I was really excited at the thought, but then Paul weighed in with a second goal: 2–0 to us. What did the headline say in the local paper? 'Mariner clinches win', I think it was.

To fully grasp the significance of Osborne's monumental contribution it is necessary to drift back in time – not just seven days but seven years, to when he became a professional footballer. He did not follow the usual, straightforward career path of signing schoolboy forms, becoming an apprentice and finally, perhaps as early as his 17th birthday, completing the paperwork to become a fully-fledged professional. Osborne's route saw him leave Farlingaye High School in Woodbridge and at the age of 21, by which time most footballers probably expect to have clocked up their first century of appearances, he was working on a building site. He drifted into the professional game via the back door, accompanying his younger brother to midweek training sessions at Portman Road. It was David, several years his junior, who had attracted the attention of the club scouts – Roger was acting as his chauffeur. However, an amazing twist of fate intervened. Town were down to the bare bones at reserve level thanks to an unprecedented casualty list, and one of the young pros, Geoff Hammond, suggested to manager Bobby Robson that it might be an idea to give Roger a chance. Osborne recalled:

Geoff told them I was fit and played at a decent local level. That was the start – and I had absolutely no idea where it would lead. If you'd suggested then that I would go on to score the FA Cup-winning goal at Wembley I couldn't have taken you seriously. But it was brilliant to be playing against Arsenal and Tottenham's reserves in the Football Combination. It was such a different world to what I was used to. I was paid £25 a week on the building site and the club were giving me £15 to play in the reserves. When I became a full-time pro I was on £25 a week, and there was no big signing-on fee, although we did get a £2 bonus for a win and £1 extra for a draw. Obviously my salary went up as I became more established and played more games. I think I was on about £12,000 a year when I finished at Ipswich. I was thinking about it one day when I was reading about the salaries of today's best-paid players. I reckon someone like Frank Lampard takes home more in a week than I earned in my whole career.

Osborne's incredible journey took him from Westerfield United, a Suffolk and Ipswich League club so far down the football pyramid that they were not even entitled to enter the FA Cup, to the absolute pinnacle of the competition. Yet just seven days prior to his Wembley winner, Osborne was a deflated figure after Robson revealed the team that would do battle with Aston Villa. Osborne remembered:

It wasn't a nice thing to happen. I could understand Bobby bringing Colin Viljoen back because he had been a loyal, excellent player for the club for 10 years. But to my mind he brought him back for the wrong reasons. Did he think that Colin, as a good passer of the ball, would exploit the open spaces of Wembley? On the other hand, are you going to allow Liam Brady to run riot simply because Colin didn't want to pick him up? That was the bottom line as far as I was concerned. Most people felt we were a stronger team with me. To be honest I had taken it for granted that I would be playing against Arsenal and what happened at Villa Park the week before was a bolt from the blue. The boss read out the team and to be honest I think I went into shock. Everyone else was stunned too. It's hard to describe how I felt. One minute I'm thinking about getting tickets for about 60 relatives and friends from as far afield as Birmingham and Cornwall, who were coming to see me play at Wembley, the next I'm convincing myself I won't even be playing. All of a sudden the biggest day of my life wasn't going to happen, or so I thought. At that moment it was as plain as the nose on my face that I wouldn't be playing. The boss wasn't resting me or protecting me. He wanted Colin in the team. I even told myself: 'You won't be on the bench either'. It was just one sub in those days and I expected he would go with Mick Lambert, who was an attacking player.

However, after a terrible beating for a Town team containing 17-year-old goalkeeper Paul Overton, in what turned out to be his only senior outing, Roger was considerably more optimistic about his chances of making the starting line-up. He said:

I sat in the dug-out the whole game and the boss never said a word. But when we got into the dressing room he said: 'Roger is the only one to come out of this with any credit.' It was quite heated in the dressing room, to say the least, with a lot of people having their say. Looking back, I think Bobby was in danger of falling into the same trap that I believe Steve McClaren fell into as England manager. Do you play your best players or your best team? On the training ground I wasn't as good a player as Colin Viljoen, but it was different come match day because I was doing a job. The strange thing about the Villa game was that Bobby didn't just leave me out to accommodate Colin. He also switched John Wark to the right side of midfield, which was a strange thing to do because Warky had never played there before.

In the space of little more than 90 minutes Roger's world had been turned upside down and back again. The 6–1 scoreline was confirmation that Robson's gamble had backfired and he was left with little alternative but to revert back to plan A. Osborne said:

Because of the result at Villa Park it took all the fire out of the argument. There wasn't an argument any more, in fact, but the boss never did say to me: 'You're playing.' It was just assumed because of what had happened at Villa Park. People go on about player power…well it was and it wasn't, really. The boss didn't have to tell me. I knew I would be playing and in the days before Wembley it was obvious because we were doing drills about who would be marking who and how we were going to play, that sort of thing. It was decided to bring in David Geddis to play wide on the right and if that hadn't have happened I couldn't have tucked in to mark Liam Brady. David was doing my old job but doing it further forward. Normally I would switch between their midfield player and their full-back, and George Burley would do the same. As a result of bringing David into the side we became stronger down that side of the pitch. It meant playing Paul Mariner through the middle rather than two up front, but PM was good enough to do that. In a way it made my job easier in that I could pick Brady up, whereas in the old system I would have had to disengage myself every now and again. It was a new plan and we had to work on it but I was playing against good players every week, and although Brady was better than most it was clear that he wasn't fully fit. You could see he was struggling and he probably shouldn't have played, but we didn't know any of that beforehand.

Whether it was his lack of fitness or the close attention of Osborne, or a combination of both, Brady was nowhere near his most effective for the Gunners. With almost 90 per cent of normal time having passed and Ipswich unable to get their noses in front, Osborne and the team were beginning to wonder if the vital breakthrough would ever come. He added:

The only good thing was that Arsenal didn't really look like scoring. It wasn't an end-to-end Final. We were totally dominating the game, although I have to admit that it did cross my mind that we might have to go to extra-time. I couldn't see them scoring so the big question was whether we could get one before the 90 minutes were up. We had about 12 to 13 minutes left, so it was getting pretty late. At half-time the manager had told us to keep doing what we were doing. Arsenal only really got into our box a couple of times and they were isolated occasions. We were the side controlling the play and to be fair they weren't offering too much by way of a reply. The thing I remember about the move that led to the goal is that Clive Woods got the ball a few yards over the halfway line. He passed it forward – I think it was intended for me – but it rebounded off Alan Hudson straight back to him. What that did – the delay – was to allow us to get that bit further up the pitch. Woodsy stuck the ball out to David

(*Photograph courtesy Offside Sports Photography Ltd*)

Wembley goal hero Roger Osborne is in seventh heaven as he gets to grips with the FA Cup.

Geddis and he got the better of Sammy Nelson. By the time he got the ball over we had bodies in the area – that was the key to it. That type of ball is so difficult to defend against. Having said that, it wasn't actually the best cross in the world – it was a bit too straight. Ideally, David would have wanted to pull it back a bit more than he did. The fact that Willie Young got a foot to the ball was good. The ball came off him to me and I only had a split second. I had no time to think. Had I had longer I'd have been thinking: 'Where do I put it?' It all happened so quickly, but I do remember the thought going through my head that I had to keep my shot low. 'Keep it low, keep it low,' I was telling myself. The last thing I wanted was to hit the ball over the bar.

Osborne managed to keep his shot low and it had too much pace for Arsenal goalkeeper Pat Jennings. Osborne said:

If you look at the pictures of the goal the one thing that is so obvious is how I am concentrating on keeping the ball low. I hit it with my left foot and I don't honestly remember scoring another goal with my left foot. I didn't get many goals so the chances are I would probably remember if I had done. Bobby Robson spent the best part of 10 years telling me to use my left foot more, so he deserves a large chunk of the credit. As it flew into the net everything just became a blur because the lads piled on top of me.

It took a few seconds, perhaps even as long as a minute, for those present and the millions watching on television to realise that the goalscorer was overcome with a mixture of exhaustion and elation, and was unable to continue. But Osborne emphasised:

Had we not had a substitute I would definitely have carried on. I'd have been groggy for a couple of minutes, perhaps, but I would have been able to continue. But you are always aware that you have a substitute. I look back over my Ipswich career and I was taken off about once every three games, so it was nothing new to me. It wasn't really as dramatic as people seem to think or thought at the time. There is absolutely no way that I would have allowed us to be reduced to 10 men. I would have recovered sufficiently to play the last 10 minutes or so, but with Mick on the bench there was no need to do that. Besides, he was having his testimonial game a couple of days later and he promised me a few bob if I went off and let him on – that's a joke, in case anyone believes it! The bottom line is that I felt I could have recovered but there was no point with a substitute only too willing to give it a go. Mind you, it was really quite terrifying to have to sit there for the last few minutes. It was in that time that Arsenal had one of their better chances to score, but Paul Cooper did well to hold on to Malcolm Macdonald's shot. It was about the only time Macdonald had a shot or did anything of note. He just managed to get away from Kevin Beattie but, although he hit the ball well from about 25 yards, Coop was right behind it and held it. That was as close as they came to scoring in the entire game but you worry that they are going to sneak an equaliser. I spent the last few minutes wondering: 'Have I just scored the winning goal in the FA Cup Final or is it going to extra-time?' When the final whistle finally went I realised I had made history. It was such a huge, huge thing for Ipswich Town and even bigger for Bobby Robson. We had been a good side for a few years without actually winning anything, always going close in the League. But now we had something to show for it and the boss got an awful lot of credibility for leading a side to a Wembley win, which is a big thing to have on your CV.

As a local boy and a Town supporter all his life, Osborne knew exactly what it would mean to the fans. Great achievement that it undoubtedly was, the League Championship success under Alf Ramsey had been 16 years ago – a generation earlier – and it was not as if Ipswich were used to winning the major trophies. Osborne added:

The fans had experienced nothing like it and I was extremely proud to have scored such an important goal, one that they would talk about for the rest of their lives. As I went up to get my medal and we were going around the stadium with the trophy I couldn't stop myself thinking: 'Is this really happening?' I had just scored the winning goal in the FA Cup Final, yet only a few years earlier I was playing for Westerfield, a club so far down the pyramid that

At last! Roger Osborne watches as his low shot beats Pat Jennings for the Wembley winner.

they couldn't even enter the competition. It was a lot to take in. People asked me later if I got drunk at the official banquet but I was on such an incredible high without the booze. It was one of those evenings I didn't want to end.

For the past decade Roger has managed the Rushmere Sports Club but freely admits to being a jack of all trades. There are even some regulars who know little of his glamorous background and his special place in football folklore. He said:

We had some kids in here one day – I think they were about 13 years old – and I heard one of them say: 'If he's an ex-footballer what's he doing sweeping out the changing rooms?' and I just had a smile to myself. Also, when I was coaching at Northgate a few years ago, I took a coach full of youngsters to Wembley to do the stadium tour. The guide wasn't very good. I know it's no excuse but he had probably done a fair few of them that day and his enthusiasm wasn't what it might have been. I was itching to say: 'Look, it's better than this,' and tell them my story but I kept my mouth shut. There was so much more to it than what the guide was telling them. He could have excited them more and, looking back, I wish I'd said something.

Referee Derek Nippard signals a goal as Roger Osborne literally jumps for joy to celebrate his crucial strike.

As BBC TV commentator David Coleman pointed out when the Town players climbed the steps to receive their medals from HRH Princess Alexandra, the man of the moment was from a family so large that they hired their own bus to transport them to Wembley. Not strictly true, since there were also a number of friends making up the numbers but, as one of 12 children, Osborne was definitely not short of support on the day. His father made the trip but his mother stayed at home. Osborne said with a smile:

My mum never saw me play – I'm talking local football as well as professional – and I reckon my dad only saw about four or five of my games. He used to say that he couldn't understand why people would want to run and chase a bag of wind! The funny thing is that all my brothers and I were football mad. When we were growing up, all we ever did was play football. I would imagine I was Ray Crawford or Ted Phillips when we had a game in the village.

Around 1978 the youngsters were all pretending to be Roger Osborne, such was the impact he made, and 30 years on our modest hero still enjoys basking in the glory of his special moment. He said:

I think it's actually now, with the big four tending to dominate the FA Cup, that my achievement tends to get better and better. Until this year you couldn't really see anyone other than Manchester United, Arsenal, Chelsea or Liverpool winning the trophy. They have all won it so many times and they will continue to win it on a regular basis. But for Ipswich and a few other clubs it has only happened once and who's to say it will ever happen again? It would be great if it did but you certainly can't guarantee it.

Osborne is quick to concede that Ipswich enjoyed their fair share of luck in the earlier rounds, not only with the opponents they drew but also in the key fifth-round game at Bristol Rovers. That was the one in which they were trailing 2–1 with time rapidly running out, but with just four minutes left to play Robin Turner scored the second of his two goals to earn a replay back at Portman Road...except that Turner did not score. In actual fact it was Osborne who scored the oh-so-important equaliser, but in the post-mortem that followed he willingly went along with the version that had Turner down as the marksman. He said:

People Sport

May 7, 1978   L

EE BY GUM

Roger the Tyke's won the FA Cup!

HIS arms are in the air. His teeth are in the dressing-room. And his name is down in history as the player who won the F.A. Cup.

He's Roger Osborne, the 28-year-old Yorkshire lad captured by the camera of Brendan Monks in the moment of his greatest triumph.

He's just scored the goal that has given Ipswich their 1—0 Wembley win over Arsenal.

That was the last thing he did before collapsing with exhaustion.

He spent the last 15 minutes sitting on the bench with an ice-pack on his head.

"I was exhausted mentally and physically. I realised I had nothing more to give," he explained later.

As far as Ipswich are concerned he'd already given enough. By gum, he had!

The Cup is in East Anglia for the first time—and he's the Tyke who put it there.

ARSENAL . . . 0
IPSWICH . . . 1

THE TOP ACTION FROM THE CUP

See Pages 42 and 43

EE BY GUM

The back-page headline in a national newspaper, the day after the FA Cup Final screamed out 'EE BY GUM' alongside a picture of the man who decided the big match. There was a further message – 'Roger the Tyke's won the FA Cup!' However, the sub-editor on the *Sunday People* got it horribly wrong in thinking our hero hailed from Yorkshire. When he was given the superb picture taken by staff photographer Brendan Monks, he no doubt reached for his *Rothmans Football Yearbook*. Inside the volume renowned as the 'Bible of football' he found what he thought was a golden nugget of information – that the Wembley goal hero was born in Otley. Hence the clever headline, except that it was not really clever at all, because it was in the village of Otley, Suffolk, and not its Yorkshire namesake, that Roger entered the world.

When Monks snapped the magic moment as Roger leapt off the ground, arms in the air, to celebrate his all-important goal, it was clear he was without his false front teeth. He smiled: 'I wore them before the game but after we had been introduced to Princess Alexandra I gave them to physio Tommy Eggleston and he looked after them for me. When I came off after scoring I put them back in so that I'd look better for the pictures and the medal ceremony. Back then I didn't make a habit of putting my teeth in and out but I thought the FA Cup Final was a bit special.'

There was a bit of confusion at the time about who had actually put the ball over the line. Funnily enough, their goalkeeper knew the truth and swore blind I'd scored it. He was right, I had, but it would have gone in anyway. It was virtually on the line and I just kicked it over. Nowadays if they are within 10 yards they claim it, but I was quite happy for Robin to get the credit as the ball was going to go in. He didn't know any differently. I can't remember anything about the build-up, just kicking it over the line. To my mind it didn't really matter who scored as long as it was a goal because we were very, very close to going out. The luck of the draw is a big thing in any Cup competition and there's no point denying we had a bit of good fortune along the way. But it's also true about having to beat good teams at some stage and that's what we did in the semi-final and at Wembley. When we played West Bromwich Albion at Highbury I was confident we would win. Three years earlier we had been beaten at the same stage by West Ham and that taught us a very important lesson. To be honest, we thought we would beat West Ham. We even allowed ourselves to look ahead to Wembley. We were wondering what the bonus would be for winning the FA Cup and that was unprofessional on our part. The disappointment in 1975 was huge and I believe a lot of clubs have suffered in the same situation. Yes, we were affected by injuries and refereeing decisions too, but there's no way we did ourselves justice and we were anxious not to make the same mistake again. Our mindset in 1978 was totally different. We knew how it would feel to lose the semi-final – it must be the worst feeling in the world. We were so focused and kept reminding ourselves that we hadn't done anything yet. The naivety of three years previously was replaced with total professionalism and nothing – not an early injury to Brian Talbot, not giving away a penalty to make it 2–1 – was going to get in our way. And once we got to Wembley it was pretty much the same story – all over again. We went there to win.

Once Ipswich were in possession of the famous trophy – the original, not a copy as is often the case today – they did their utmost to share their success with the people of Suffolk. Osborne found himself in greater demand than ever and remembers travelling out to Leiston High School for a pre-arranged event. His return journey took him past his former school, Farlingaye High at Woodbridge, and he could not resist the temptation to pay them a visit. He said:

I was driving past and I just thought 'bugger it' and turned in. The security surrounding the trophy was supposed to be tight but at that precise moment I wasn't the least bit

CHARITY CHAMPION

In an extraordinarily generous act, Roger Osborne donated the shirt he was wearing when he scored the winning goal at Wembley to charity. It was auctioned through a local newspaper and the highest bidder paid £5,500, the money going to Breast Cancer Care, the UK's leading provider of information, practical assistance and emotional support for anyone affected by breast cancer. Osborne says: 'I wore two shirts at Wembley – a long-sleeved one in the first half and a short-sleeved one in the second. After the game I swapped my first-half shirt with Liam Brady and his shirt is on display in the boardroom at Portman Road. I kept the one I was wearing when I scored the goal but after a few years I decided to put it up for auction and I have absolutely no regrets. The money went to a very good cause.' But what happened to the famous left boot with which Osborne scored the all-important winning goal at Wembley? Was it, too, auctioned to raise vital funds for charity or has he had it mounted in a special display box? Osborne laughed:

You might not believe it, but both the boots I wore at Wembley were binned. These days an FA Cup Final goalscorer's boots would probably fetch thousands but it's the gospel truth – mine were just thrown away. What happened is this. I wasn't playing much the following season and one day Allan Hunter came to me and asked to borrow my boots because one of his own had split. I let him have them and that was the last I saw of them. Allan wore them until they were no good and then they were chucked out. I certainly don't blame Allan. He did nothing wrong. It's just that at the time I never even thought of putting them up for auction or hanging on to them. As for Wembley souvenirs, I have a print of me scoring the goal from a watercolour that an artist did and a pewter plate that carries all the signatures of the Town squad, plus my winner's medal, of course. No matter what I have and haven't got, the one thing that nobody can take away is that I scored the only goal. That's the most precious thing of them all and you can't put a price on it.

Incidentally, on the subject of money, Osborne revealed that he and his teammates were each paid a bonus of £4,000 by the club for their FA Cup success – £2,000 for reaching Wembley and the same again for winning.

(Photograph courtesy of Owen Hines)

Goalscorer Roger Osborne and skipper Mick Mills with the FA Cup.

concerned about that. No one had a clue I was going to turn up. I went in with the FA Cup, told them who I was and asked to see the headmaster. They were so taken aback. The headmaster called an assembly so that every single pupil would get to see it. Things like that made me realise what it meant to people. It was a truly magical moment for me, and for so many thousands of people to get so much pleasure out of it made me feel that I had done something really worthwhile.

BRIAN TALBOT

FULL NAME: Brian Ernest Talbot
DATE OF BIRTH: 27 July 1953
PLACE OF BIRTH: Ipswich, Suffolk
IPSWICH TOWN APPEARANCES: 227
IPSWICH TOWN GOALS: 31

Little did Brian Talbot realise, as he proudly collected his FA Cup-winner's medal from HRH Princess Alexandra in 1978, that it was merely the start of a lengthy link with the famous competition that would see him go on to make three Final appearances at Wembley in as many seasons. Fate decreed that the industrious midfielder would return the following year with the team he had helped to defeat and earn himself a place in the record books, thanks to Arsenal's dramatic defeat of Manchester United, for his feat of winning the competition in successive seasons with different clubs. It might even have been a hat-trick of consecutive victories but for Trevor Brooking's rare headed goal, which resulted in an unexpected, but nevertheless fully merited victory over the Gunners. It was the only goal of the 1980 Final when Second Division West Ham were led by future Ipswich boss John Lyall.

Talbot's move to the capital came about as a result of Arsenal going ahead with a transfer that their persistent management duo of Terry Neill and Don Howe had first proposed in the summer of 1977, although at that stage their approach had been instantly rebuffed by Ipswich boss Bobby Robson. However, eight months on from Ipswich's FA Cup success the situation had changed and Robson happily sanctioned Talbot's switch to North London, the main reason being his own successful pursuit of Dutch midfielder Arnold Muhren and the impending purchase of Muhren's friend and former FC Twente colleague Frans Thijssen to further bolster an engine room in which Talbot had previously been a vital cog. Robson's team was taking on a new look, down not only to the arrival of Muhren and Thijssen but also the manager's desire to accommodate the burgeoning talent of Eric Gates in the side, in his speciality role behind the front two. It was a deal that made sense from both a football and financial standpoint, with Robson paying out a total of £250,000 for his two Dutch gems and Arsenal willing to pay £450,000 for the workaholic Talbot – a £200,000 profit on the triple transaction. It was shrewd business by Robson, who often said he spent the club's money as if it were his own, and Talbot was also pleased to be given the chance to join the playing staff at one of the country's leading clubs, remaining at Highbury for six and a half years. He rarely missed a game and proved a tremendous value-for-money acquisition as he clocked up 327 appearances and scored 49 goals.

Renowned for his stamina and fitness, Talbot actually played every one of the 70 games that comprised Arsenal's marathon 1979–80 season, his first full campaign on the Highbury payroll. The Gunners reached the FA Cup Final and European Cup-winners' Cup Final, only to lose to West Ham and Valencia, the latter by the narrowest possible margin – 5–4 on penalties.

However, it was at Portman Road that Talbot, the only Ipswich-born player in the victorious Town side, first rose to prominence – although had it not been for legendary manager Ron Greenwood, he might have slipped through the net and missed out on a highly successful career that also earned him six international caps, five of which he won during his time in Suffolk.

When Bournemouth enquired about Talbot's availability at a time when he was in the Ipswich reserve side and appeared unlikely to dislodge Peter Morris from the first team, Robson did nothing to discourage an £8,000 bid and it seemed the player was destined to drop down a level or two to launch his career. But then the Town manager remembered a sound piece of advice passed on by Greenwood, whom he was later to succeed in charge of England, that he should not sell anyone without seeing him in action at first-team level. On the spur of the moment, and fearing Talbot might return to haunt him, Robson decided not to take the proposed transfer any further.

In time, Talbot's big chance came along and he grasped it. Morris became surplus to requirements and was sold to Norwich, allowing yet another home-grown talent to graduate to first-team level. He became part of a tremendously effective left-sided triangle, along with skipper Mick Mills and winger Clive Woods, which was a key part of the side and reached amazing levels of consistency.

While other players were reluctant to discuss the so-called player power that led to Robson changing his Wembley line up after the previous week's debacle at Villa Park, Talbot was refreshingly forthright about the remarkable events that provided a fascinating backdrop to the team's glorious FA Cup triumph. Indeed, he revealed just how close his part in the 6–1 defeat came to costing him his own place at Wembley. Such was Robson's anger with Talbot in particular that he considered leaving him out of the side to face Arsenal, which would have been the ultimate in disciplinary measures. Talbot recalled:

Several players were annoyed that the boss changed the team for the game at Aston Villa, bringing in Colin Viljoen for Roger Osborne, but I was the one who piped up. I got into trouble because I was honest. Viljoen was the best passer of a ball at the club. There was no argument about that. He was quick, too, but when he lost the ball you wouldn't see him chasing back. I don't want to harp on about this, but I haven't spoken to the bloke since 1978. He blamed me because he didn't play at Wembley. I was also concerned about my own position. If Viljoen had played it would have meant me switching to the right and I didn't want that. I admit it – I was selfish. We had a lot of strong characters in the side at the time and most of us thought about ourselves first and foremost. Not Roger. He was the nicest lad in the team, so easy-going, and we didn't want to see him dropped for the FA Cup Final. I made it clear I didn't want Viljoen in the team. Others felt exactly the same but they said nothing. Because I spoke up, Bobby Robson had me in his office on the Monday. He was dead right to do what he did. He was angry that we had questioned his decision and he told me: 'If you do that again I'll leave you out.' But Bobby was a good manager. It was him – not me, not anyone else – who picked the team. In the end he made a tremendous decision and it won us the FA Cup. You have to feel sorry for players who are not in the side at Wembley because there can't be many teams, if any at all, who get there having used just 11 players along the way, but that's all the manager can pick and somebody is always disappointed.

Thirty years on from that special victory, Talbot still remains puzzled as to why Ipswich were such rank outsiders to win at Wembley, the bookmakers making Arsenal red-hot favourites and virtually dismissing Town as no-hopers by naming them as 5–2 shots. It is no secret, of course, that Talbot and the team took full advantage of the bookies' generosity to collect some useful bonus money. He said:

It amazed us to see how little chance we were being given. It seemed as if we were not only wasting our money – we were written off to such an extent that we also seemed to be wasting our time even turning up for the game! It was all based on the fact that we had not had a good League season, but that didn't matter to us. We knew it was all about who performed on the day and the reason for us feeling confident that we would win was that we knew how good we were and that Arsenal didn't have players who were any better than ours. When you look back at our squad we had international full-backs, international midfield players and an international centre-forward. Everywhere you looked we had quality. We knew we had nothing to fear and we were quietly confident. Kevin Beattie was probably our most influential player. He played in the semi-final and then we rested him until the Final. We knew what we had. It wasn't like Sunderland against Leeds five years earlier. Everyone – even Sunderland if they are honest – probably thought Leeds would dominate that game from start to finish. We didn't see ourselves as underdogs. We were saying to ourselves: 'At long last we are doing something.' We felt that winning a major prize was long overdue. We should have won the League Championship and FA Cup double three years earlier and the title again in 1977. What I'm saying is this: we were a good side!

Talbot, whose father Ernie paid him a visit in the Wembley dressing room after the win over Arsenal, has no regrets about speaking up in 1978. His own experiences in a see-saw managerial career, however, have made him far more understanding of the dilemma facing Bobby Robson at the time. He added:

When I made my feelings known in 1978 I was only thinking of one thing – winning the game – and when the boss made his decision as to who should be in the team for the Final he was thinking exactly the same. Bobby Robson is clever. He was a good manager for more than 30 years. He got good players together and made good teams, not just at Ipswich but everywhere he went. It wasn't good luck, it was good judgement. He was clever back in 1978 too. He listened to his coaching staff, people like Cyril Lea and Bobby Ferguson. It was a team effort in more ways than one. It was Fergie who looked at Arsenal and came up with the idea of putting David Geddis out on the right to block the service to Sammy Nelson and, ultimately, Liam Brady, who was one of the best playmakers around at the time. The move worked a treat. We were always in charge and everybody felt it was only a matter of time before we scored. For Roger to pop up with the winning goal was as good as it could have been. All the other members of the team felt the same. It was perfect, absolutely perfect.

Talbot was one of just five Town players, alongside Paul Cooper, Mick Mills, Allan Hunter and Paul Mariner, who were ever present in the successful FA Cup campaign – although his semi-final involvement, albeit telling, was painfully brief. Just eight minutes into the game at Highbury the all-action midfielder dived full length to make contact with Mick Mills' superb left-wing cross, directing the ball past goalkeeper Tony Godden and into the net to give Ipswich a dream start. However, he lay motionless as teammates rushed to congratulate him and it was clear all was far from well. As well as making contact with the ball, Talbot's head collided with that of West Bromwich Albion skipper John Wile, and it was the Town star who came off worst. Blood gushed from a wound above his right eye, which later required three stitches. Talbot was patched up, but his eye was almost completely closed by the swelling, and although he wanted to continue he had to admit defeat and be replaced by Mick Lambert. He said:

I just couldn't distinguish anything. It was all out of focus and I would have been cheating myself, the team and the supporters to have gone back on. I desperately wanted to carry on but after a jog up the touchline I just knew it was hopeless and signalled that I was finished. I went back to the dressing room, laid down and fell asleep. At half-time I had a cup of tea with the lads and I intended to go out and watch the last half an hour or so. But I had another lie down and the next thing I knew our physio, Tommy Eggleston, was telling me that Albion had scored from a penalty and it was now 2–1 to us. Tommy helped wake me up and I got up to watch the closing stages. I just got to the end of the tunnel when John Wark scored our third goal but at the time I was still affected by the clash of heads and I couldn't actually make out who had scored it. My memory was affected. All I could recall about my goal was seeing the cross come over from Millsy. I knew I could get to it and I can vaguely remember making contact with the ball – but after that everything went blank. I didn't even know I had put us ahead. All the other lads were congratulating me but I hadn't a clue what was going on. I must have been the only person at Highbury that day who was wondering what all the fuss was about.

The injury saw Talbot sit out Town's next two games, denying him the opportunity of clocking up 100 consecutive appearances within the space of two years, confirmation of how the one-time reserve player's stock had risen. But there was no way he was going to miss out on the FA Cup Final and he took the field sporting his tell-tale scar before turning in a typically honest and wholehearted performance full of running and endeavour, and with no little skill. By his own admission, Talbot's was a fetch-and-carry role, providing a link between defence and attack, but he also weighed in with a number of useful goals throughout his career, including three in the successful FA Cup campaign against Hartlepool, Millwall and West Bromwich Albion.

Watch the Wembley win again on DVD and his display is a real eye-opener. Socks down near his ankles, shin pads exposed, he popped up on both the right and the left of the pitch in a tireless display. He also took off on surging runs through the middle, making light of the strength-sapping conditions and rarely wasting a pass. Talbot started the 1977–78 season as captain because regular skipper Mick Mills was sidelined after a cartilage operation and missed the first nine games. He began to dream about the possibility of reaching the Final when, having disposed of Cardiff City and Hartlepool United in comfortable fashion, Ipswich came out of the fifth-round draw alongside another team from a lower division in Bristol Rovers. He said:

I looked at the other ties and most of the bigger sides seemed to have been drawn together. To be honest, I think every player starts every FA Cup campaign wishing it is going to be his year, but the luck of the draw is such a massive factor. After beating Bristol Rovers we were drawn to play Millwall, and you realise then that you are just one game away from the semis. At that stage I doubt if anyone – players or supporters – wasn't allowing the thought of going to Wembley to cross their minds. I wasn't overly concerned at the prospect of facing West Bromwich Albion in the semi-final. I felt we were carrying enough experience to be too good for them on the day and we were also hungry for the glory. That's what the FA Cup is all about – the glory. Just the thought of going to Wembley had the adrenalin pumping. It was the latest chapter of a story that started when I left Tower Ramparts School and signed for the club. I set myself targets, like getting into the reserves and then the first team, and once I was established I wanted to play for my country. Reaching the FA Cup Final was always an ambition, and being a local boy I knew what it meant to our fans because not many years earlier I had been one of them. I used to stand on the terraces at Portman Road long before I signed for the club and I knew how much it meant to the supporters to be at Wembley. I know they always say that the League Championship is the more prestigious prize, but to a club like Ipswich an appearance in a Cup Final meant so much. We did the fans proud, I think. It was a terrific occasion all round. I couldn't believe how good the support was and there's no doubt they helped us out there on the pitch. We were all genuinely surprised that the Ipswich fans were

Brian Talbot comes out on top in this challenge with David Price as John Wark looks on.

Another surging midfield run by Brian Talbot with Arsenal striker Malcom Macdonald in pursuit.

making so much noise and creating such a great atmosphere. We had a reputation in Suffolk for being a bit sleepy but at Wembley we came alive, both on and off the field.

Talbot, 24 at the time, was only too aware of Arsenal's initial interest in signing him – there were even suggestions that it surfaced again before the FA Cup Final – and of Bobby Robson's reluctance to let him go. He said:

*I found it extremely flattering that a club like Arsenal were prepared to pay so much money for me. I had always considered them to be **the** club in the country. I had one or two chats with the manager and he made it clear he didn't want me to go and although I was interested in hearing all about the deal I didn't really want to leave either. I remember we were coming back on the bus from a game at Middlesbrough. The atmosphere was so friendly and everyone was laughing. I looked around me and realised I had to stay. I signed a new contract and at the time I couldn't have been happier. But what I didn't realise was that all the talk of a transfer was affecting my game. The fans were quick to have a go because to them it must have appeared as if I wanted to leave the club.*

Just a few months later everything changed and Talbot was on his way to Arsenal after all. The Gunners persisted and once Ipswich had Muhren in place and Thijssen lined up they decided to accept the offer. Talbot arrived at Highbury just in time to launch the 1978–79 FA Cup campaign with his new employers and, after scoring in their fourth-round win over Notts County, he was on target again with the opening goal in the Final, although he had to convince a Wembley full house, as well as a global armchair audience of millions, that he had got the last touch as he and Alan Sunderland appeared to make contact with the ball simultaneously. At the time the Arsenal players clearly seemed to think Sunderland was the scorer, judging by the way they mobbed him, but in fact the goal was later credited to Talbot. His teammate, who was to join Town five years later, went on to net the late winner to secure a 3–2 win in what is generally acknowledged as one of the most thrilling FA Cup Final climaxes of them all.

Talbot experienced a very different feeling in 1980, although he was on a real high after scoring the vital goal that eventually decided a marathon semi-final against Liverpool. Their first meeting ended goalless and the stalemate continued as two replays at Villa Park both resulted in 1–1 draws. So to Highfield Road for the third replay, just nine days before the

Final, when Talbot finally broke the deadlock to separate the sides after seven hours of football. Talbot was more than just a midfield driving force. He scored in Arsenal's 2–0 win over Brighton in a fourth-round tie that year and was also on target at Anfield in a League meeting with Liverpool which, like the corresponding fixture at Highbury, ended all square. Since Bob Paisley's team won the League title that year, to eliminate them in the FA Cup semi-final was no mean feat, even if it took them four games to come out on top. Rather than collect a third winner's medal, however, Talbot was on the losing side and definitely did not enjoy being second best on the day. He said:

Basically, Wembley is for winners and no one really wants to know about the runners-up – I really can't think of a greater contrast in emotions. Players have to find out for themselves what it's like to win and lose. You can't tell them. I'll be honest and admit that when I was a winner in 1978 and 1979 I didn't stop to think about the other lads. I was too wrapped up in my own feelings. But in 1980 I realised what it was like. After we lost to West Ham our dressing room was like a morgue. No one spoke. In these moments, when you're really down, you don't stop to recall the great achievement of actually getting to Wembley. All of a sudden it means nothing.

Indeed, it proved to be such a shattering experience for the two-time winner that he collapsed on the bus transporting the Arsenal team to what they had hoped would be a victory celebration at London's plush Grosvenor House Hotel. He added:

I can only remember feeling very hot and tired, as if I was going to faint. I had to have mouth-to-mouth resuscitation and the lads told me later how concerned they were for me. The club doctor was with me and ordered me to rest. I spent about three or four hours in bed at the hotel and got up to have one fruit juice before the bar closed. It was only after an examination on the Monday confirmed there was nothing wrong with my heart that I was given the all-clear.

Talbot continued his playing career at Watford, Stoke, West Bromwich Albion, Fulham and Aldershot until it finally came to an end, and he moved into management after spending four years from 1984 as chairman of the Professional Footballers' Association. Coincidentally, West Brom and the FA Cup featured prominently in Talbot's life, starting in 1968 when he went to Wembley and cheered them on to victory in their Final clash with Everton. The game went to extra-time before Jeff Astle scored the only goal, maintaining his

WEMBLEY DOUBLE

Brian Talbot was one of five members of the FA Cup-winning side who celebrated a Wembley double in the 1977–78 season. Along with Paul Cooper, Paul Mariner, Clive Woods, skipper Mick Mills and Russell Osman, he was in the six-man squad that triumphed in the *Daily Express* five-a-side Championship, six months before the FA Cup Final. Talbot played a key part, netting from the spot with just 20 seconds left in the 1–1 draw with Newcastle. Talbot got Ipswich off to a flying start in the penalty shoot-out and the Geordies went the way of Wolves and West Ham in being knocked out by the men from Suffolk. Talbot was again on target in the Final with his side's second goal in a 3–1 defeat of Coventry.

The action was lapped up by an 8,000 capacity crowd at the Empire Pool, Wembley, and the highlights by millions of armchair viewers. Talbot said: 'At the time I remember captain Mick Mills saying we would all be going back to Wembley for the big one at the end of the season. How right he was.'

feat of having scored in every round of that year's competition. What was Talbot doing there? He said: 'I only went to that game because a mate of mine was an Albion fan and he got me a ticket. I didn't really care who won but I joined my friend in cheering for Albion.'

His goal in the semi-final dented Albion's hopes of returning to Wembley and it was with the Midlands club that he had his first taste of football management – a natural step for someone so totally immersed in the game. Talbot succeeded Ron Atkinson in November 1988, initially combining the role with playing. Following an embarrassing 4–2 FA Cup defeat at the Hawthorns by non-League Woking in January 1991, Talbot was sacked. His next move was to Aldershot, where he stayed until November of that year before moving to Malta and winning the Premier League title there twice with Hibernians, in 1993 and again the following year. He returned to England to join Conference side Rushden & Diamonds in 1997 and led them into the Football League in 2001, reaching the play-offs a year later and then, in 2003, winning the old Division Three Championship. He left in March 2004 to join Oldham, while Rushden, for whom his son Daniel played a number of games, were subsequently relegated.

In May 2005 he joined Oxford United but was sacked in March the following year as the club slid towards the Conference. He was not out of work for long, however, and returned to Malta, where his former Arsenal teammate Alan Sunderland resides, joining Marsaxlokk and leading them into the Champions League on the back of the first domestic title in their 58-year history.

Justifiably proud of his achievements in a career that is far from over, Talbot agreed he was privileged to not only play for his home-town club but also Arsenal, one of the true giants of the English game. He said:

At Ipswich we were like a big happy family. We were all hard workers, we were all down to earth and we were all good mates. There wasn't the same sort of camaraderie at Highbury because it was a much bigger family. The very fact that Ipswich have organised reunions to celebrate the 1978 win tends to say it all. Arsenal wouldn't do the same thing because they have had more success over the years. If you think about it, they would have to hold one every few years. We should have had other successes in my time at Portman Road but it just didn't work out, although that is what makes 1978 such a huge landmark for the club. The first time is always special and I am just as proud now as I was back then to have been a part of something so very special for Ipswich.

Brian Talbot (left) joins Clive Woods to show off the FA Cup at Wembley.

John Wark

FULL NAME: John Wark
DATE OF BIRTH: 4 August 1957
PLACE OF BIRTH: Glasgow, Scotland
IPSWICH TOWN APPEARANCES: 679
IPSWICH TOWN GOALS: 179

(Photograph courtesy of Owen Hines)

Ask Ipswich fans to nominate their favourite player of all time and there would be a flood of votes for John Wark, the midfield marksman extraordinaire who converted to defensive linchpin for the final chapter of a fabulously successful career.

There are few, if any, former stars to rival ex-skipper Mick Mills for the title of Mr Ipswich but Wark runs him close, finishing second only to Mills in terms of appearances and also playing a leading role in the club's FA Cup and UEFA Cup triumphs. When it comes to goals scored, Wark is in third place behind Ray Crawford, the most prolific marksman in the history of the club, and Ted Phillips, which is some achievement by the moustachioed Scot given the fact that he played mainly in midfield and the rest of the time at the back. The fact that he was regularly the scourge of the traditional derby enemy – no one has featured in more games or scored more goals against Norwich City – is also guaranteed to maintain his status as a firm fans' favourite for many years to come. Add his Scottish international honours – he scored twice in the World Cup Finals in 1982 and also captained the Youth and Under-21 sides – and the fact that he was voted the PFA Player of the Year the previous year, the only Ipswich player to have won the prestigious accolade, and he has plenty upon which to reflect as he looks back on 20-plus years of active service. However, he needs only a split second to declare that the highlight to beat all others was the FA Cup Final of 1978, even if he was the very last of the 22 players on the pitch to touch the ball and, until Roger Osborne's match-winning strike, he was by far the most frustrated, since two replica second-half shots both came crashing back off the same upright. Wark remembered:

Not only did they rebound off the same post, but I wouldn't mind betting the ball hit the same spot each time. The only difference was that one drive was from outside the area and the other was from just inside the 18-yard area. I can actually remember the exact moment when I took aim on both occasions. As I prepared to shoot I was thinking to myself: 'Remember, you've got Pat Jennings to beat' and I was determined to score. I struck them well – perhaps too well – and I was sure at least one of them was going to hit the net. I even managed to bend them slightly so I couldn't have done much more. Big Pat was beaten each time, no doubt about it. I had trouble sleeping the night before at our hotel. I was sharing with Paul Mariner and he went out like a light. He could have snored, never mind scored, for England and I was just lying there thinking about the next day's game. I could see Wembley in my head, the game was under way and I popped up with a goal. In my dreams! You have to remember I wasn't much more than a boy back then. I hadn't turned 21 and in one way I couldn't really believe what was happening to me. Even now I look back on my career and I realise how fortunate I was to get an FA Cup winner's medal at such a young age. No matter how old I was I still count myself lucky. I mean, some players go through their entire career and they don't get one. And top, top players, too, people like George Best and Alan Shearer – that's just two names off the top of my head who never did it.

Wark's late header in the semi-final win over West Bromwich Albion was one of the more magical moments of Ipswich's run in the competition, ending any fears that the Midlands outfit would level and take the game into extra-time and clinching the club's first-ever Wembley appearance. 'That was some day,' laughed Wark, recalling the extraordinary events at Highbury as Town raced into an early two-goal lead and were comfortable until Allan Hunter conceded a penalty. Wark added:

When Big Al stuck his hand up and touched the ball as it came over I don't think any of us could quite believe what we had seen. Some of the senior players had a go – Millsy gave him a real ear-bashing – but me and George didn't say a word. In all honesty we were scared of the big man so we stayed silent. They scored from the penalty and all of a sudden we're not just seeing out the game. But we're in a bit of a fix because we don't want to go chasing a third goal and leave

---

TEAM CONFIDENCE

John Wark was just as confident as his Ipswich colleagues of beating Arsenal to win the FA Cup, but it was shortly after the kick-off that he knew 'for sure' that the trophy was destined for Portman Road. He said:

Allan Hunter went into a tackle on Frank Stapleton in the very first minute and it was one of those challenges that took the ball and also sent the player up in the air. I had a bit of a smile to myself because it showed Allan's determination not to be second best at anything on the day – it summed up the way we had been feeling all along. He got it in nice and early to make his mark and in a way it set the tone for the game. Funnily enough, everybody seems to think the tackle was on Malcolm Macdonald but that didn't happen until midway through the first half. That was a real cruncher as well. It proved two things – that the big man's knee was okay and that he more than had the measure of Supermac, who talked a good game beforehand but got no change out of Allan and Kevin Beattie in the entire 90 minutes. But that first-minute tackle on Stapleton is the one I remember best of all. It was as if he was sending out a signal to the other lads and we all got the message loud and clear.

---

ourselves exposed, but nor do we want to sit back and try to hang on to what we've got because that wasn't our way and it might have been asking for trouble. In the end everything was fine but it was a long 15 minutes or so until I headed in a corner. Of all the goals I scored for Ipswich that was probably the one that gave me the most pleasure, the greatest thrill. It was so important and you could tell what it meant to the rest of the lads, too, the way they all piled on top of me. It was just like a rugby scrum, with me right at the bottom. The sheer relief is something I can't describe. It was a killer for them because they knew the clock was against them, but for us, well, it was a case of 'Wembley here we come'. We had a couple of minutes to play and then it was absolute bedlam as we got the celebrations under way. Once we got to the dressing room we really got stuck in – we were drinking champagne in the bath.

Wark had also weighed in with a goal in the 6–1 mauling of Millwall at the quarter-final stage, and he was very grateful to end the season on such an incredible high since it had started with him sidelined with a hamstring injury he sustained on the club's pre-season tour of Holland. He said:

Wembley was the only good thing about the season, to be honest. Had it not been for the FA Cup win it would have been a non-event – and I wouldn't have been the only one to say that. A lot of the lads were in and out with injury and we never did enough to challenge for the League, which was something we used to do every single year in those days. I didn't make my first appearance that season until January and in the third-round game at Cardiff. How lucky was I that I got back in time for the FA Cup campaign? Mind you, I played at Ninian Park and I reckon I was only about 60 per cent fit. I could have done with another week or two but we had a lot of injuries at the time so I came back before I was fully fit. The torn hamstring troubled me quite a lot. Even at Wembley I could feel it wasn't perfect, although it didn't stop me from doing what I was asked to do on the day. But I had to pull out of the Scotland squad for a game in East Germany and that cost me my first senior cap, although I managed to win a few later on. I was also close to going to the World Cup Finals in Argentina with Scotland. The manager was Ally MacLeod and he picked me for his first squad of 40 but when he had to cut it down to 22 in the end my name was one of those that disappeared. Again, though, I got there in 1982 in Spain and none of the players who went to Argentina look back on it with any great memories. I was lucky that I got myself fit enough to get involved in the Cup run. Poor old Trevor Whymark got injured in December and couldn't get back in time, which was cruel luck for him. Football's like that, so I thank my lucky stars for what I was able to achieve. You are always at the mercy of injuries but I had fewer problems than others. The odd thing about that hamstring injury was that I kind of had it with me for the rest of my career. I used to run with a sort of limp, if you remember, and that was why. The way I ran, I was doing my utmost to make sure it never went again.

Wark loved the build-up to the Final, and the Ipswich squad followed the same route as all FA Cup Final teams in those days, taking part in a host of goodwill visits as part of a packed commercial programme that included a visit to the recording studios. He explained:

It was all great fun, but none of us got too carried away – we just did what every Wembley team did. We tried to make a few bob out of it, but we never lost sight of the fact that there was a game to be won. And to be perfectly honest, I doubt if there has ever been a more confident team in the FA Cup Final than us that year. Too many people, including the bookies, made a big thing of our League position. But anyone who knew us knew we were better than that. We kept telling people that on our day, with our strongest line-up, or at least close to it, we were more than a match for any side. We proved it in the semi-final, I thought. It wasn't just the fact that we won it, but the way we won it. We played some great football on the day and that's what it is all about in a Cup competition – what happens on the day.

Wark still shudders at the memory of what happened a week before Wembley, when events at Villa Park threatened to throw a spanner in the works. A 6–1 defeat was bad enough, but it was an eye-opener for the young Scot as several of his senior colleagues took matters into their own hands. Manager Bobby Robson's decision to allow fit-again midfielder Colin Viljoen to stake a claim for a place in the Final, at the expense of Roger Osborne, went down like a lead balloon in some quarters and Wark witnessed something that day he never saw repeated in any other game he played for Liverpool, Middlesbrough or Scotland, never mind Ipswich. He remembered:

The manager's team selection at Aston Villa provoked an amazing reaction among the players. Some of them just went through the motions – there is no other way I can describe it. Half of them didn't try so it wasn't surprising that we got thumped by Aston Villa. Actually, they could have got double figures, that's how bad we were. If it hadn't been for young Paul Overton, making his debut in goal, we'd have conceded more than 10, I'm convinced of it. I was doing my best and putting in the effort but I looked around me and I couldn't believe that some of the players clearly weren't bothered how many we let in. The papers called it player power and that's exactly what it was. You couldn't call it anything else. The senior lads challenged the manager's decision and he changed his mind. It was weird that day. I just sat there in the dressing room and the row was going on around me. I must admit that I felt sorry for Colin Viljoen. It's what I was saying earlier about injuries that season and how so many players were affected. In the end, he wasn't fit enough and it was right that Roger should play. Colin took it badly and I felt for him, but had he played against Arsenal I'm not sure how we would have fared. The upheaval might have really cost us. When he came into the side at Villa it wasn't just a simple one-in-one-out switch. There were positional changes as well and it was all a bit much with the FA Cup Final just a week away. It meant things were up in the air and the players who complained couldn't really see the point. I played out on the right of midfield and that wasn't really my scene. I never felt I was suited to that role, although I did play wide, both right and left, for Scotland – in 28 of my 29 games to be honest – but that was because I was up against the likes of Graeme Souness, Bruce Rioch, Archie Gemmill and Asa Hartford, all of them established players, for the central places. I was much more useful in the middle for Ipswich and I think my record proves it. I liked to win the ball, spread it wide and then take up positions on the edge of the box. I would get in a shot whenever possible. I would time my runs to get there and pick up knock-downs from the likes of Paul Mariner or I would get on the end of crosses myself. That was my game.

Wark was a central defender of huge potential when he first made the long trek south to Suffolk from his native Glasgow. It was in that position that he made his senior debut in the third, and decisive, replay of the FA Cup quarter-final tie with Leeds in March 1975. In a sense, although he did not establish himself straight away, he never looked back. That was a baptism of fire and he featured again in the semi-final replay against West Ham at Stamford Bridge a few weeks later, a night he will never forget for all the wrong reasons as luckless Town crashed out of the competition in the cruellest possible circumstances. He added:

I was 17 at the time and a real novice but that defeat hit the senior lads hard. There were a lot of tears in the dressing room and on the bus home. That experience – it was absolutely horrible – has lived with me forever, and when we won at Highbury I was delighted for Millsy and others as they experienced the opposite side of the coin. Semi-finals are great occasions when you win but it's a horrible game to lose. We did it again in 1981 and we were kicking ourselves. Had we not won in 1978 I'd be sitting here now as miserable as sin because I wouldn't have my FA Cup medal. On the other hand, I could have three.

Wark recalls how he 'froze' in front of the BBC cameras at the team's hotel on the morning of the game, when John Motson conducted live interviews with all the players. Old hands like skipper Mick Mills may have taken it all in their stride, but it was a different story for their young teammate. He remembered:

I see young players now and they are just the same as I was then – a bit uptight. I fluffed my lines – a bit like in Escape to Victory. I had only one thing to say in that film and they dubbed a voice over mine. I've had some stick for that over the years. I always get the mickey taken out of me when we get the 1978 team together. They can't wait to remind me that it took me 18 minutes to get a kick and that was when I ran a long way, about 60 yards I think it was, to stop the ball going out for a corner. It hardly seems possible but I'm afraid it is true. Basically, this is what happened. Just as Roger Osborne was told to mark Liam Brady I was told to stay close to Alan Hudson. They were both talented players who would soon start to influence the game if they had the time on the ball. I took the instructions literally and stuck to Hudson like glue. When he went deep and picked the ball up from David O'Leary or Willie Young, I was there. He played little passes here and there but not once did he get the other side of me. In other words, he wasn't hurting us and shadowing him the way I did made perfect sense. I was making a nuisance of myself but I wasn't actually getting a kick. But when the lads start taking the mickey I have the perfect answer. As far as I'm concerned there are only a few things people remember about the FA Cup Final – first and foremost Roger's goal, PM hitting the bar early doors, an unbelievable save by Pat Jennings from George Burley's header and my two shots against the same post. It tends to shut them up when I remind them about that!

This book would not be complete without Wark's classic tale about his family – parents, brother, sister, aunts, uncles and cousins galore – hiring a small bus to make the journey south of the border for their very first FA Cup Final. He said:

I've told this story a few times but even I still have to laugh when I tell it. There were about 24 of them in all and it was a big, big adventure for them. It's not every day that ordinary folk from Glasgow head for Wembley to see a family member playing in the biggest game of the season and they were determined to make the most of it. I've no idea how many stops they made on the way but it was a few. They said they had to refuel – and buy petrol as well – if you see what I mean. I think they left on the Thursday and had bed and breakfast along the way but it would be fair to say they were in a reasonably merry state by the time they reached London. Come the end of the game, and after we were presented with the Cup and our medals, we were off on the traditional lap of honour. As we got to the point where the Ipswich fans were sitting I spotted my sister, Wilma, on the other side of the fence. Then I saw my mother, father and the rest of them. I jumped over a small perimeter fence and went running up to them. Without the fence I'd have been in there with them and I don't think another FA Cup Final player has ever done that. As I got really close I couldn't believe my eyes. No joking, their faces were just about tripping them. I was over the moon but they all looked bloody miserable. 'What's up?' I asked and they explained that they had all placed bets at odds of 20–1 that I would score the first goal. To be fair, that seemed a bit generous when you think I'd got a goal in both the quarter-final and the semi-final. Anyway, I've got an FA Cup-winner's medal in my hand and all they could say was: 'Why didn't you score?' and I said something about doing my best and carried on my way. I couldn't believe the reception they gave me. It was alright in the end because although the bulk of them carried on back to Glasgow, some of them came out to Ipswich and were there for the open-top bus ride and the party that followed. It was great to have some of my family around me, even if they felt I had let them down by not scoring. By that time we were all on the same wavelength – I mean, we weren't exactly stone-cold sober. I was determined to make the most of it and what surprises me now, 30 years on, is that I can remember so much about it. The scenes in the town centre on the Sunday were really something and brought a lump to my throat. I didn't know there were that many people in Ipswich.

Wark hardly missed a game for the club over the next six seasons, his remarkable contribution of 14 goals in 12 games in the UEFA Cup success of 1981 equalling the European record set by Italian ace Jose Altafini, who scored the same number as AC Milan won the European Cup in 1963, when they also happened to eliminate Ipswich along the way.

It was quite a season for Wark, as he took his overall goal tally to 36 in 64 games, scooped the PFA Player of the Year award ahead of club colleagues Frans Thijssen and Paul Mariner, came third in the Football Writers' Footballer of the Year poll behind winner Thijssen and runner-up Mick Mills and also earned the accolade of Top Young Player in Europe in a contest organised by an Italian sports magazine. He completed a British hat-trick behind previous winners Jimmy Case and Garry Birtles, and he was awarded an all-expenses-paid fortnight's holiday in Italy to coincide with collecting his solid gold award at a glittering ceremony. Ironically, however, it was only when he returned to Portman Road for two spells later in his career that he actually won the supporters' Player of the Year trophy, although doing so an unprecedented four times in the space of five seasons emphasised the impact he made under managers John Duncan and John Lyall.

With Ipswich on the slide since Bobby Robson's departure to take charge of England in the summer of 1982, Wark departed for Liverpool in March 1984, and after scoring on his debut at Watford he did not have long to wait to collect his one and only League Championship medal. Sadly, the rest of his stay was a tale of finishing second or being sidelined through injury. He explained: 'At the end of my first season we won the League and although I only played the last 12 games I was awarded a medal. I think the rule at the time was that you had to play 14 games but Liverpool argued on my behalf and won. In my second season I was top scorer with 27 goals and I think I'm right in saying it was the only occasion in Ian Rush's time with the club that he didn't finish top.'

Wark was in the Liverpool side that lost to Juventus in the 1985 European Cup Final, a game completely overshadowed by the horrific events at the Heysel Stadium, and also when Arsenal defeated them in the Littlewoods (League) Cup Final of 1987. In between, when they defeated Everton 3–1 in the FA Cup Final, he was in plaster for the second time that season due to a broken ankle and a ruptured Achilles tendon.

Perhaps the most remarkable episode of Wark's career came in 1991. The previous year, when Lyall succeeded Duncan, Wark had been allowed to move to Middlesbrough, who released him after one season as part of then manager Lennie Lawrence's insistence that all players be permanently based in Teesside. Wark said:

(Photograph by Peter Stack)

John Wark scores Ipswich's fourth goal in the 6–1 FA Cup quarter-final win over Millwall at The Den.

I had been renting a place up there and coming back when I had time in between games. I still played 40 games for them that season but I accepted the rule that Lennie brought in and I came back to Ipswich and waited for the phone to ring. I waited and waited. One of the clubs who rang were Falkirk and they invited me up there for a trial. I didn't think I had anything to prove at that stage of my career and politely declined. But for a few weeks I was kicking my heels and wondering if that was it; the end.

Ipswich invited him to train at Portman Road so that he would at least be fully fit once another club came on the scene but when he was still unemployed some weeks later, and Town were short of players for a reserve game, he was invited to fill a defensive gap. He performed so well that Lyall gave him another game, then another, and finally signed him on a contract until the end of the season. The fact that Ipswich won the Second Division title, having been dismissed as no-hopers with pre-season odds of 25–1, and that Wark was crowned Player of the Year, says it all. Now the brand new Premier League beckoned and the veteran was relishing the challenge, so much so that he featured prominently in Sky Sports' advertisements aimed at attracting subscribers. He even had a spell alongside Paul Goddard in charge of the first team, which he combined with playing, and it was quite an achievement that Town survived for three seasons with very little invested in squad strengthening. When Lyall resigned in December 1994, to be replaced by George Burley, it meant Wark was playing for his fifth Ipswich manager.

Wark celebrated a testimonial in the form of a pre-season clash with Arsenal, and it was on 30 November 1996 – St Andrew's Day – that he made what was to be his final appearance in an Ipswich shirt, when he was replaced after 80 minutes of a 3–0 League defeat at Tranmere. At the end of that season, with his 40th birthday in sight, he officially retired.

Wark was chief scout at both Portsmouth and Coventry but now acts as matchday host in the Sir Bobby Robson Suite at Portman Road, his only official connection with the professional game. However, despite celebrating his 50th birthday in 2007, he continued to play in the Licensed Trades League for SophtLogic and also for the Liverpool Legends side in games both in this country and abroad.

CLIVE WOODS

FULL NAME: Clive Richard Woods
DATE OF BIRTH: 18 December 1947
PLACE OF BIRTH: Norwich, Norfolk
IPSWICH TOWN APPEARANCES: 338
IPSWICH TOWN GOALS: 31

(*Photograph courtesy of Owen Hines*)

He may have turned on a Man of the Match display in the FA Cup Final but Clive Woods is adamant he played better games for Ipswich than at Wembley on 6 May 1978. The fact that he was capable of improving on a display in which he tortured Arsenal full-back and captain Pat Rice, now Arsene Wenger's right-hand man at the Emirates Stadium, underlines what a fabulous player he was – fit to compare with football's first knight according to another, Sir Bobby Robson. When Robson introduced one of his players to the crowd as 'Stanley Matthews' on the Cornhill the day after Ipswich won the famous trophy, each and every one of the massed throng knew he was referring to Woods. For his manager to compare Woods with the one and only Sir Stanley, nicknamed the Wizard of Dribble, was an accolade in itself, while to be officially named as the best player on the pitch put him alongside some other all-time greats who had graced the showpiece occasion over the years.

Wembley was the perfect stage for a player who had plenty in common with several of his teammates that day. Many had taken an unconventional, almost fairytale-like route to stardom, that had seen them employed outside the game before football came calling, at a time when they feared the opportunity had passed them by.

They still call the 1953 showdown, when Blackpool defeated Bolton Wanderers 4–3, the Matthews Final and it was not until Woods turned on the magic, 25 years later, that another winger dominated the event to such an extent. It seemed he was playing the game of his life as he tied Rice up in knots, twisting one way and then the other to leave the defender in his wake as he ran riot on Town's behalf. No other player appeared to be enjoying the occasion quite as much as Woods, who knew that since he was in his 31st year he might never have another chance to grace such a grand stage. He said:

To be named as Man of the Match in an FA Cup Final is a magnificent honour but I just went out to play my normal game. I always did. Sometimes it didn't come off but I knew I'd played really well at Wembley, although I don't believe it was my best game for the club. That very season, for example, I believe I played better in the UEFA Cup tie against Barcelona over in Spain. We were leading 3–0 going into the second leg at the Nou Camp and we were very unlucky to go out on penalties. I was one of the players who missed in the shoot-out but I know I played well in the game itself. I loved the European games – a change of scenery and different opponents, I always looked forward to them. We played in Holland against Feyenoord and I just know I had a better game that night than at Wembley.

As soon as he helped clinch victory over West Bromwich Albion in the semi-final at Highbury, Woods set about planning a no-expense-spared family reunion to coincide with the Final, that involved bringing his parents, three brothers and twin sister together for the first time in four years. One of his brothers, Denis, a former player with Cambridge United and Watford, was based in Norway but that did not matter and Woods footed the bill for a family knees-up, the celebrations being completed by Ipswich's win and his own fantastic contribution on the day. He recalled:

All through the FA Cup campaign that year I remained confident that we would go all the way. To play in a Final had been an ambition of mine for years and I just had a feeling that year would offer my best-ever chance of doing it. When we won the semi-final I was absolutely certain we would go on and beat Arsenal in the Final. I wasn't getting carried away, I just knew. When we came out of the hat with Albion in the semi-finals I was sure we would be going to Wembley. My confidence was based on the fact that I felt we were a much better all-round side than they were, especially down the left side, which was supposed to be their strong point.

Woods missed the third-round trip to Cardiff with a groin injury but was ever-present thereafter and made a vital contribution at Highbury, filling in for midfielder Brian Talbot, who was forced to quit after putting Town ahead in the eighth minute with a diving header. There was no way Talbot could continue after an ugly clash of heads with West Brom skipper John Wile. Woods said:

As soon as I saw the extent of Brian's injury I knew he would have to go off and stay off. Because our substitute, Mick Lambert, was a winger, I realised I would have to drop back and plug the gap caused by Noddy's early departure. It can be a difficult job switching roles like that but I was pleased with my game. I tried to do things simply and having so many good players around me was a big help. It was a bit like that at Wembley as well because we were simply too good for Arsenal on the day. Our players were better than theirs, both individually and as a team.

When he started out, Woods did not even dare to think he might one day be an established top-flight star, never mind upstaging colleagues and opponents in an FA Cup Final at Wembley and earning a call-up to England's senior squad. It was, to coin a phrase, a rags to riches story. When he left school in his native Norwich he worked as a delivery boy for the local Co-op, which involved setting off from the store on his bike to drop off groceries around the area. He laughed: 'You know David Jason's character, Granville, in *Open All Hours*? Well, that was me. One day there was so much packed into the box on the bike that when I got off the saddle the thing tipped up.'

Before long his displays in local football attracted the attention of scouts representing clubs all over the country. When he accepted an invitation to go on trial to Scunthorpe he found himself sharing digs with a dark-haired lad, small in stature but big in talent and application. Kevin Keegan was taken on, unlike Woods, and did not do too badly for himself. The next time the pair met, years later, they were both in the same England squad.

Woods was 21 and playing in the Norwich Business Houses League when Ipswich first took an interest. They asked him to play in a reserve fixture at Northampton, and he remembered:

It was only the Football Combination but that was a huge leap from where I was playing at the time. Mick Mills, Gerry Baker and Eddie Spearritt were in the Town side and I hardly had a kick the whole game. When we got back to Ipswich everyone piled off the bus and headed home. There was only myself and a director, Mr Robinson, left on board. I asked him if I got anything for coming along and he put his hand in his pocket, pulled out a quid and gave it to me.

Norwich were not taking a complete back seat but Clive, despite being a Canaries fan, was less than enthusiastic about going to Carrow Road. He also made a wasted trip to Wolves for another trial match that came to nothing. It was when Ipswich came knocking at his door for a second time that things really started to happen. He recalled:

They asked me to play in the reserves at QPR and we won the game 4–1. It was one of those games where everything I tried came off. Bobby Robson was in the stand and I stayed on to play about another nine or 10 games. I was working full-time in a shoe factory at the time and I was playing for nothing. Ipswich gave me my train fare from Norwich – about 15 bob (shillings, 75 pence in today's currency) I think it was. Trevor [Whymark] was in exactly the same boat. We played against Chelsea reserves at Portman Road one night and were waiting at the station to go home when a chap popped his head out of the train going to London and called us over. He handed me a card and said: 'Give me a call in the morning.' After the train had gone I looked at the card and it said: 'Jack Mansell, Manager, Reading FC.' He had obviously been at the game and liked the look of us but, as it happened, we were summoned to the manager's office at Ipswich the next morning and offered full-time professional contracts. I packed in the job at the shoe factory, where I was on £19 a week, and Ipswich paid me £20 or it might have been £25. But whatever it was, I didn't become rich overnight.

Woods was on his way but given the way he regularly made life miserable for opposition full-backs it comes as a shock to learn that he was not operating as a winger in those days. In fact, he played in midfield and up front before moving out wide. He said: 'I honestly don't know how I came to be stuck out there. As a kid I was no ball-playing winger, I can assure you. But I knew where to run and I knew how to find space so that might have had something to do with it.'

The emergence of Woods and Whymark coincided with Robson getting to grips with the task of managing Ipswich, and to have two such good players virtually on his doorstep was a godsend. They signed professional forms in May 1969, just four months after his appointment. However, Woods made an unsteady start. From making just one first-team start and two substitute appearances in his first full season, he went on to have 36 senior outings in the 1970–71 campaign and seemed to be well on his way. But he managed just 14 in the following two seasons, including a mere two starts, so he was certainly no overnight success. He made a much more telling contribution as Ipswich finished fourth in 1974 and it was often a question of whether Woods or Lambert was the player in form when Robson got round to selecting his team, and the statistics support the theory that they more or less shared the number 11 shirt for several seasons.

Woods' ability to skip past defenders' challenges was by no means his only asset and, while he was hardly a prolific marksman, a number of his goals stayed in the memory for a long time. Like the one that decided the marathon quarter-final tie with Leeds in 1975, when he cut in from the left at the neutral venue, Filbert Street, Leicester, and buried a rising right-foot shot that curled around the 'keeper and inside the far post.

Continuing on the subject of Wembley in 1978, he said: 'I have watched the video and DVD of the match over the years and it is almost as if it is slow motion compared to the game today. On the day I was totally relaxed beforehand with no sign of nerves. It was one of the few times I wasn't nervous. Most of the lads were the same. Maybe it was because we were just so pleased to be there after a terrible let-down three years earlier. The other players will tell you the same – after that disappointment we didn't want another one.'

It was in March 1980 that Woods went 'home' and signed for Norwich, after manager John Bond willingly handed over an £80,000 fee to tempt Robson to sell. But although he threw himself headlong into the challenge, he did not have the best of times at Carrow Road. He added:

I remember being at home painting one day when Bondy called me. They had agreed a fee with Ipswich and wanted to get things moving. I arranged to meet him and signed straight away. But when Bondy left and was replaced by Ken Brown my days were numbered. There was one game at Watford when I genuinely thought I was our best player. The papers gave me a good write-up, too, but on the Monday morning I went in and Brown said I would never play for Norwich again. He said he would give me a free transfer and paid me up. That was that; the end of my career. I did get an invitation to go over to Holland and talk to FC Twente so I decided to give it a go and went over for a week to see how things were. In the end it wasn't worth uprooting my family for the money they were offering.

Woods took a job managing a sports shop in Norwich city centre but his playing days were actually far from over. He may have turned his back on the professional scene but in a sense he went back to his roots, signing for village team Newton Flotman of the Anglian Combination Premier Division and continuing at that level until he was in his late 40s, by which time he had become a full-back. Incredibly, he moved to Diss Town and was still playing for their reserves at the age of 50.

Just as his display in the FA Cup Final showed, Woods enjoyed playing football for a living. He said:

When I think back to my time with Ipswich I realise what great fun it was. Allan Hunter was some character and I can see him grabbing the microphone on the bus and taking the mickey out of everyone. No one was safe from the big man. He would have a go at the directors and they just laughed. None of the rest of us would have dared and you couldn't see it happening at any other club. We were all different. There were a few local lads and the outsiders were all lively characters. There were no real cliques – we all got on well. When people ask me about the highlight of my career I say it was the time I spent at Ipswich – all of it.

Clive Woods (left) and captain Mick Mills show off the FA Cup during a lap of honour at Portman Road.

CRUCIAL GOAL

Clive Woods scored a goal in the FA Cup-winning season that was worth its weight in gold. However, it was not his team's third in the 3–0 home win over Bristol Rovers in the fifth-round replay, although that was certainly welcomed at the time. The one that mattered more was the only goal of a League game at Newcastle, which took place between the two FA Cup clashes with the West Country side. Its significance? It clinched Ipswich's only League success on their travels that season and went a long way towards securing their First Division status. Woods said: 'Even by the time we won the semi-final there was still a danger we might get relegated but we managed to do just enough to stay up. We couldn't get going in away League games but thankfully it was a different story in the FA Cup.'

For several years Woods has been a distribution manager for electrical retailer Bennetts, ensuring goods leave the warehouse on time and arrive at the proper destination. His football fix comes courtesy of Sky Sports, rather than what is on offer at either Portman Road or Carrow Road, where he used to thrill the crowds. Casting his mind back 30 years, his face lights up at the memory of how he turned on the style in front of a live audience of 100,000 and millions more around the globe following the action on the box. Almost looking embarrassed, he admitted:

I can't remember too much about what was happening beforehand – not even the manager's team talk. This may sound silly, but it was just like any other game in a way. We had a pre-match meal at the hotel and did a few TV interviews, but you could see that none of us was nervous. We were like a bunch of lads on holiday, rather than a team preparing for the game of their lives. It is often the case that a player will go out of his way to show he is not nervous but it's actually all an act. It was totally genuine with us. We were all relaxed and, considering the importance of the occasion, I found it really strange that it was one of the very few occasions when the butterflies stayed quiet in my stomach. I had a massage, just as I did before every game. The night before the Final there was a massive storm and the rain didn't stop. I was sharing a room with Brian Talbot and we started to wonder if the game might be in danger of being called off because when we woke up in the morning it was still coming down and it didn't look as if there had been a break in the weather. When we got to the stadium it was still very damp. The pitch was playable but it was a bit heavy, which was hardly surprising. The sun came out around kick-off time and it was beating down on us throughout the game. I was completely knackered at the end and so were most of the players because we had really worked hard to get the win. For what seemed like several minutes I was begging the ref to blow his whistle for full-time. When he did we just hugged each other. When we went up to get the trophy I was right behind Millsy and it wasn't until I actually had that winner's medal in my hand that I believed what we had done.

One of Woods' main highlights of the occasion came right at the start, when he emerged from the tunnel prior to kick-off and was able to pick out his mother in the crowd. He said:

Mum's dead now, bless her, but she suffered from multiple sclerosis and never went very far in those days. But I was determined that she would be there at Wembley to see me play. We managed to get her a special place, in her wheelchair, behind the goal and when I spotted her I had a huge lump in my throat. That was a very emotional moment for us both. At the end of the game my brother managed to gatecrash the dressing room. I don't know how he bluffed his way past the stewards. We had a picture taken in there with most of the players together with the Cup and he's right in the middle alongside me. Some people still haven't worked out the identity of the bloke with the big cigar!

Nowadays the FA Cup Final is still a fixture Woods looks forward to every year and he has a ritual to which he adheres. He skips most of the build-up but ensures he is in his seat five minutes before the start – with his winner's medal on its chain around his neck. He explained: 'I'll have a couple of mates with me, we'll open a few lagers and away we go. By half-time everybody's having a great game. It's still a big game, even if some managers try to make out the FA Cup is no big deal any more. I just sit there and the goosebumps are out. I consider myself very fortunate to have played in it and won.'

Woods could hardly have come closer to winning an England cap since he was named in Ron Greenwood's squad for a World Cup qualifier in Luxembourg alongside club colleagues Mick Mills, Brian Talbot, Kevin Beattie and Trevor Whymark. But instead of playing, he ended up just going along for the ride. He recalled: 'I didn't expect to be in the starting line-up but I felt I had a chance of being on the bench because it was a game we needed to win and ideally with a few goals to spare. But I didn't make it on to the bench and when the next game came round I didn't even make the squad, so my international career, if you could call it that, was over and done with.'

Along with his Town teammates, he also came close on more than one occasion to winning a League Championship medal but again it was a case of so near and yet so far as Ipswich mounted a firm challenge only to fall short over the final lap, in the main through a lack of depth in their squad. However, Ipswich's home form was so good for a while that supporters used to turn out wondering not whether they would see their team win but by how many they would achieve victory. That led to visiting teams revising their tactics and Woods would often come in for extra special attention. He remembered:

There were a lot of times when I would be marked by two players and it was difficult just to get on the ball, never mind do anything with it. I used to get a fair bit of stick from the supporters because a lot was expected of me as the only winger in the side, and people looked to me to supply most of the ammunition for the strikers. I would drop back and try to create more space for the strikers but the crowd didn't seem to realise what I was doing and would get on my back. As I got more frustrated my game would suffer but on the really big occasions, like at Wembley, I seemed to perform. The big pitch at Wembley appealed to me and I enjoyed

[Photograph courtesy Offside Sports Photography Ltd]

Clive Woods on the ball at Wembley with direct opponent Pat Rice struggling to keep up.

the extra space I seemed to have. It was quite an open game, as I recall. We had David Geddis out on the right to contain Sammy Nelson and we didn't really have too much bother carving out chances for ourselves. I had one myself when Paul Mariner knocked the ball on for me but I jumped a fraction early and my header was off target and too weak. Of course I would have loved to have scored, but so would George Burley, John Wark and Paul Mariner, who all went close. The main thing, at the end of the day, was to ensure we won a game we dominated and not get done by a sucker punch. No one could say we didn't deserve our win. Even the Arsenal lads knew they were second-best on the day. We got the goal thanks to Roger and it was just utter relief when the referee finally blew his whistle to signal the end of the game. We had felt all along that we would win but when it became a reality there was no danger of it being an anti-climax. We celebrated in the dressing room with some champagne and the party went on for about another 24 hours. It was typical of Ipswich – great fun!

THE SUPPORTING CasT

No tribute to the Wembley '78 heroes would be complete without acknowledging the contribution of those who played their part in Ipswich's progress, even if they were not involved in the Final. Town used a total of 19 players to negotiate their route to the national stadium, while runners-up Arsenal were able to rely on the same 12 individuals throughout the competition.

In the FA Cup Final programme, interestingly enough, Arsenal's team group featured just 14 players – the Wembley dozen plus future Sudbury manager Richie Powling and defender John Matthews – and one wonders how current boss Arsene Wenger might view the prospect of coping with a similar-sized squad today. Towards the back of the programme – it was clear from the layout that even the publishers viewed Arsenal as firm favourites – the Ipswich team picture featured 19 players alongside manager Bobby Robson and first-team coach Cyril Lea. Curiously though, there was no sign of Alan Brazil, his 15-minute part in the 3–0 fifth-round replay victory over Bristol Rovers apparently overlooked, while reserve 'keeper Laurie Sivell, who had played no part at all in the journey to Wembley, was included. Similarly, while Trevor Whymark appeared in the picture but not in any of Town's six games prior to Wembley, there was no place for Tommy Parkin, whose seven-minute cameo at Cardiff marked his senior debut for the club.

Along with Brazil and Parkin, the other five Town players who featured at some stage before the Final were Robin Turner, Russell Osman, Les Tibbott, Colin Viljoen

Trevor Whymark

149

and Eric Gates. Turner actually started five of the six games Robson's men had to negotiate before the Final, and also weighed in with two goals as the record books report. However, even allowing for Roger Osborne's frank admission elsewhere in this book that it was him, and not Turner, who scored the oh-so-vital late equaliser at Bristol Rovers, the simple truth is that Ipswich would have gone out at snowbound Eastville had Turner not also netted a 27th minute opener.

Right back at the start of the competition, Ipswich were forced to field several fringe players in the third-round tie at Cardiff, where Messrs Tibbott, Osman, Viljoen and Gates took the places of eventual Wembley heroes George Burley, Kevin Beattie, Roger Osborne and Clive Woods.

Parkin's late introduction at Ninian Park was one of two substitute appearances he made that season – the other came in the final League fixture at home to Wolves – and ironically it was at Wembley for the Charity Shield game against champions Nottingham Forest that he made his first senior start. The Gateshead-born midfielder, whose best run in the side came after Bobby Ferguson took charge in 1982, clocked up a total of 60 first-team outings, 20 of which were as a substitute, during 13 years on the books.

In the case of Osman and Gates, who helped Ipswich to a 2–0 win at Cardiff, their best years were ahead of them and they not only helped bring the UEFA Cup to Portman Road in 1981 but also went on to win England international honours.

Central defender Osman who forged a formidable partnership with Terry Butcher for club and, to a lesser extent, country, made four FA Cup appearances in 1978. Apart from Cardiff, he also appeared in both games against Bristol Rovers and in the 6–1 rout of Millwall at the quarter-final stage. Osman, who won 11 senior caps to add to those gained at Youth, Under-21 and B levels, features among the top 10 all time Ipswich appearance makers, playing 385 games and also contributing 21 goals during his nine years as a professional at Portman Road.

Gates found a niche for himself as manager Robson reshaped his team post-Wembley. He operated behind front men Paul Mariner and Alan Brazil as Town used Dutch players Frans Thijssen and Arnold Muhren either side of John Wark in midfield. It presented opposition sides with a real conundrum in how to mark the diminutive Gates and he thrived on it, making long-distance strikes something of a trademark and using his low centre of gravity to swivel and create space for himself. In his youth, Gates once went on 'strike', and said he would rather go potato-picking in his native North East than continue with Town, but thankfully he had a change of heart and went on to make 384 appearances and score 96 goals in his 13 years as a valued professional. Meanwhile, he won two England caps.

Back in 1978, Brazil was also a star in the making. The day after witnessing his club lift the FA Cup he jetted across the Atlantic to guest alongside Trevor Francis for Detroit Express in the North American Soccer League, and upon his return he was determined to challenge for a regular first team place. He achieved his aim in the second half of the following season and in the 1981–82 campaign he scored all five of Town's goals in a 5–2 home win over League leaders Southampton, which helped him become the club's leading scorer with 28 in all competitions. Brazil was also the Ipswich fans' choice as Player of the Year in 1982 and he went on to represent Scotland at the World Cup Finals in Spain that summer. He won 11 full caps and, by the time he left to join Tottenham in 1983, he had scored 80 goals in 210 games for Town.

Although Tibbott's involvement in the FA Cup campaign of 1978 began and ended with the third-round trip to Cardiff, he made a total of 36 first team appearances for Ipswich that season. It was by far the Welsh international full-back's best tally in his six years as a professional with Ipswich, during which he made 72 appearances and scored once before moving to Sheffield United in 1979.

Finally, Viljoen played in the first four FA Cup games 30 years ago, and although Robson gave him an opportunity to prove his fitness ahead of the Final in the 6–1 League defeat at Aston Villa, it did him no favours. If anything, that result only convinced Robson not to gamble on the Johannesburg-born England international midfield man and it turned out to be the last of his 372 games for the club. Viljoen, who also scored 54 goals, rejected the chance to join the Ipswich squad at their pre-Final hotel and was transferred to Manchester City in the summer of 1978.

The seven players who played a part in the club's Wembley success but were absent from the clash with Arsenal all had one thing in common: having graduated through the youth ranks, no fewer than 16 of the 19 Town players who were involved in the FA Cup that year were home grown – an incredible statistic.

THE ROAD TO WEMBLEY

CARDIFF CITY VS IPSWICH TOWN

7 January 1978 • FA Cup Third Round

CARDIFF CITY: 0	IPSWICH TOWN: 2 (Mariner 49, 73)
Healey, Dwyer, Pethard, Campbell, Pontin, Larmour, Giles, Sayer, Went, Bishop, Attley (Grapes, 73 mins).	Cooper, Mills, Tibbott, Talbot, Hunter, Osman, Wark, Viljoen, Mariner, Geddis (Parkin, 83 mins), Gates.

REFEREE: Mr J. Bent (Hemel Hempstead)
ATTENDANCE: 13,584

Bobby Robson was not one to mince his words. In the build-up to the third-round trip to Cardiff, the Ipswich Town manager was more aware than anyone that the FA Cup could rescue what was proving an otherwise drab season. So, as the visit to South Wales loomed, he labelled the game as Ipswich's most important of the season, knowing only too well that defeat at Ninian Park, coupled with the fact that his side's anticipated title challenge had not so much evaporated as never materialised in the first place, would render the campaign something of a non-event.

Established among the most powerful clubs in the country, Ipswich had emerged as genuine League Championship contenders in the previous five seasons, finishing in the top six on each occasion to secure qualification for Europe, a major prize in itself. Of course, such a high degree of success merely increased the level of expectation among supporters, who had come to regard it as the norm, so the fact that Ipswich were surprisingly subdued domestically – they occupied a mid-table slot in the First Division and had already exited the League Cup – was a major disappointment.

They were out of the UEFA Cup, too, having been eliminated by Spanish giants Barcelona in a third-round penalty shoot-out at the Nou Camp Stadium just weeks earlier, so Robson was entitled to stress the huge importance the FA Cup could play at a time when the club and its fans were undoubtedly in need of a major lift. An unprecedented number of injuries had contributed to the lack of success, with Robson confirming: 'In conversations with our club doctor and specialist they told me the situation is worse now than they have known it in almost 20 years of service to the club.'

The injuries had undoubtedly taken their toll, with Town being one of four First Division clubs – Bristol City, Queen's Park Rangers and Leicester City were the others – to reach the halfway stage of the League programme without a single away win to their credit. But despite being handicapped by their travel sickness, the trek across the border into Wales held no apparent fears for Ipswich skipper Mick Mills, ever the realist and a player for whom the game carried extra significance. Almost 12 years after making his senior debut for the club, he was chalking up his 494th first-team outing, overtaking ex-captain Tommy Parker as the Town player with most appearances to his name.

Mills, who eventually amassed 741 games for the club, only joined as a result of Portsmouth disbanding their youth system as a cost-cutting exercise in the mid-60s. He echoed the feelings of his teammates and, no doubt, thousands of supporters, as he reflected on the third-round draw. The future England captain, who celebrated his 29th birthday just three days before the game at Ninian Park, said: 'While I don't doubt we could have had a better draw, I think we've come out of it with a great chance of advancing into round four. Let's be honest, if we are to be taken seriously as FA Cup challengers then an away match to a club battling to get out of the Second Division relegation zone should not be too difficult an obstacle to overcome.' And so it proved, as an under-strength Ipswich side coped comfortably with what was seen as a potentially hazardous assignment, especially as the Cardiff players had made the point beforehand that they quite fancied themselves to pull off what would have been viewed as a noteworthy giant-killing act.

Ipswich, facing their Welsh opponents for the first time in the FA Cup, left nothing to chance and took the sensible precaution of compiling a detailed report on their opponents. The club's spy was reserve-team coach Bobby Ferguson, ironically a former Cardiff defender, who witnessed their convincing 4–1 demolition of fellow strugglers Millwall. Meanwhile, first-team coach Cyril Lea, a patriotic Welshman and second in command of the national team, had no doubt that Ipswich would triumph, not only at Ninian Park but in the competition as a whole, having confidently predicted in that day's match programme that his 13th season at Portman Road would climax in Wembley glory.

Manager Robson's main anxiety in the build-up to the game concerned which players would be fit to face Cardiff, and he had to do without several crocked regulars in the final reckoning. Long-term absentees Kevin Beattie and Mick Lambert were again missing, as was Trevor Whymark, who had been injured and stretchered off in the 1–0 Boxing Day defeat at neighbours Norwich. Although it was initially feared he had broken his leg, the big striker was actually found to have suffered damaged ligaments but was nevertheless ruled out for many weeks to come, with the Final itself even proving beyond him. Robin Turner, the player regarded as most likely to deputise in the number 10 shirt, was also sidelined with a thigh problem, paving the way for rookie striker David Geddis, who had made a scoring debut on the opening day of the season in a 1–0 win over Arsenal. He was to go on and make such a telling contribution in the Final as the Gunners were again beaten by the same scoreline. A groin injury kept out Clive Woods, with Eric Gates replacing him for what was the diminutive striker's full FA Cup debut, having made three substitute appearances in the previous two seasons. Not only that, it was to be Gates' first and last outing in the tournament that term as he joined the 'nearly' men unable to force their way into Robson's final starting XI. Meanwhile, John Wark made an earlier-than-expected first appearance of the season after tearing his hamstring in the final game of the club's pre-season tour to Holland. George Burley was also declared unfit with a hamstring injury, so Mills switched flanks to wear the number two shirt and the left-back berth went to Les Tibbott, a Welsh international making only his second appearance in the competition and what proved to be his only one en route to Wembley that season.

Ipswich wore their change strip of white shirts and black shorts and it was appropriate that Mills should have an impact on the game, setting up his side's key opening goal four minutes into the second half. Never afraid to venture forward, he followed his diagonal run into the inside-left channel with a pass that released Paul Mariner, who, in turn, steered his shot well beyond Cardiff 'keeper Ron Healey.

In the Town goal, Paul Cooper had a quiet time. His only genuine save came just before the break, when he was able to beat away a fierce drive from lively home striker Peter Sayer. However, that was an isolated effort by the Bluebirds, who went into the game positioned 19th in the Second Division but with high hopes of being able to narrow the gap between them and their top-flight opponents.

Jimmy Andrews' team never once looked capable of causing an FA Cup upset and were always second-best throughout a rather low-key fixture, no more so than in front of goal, where they were unable to create too many problems for the Town defence. Having fired Ipswich in front, Mariner exploded into action all over again to add a second goal in the 73rd minute when he leapt high above home defender Freddie Pethard to power in a header from midfielder Brian Talbot's superb left-wing centre.

Cardiff had little to offer in what remained of the contest so there were no anxious moments for Robson's men as they continued to control the game right through to the final whistle, securing a richly deserved win to delight a sizeable contingent of travelling fans. One moment of significance came seven minutes from the end when Tommy Parkin was introduced for his senior debut, with Geddis the player to make way.

Robson singled out the experienced trio of skipper Mills, defensive stalwart Allan Hunter and two-goal hero Mariner for special mention as he delivered his after-match verdict:

We had top players in key positions. I thought Cardiff battled well but they were short of ideas and lacked class. It was a deserved win and one that has restored the smile on a lot of faces at the club. In my mind the FA Cup is still very much the glamour competition and it is good to survive this opening hurdle. The outcome is never certain and we desperately wanted this result. Cardiff had not been enjoying much luck in the League but they were able to forget about their relegation worries and try to raise their game against a side from a higher level. There are shocks at this stage of the competition every year and maybe some people were looking in the direction of Ninian Park for a possible giant-killing act, which to some extent I can understand. We are relieved and delighted, especially in view of the fact that we had so many injury problems and had to reshuffle the pack more than we might have liked to book our place in the fourth round.

Robson also took time out to praise skipper Mills' feat of breaking the club's long-standing appearance record and went on:

I feel it is significant that Mick has played so many of his games at the highest level of football in this country. For the last six years he has led the side in the hunt for the game's top prizes and in that time we have been one of the most consistent sides in the First Division, always challenging for the title and giving a good account of ourselves in Cup competitions both at home and in Europe. As a club we have admired his achievements and also his loyalty, attitude and dedication. He has been a credit to the town, both on and off the field, and I am personally delighted for him.

DID YOU KNOW?

• Ipswich skipper Mick Mills enjoyed reminiscing with an opposing player, Cardiff's Paul Went, after the game. The pair had been colleagues in the England Youth team more than 10 years earlier.

• Ipswich were to come across Ninian Park referee Jim Bent later in the season. Not only did he take charge of the First Division game against Leeds at Portman Road the following month, but he was also on duty at the Wembley Final. He was one of the linesmen who assisted referee Derek Nippard, officiating at his very last game, and accompanied him on his impromptu lap of honour. Sadly, Mr Bent died in a motorcycling accident some years later.

The outcome was entirely satisfactory for Robson and eased his frustration at Town's inconsistent League form, which saw them collect a mere two points from a possible eight in the four games played prior to travelling to Cardiff. Having won through to the last 32, Ipswich then suffered a further two defeats, at home to Manchester United and at Chelsea, which left them uncomfortably close to the First Division relegation zone. At this point, the FA Cup offered no more than temporary respite from concerns over their League status, but maybe Robson had an inkling of what was to come. Writing in the club's official matchday magazine, he concluded his column in the issue for the visit of Manchester United with what turned out to be a prophetic paragraph. 'Our aim is to please,' he told supporters buoyed by the team's success in Cardiff, 'and I can assure you that we still intend to give you all plenty to cheer about this season.' Skipper Mills was clearly reading from the same hymn sheet as he reflected on almost 13 years at the club and said:

It is still the biggest disappointment of my career to date that I haven't led Ipswich to a major honour. There is still plenty of time, however, to put that right and I think we showed signs at Cardiff that we are not far short of our best. A lot of our injured players are on the way back and I am sure that with a full-strength side we could be more than a match for any side in the country.

IPSWICH TOWN VS HARTLEPOOL UNITED

28 January 1978 • FA Cup Fourth Round

IPSWICH TOWN: 4 (Viljoen 6 pen, 66, Mariner 27, Talbot 49)	HARTLEPOOL UNITED: 1 (Downing 40)
Cooper, Burley (Wark, 87 mins), Mills, Talbot, Hunter, Beattie, Lambert, Viljoen, Mariner, Turner, Woods.	Edgar, Malone, Downing, Gibb, Ayre, Smith, Creamer, McMordie (Linacre, 80 mins), Newton, Poskett, Bielby.

REFEREE: Mr J. Homewood (Sunbury-on-Thames)
ATTENDANCE: 24,207

There was no mistaking the loud whoop of delight that emanated from the home dressing room at Portman Road. The Ipswich Town players were a very contented bunch as they learned their FA Cup fate: a home fourth-round tie against lower-level opposition in the shape of Hartlepool United, struggling in second from bottom place in the old Fourth Division. Bobby Robson's squad crowded around a radio as the 16 ties were drawn at Football Association headquarters in London and there was no disguising their glee at the outcome. Whether anyone had dared contemplate the possibility of going all the way in the competition is unclear, but there was an immediate surge of confidence at the prospect of not only a home tie but the fact that it would be against the second lowest-ranked side left in the tournament behind non-League heroes Blyth Spartans.

Skipper Mick Mills, a veteran of many an FA Cup campaign who had been reduced to tears by the team's controversial exit in a semi-final replay against West Ham at Stamford Bridge three years earlier, revealed:

I have never known an FA Cup draw to be greeted with more enthusiasm. We listened intently in the dressing room as the draw came over the airwaves and as soon as Hartlepool's name was mentioned there were players cheering out loud. I don't think we could have asked for a better draw. I know Hartlepool shocked Crystal Palace in the third round but I don't think that matters because it was on their own ground.

Mills was not dismissing the opposition, however, and on the day of the match went on to add:

We all know that Hartlepool are currently in 91st position in the Football League but we are treating them in exactly the same way as we did Barcelona. Reserve coach Bobby Ferguson watched them at Torquay recently and we intended spying on them again last Friday when youth coach Charlie Woods went up to the North East, only to find that their home game with Southport had been postponed. We even forfeited our day off on Wednesday to arrange a full-scale practice match, with the reserves playing the system we know Hartlepool prefer away from home. Unfortunately, because of injuries it was not possible to field the strongest side, although it was still a very useful exercise. Beforehand, we had discussed Hartlepool in some detail and I was surprised that I knew so many of their players – people like Tommy Gibb, who appeared at Portman Road last season as a second-half substitute for Sunderland and was previously with Newcastle United. Another vital part of our preparations for this match has been an exchange of words between our manager, Bobby Robson, and Terry Venables, boss of Crystal Palace, who lost at Hartlepool in the third round. So you can see we've been doing our homework because we simply cannot afford to even think about not winning today. If we lost it could take as long as a year to get over it.

The importance being placed on the game was clear. Town had reaped just 23 points from 26 League games, of which eight were wins and seven draws, a record that put a huge question mark against their ability to qualify for Europe via a sufficiently lofty First Division berth.

Hartlepool were aiming to rewrite the history books and record their first win over top-flight opposition in 70 years and, coming right up to date, claim their first away win of the season at the 14th attempt. The odds were stacked against them and one leading firm of bookmakers appeared to have been blessed with psychic powers as the draw led them to conclude that Ipswich and Arsenal should be installed as 7–1 joint-favourites to lift the trophy.

First things first, though, and the small matter of removing the obstacle known as Hartlepool was priority. They were facing Ipswich for the very first time, having disposed of Tranmere Rovers and non-League Runcorn before pulling off a shock win over Crystal Palace. The Fourth Division side brought almost 4,000 fans to Portman Road for the game, which was baffling in itself since they attracted only about half as many to their home League games, but the healthy turnout would at least have ensured them much higher than usual gate receipts.

In right-back Dick Malone, Hartlepool had the only player on the field who could boast an FA Cup-winner's medal, which the Scot achieved as a member of Bob Stokoe's marvellous Sunderland side that stunned red-hot favourites Leeds in the 1973 Final. Ipswich boss Bobby Robson left his players in no doubt as to the importance he placed on the game and was clearly intent on ensuring there was no complacency in the ranks. Robson said:

Every game is important but today's FA Cup fourth-round tie with Hartlepool United could be classed as crucial in view of the fact that our League position has worsened and we have no further interest in any other competitions. Naturally, this is not the situation that we either expected or wanted. But the sparkle that we are desperately seeking within the club could be restored by success in the FA Cup. I think it would be true to say that we are currently having to put up with a run of non-success, the like of which I cannot recall in the last six or seven years at Portman Road. We know it is hard for the supporters to take but I would remind you that we are the professionals so how do you think we feel about it? Football is our bread and butter; we sleep and live on results, and you can be sure that everyone at Portman Road is determined that we turn the corner and get back on the rails.

Robson even took the opportunity to hit back at a section of the club's fans, adding:

It is obvious that we, like most other clubs, have our fickle supporters with short memories. They have tried to fill my postbag following last week's 5–3 defeat at Chelsea but I have also received some great letters from some great supporters and it is for them that we will try to get things right. Do I really have to remind you that it is at a time like this, when we are being deserted by good fortune and the breaks are going against us, that we need your support more than ever?

Robson was able to welcome right-back George Burley back after a hamstring injury and restore Kevin Beattie to the heart of the defence at the expense of teenager Russell Osman, whose exclusion prompted an explanation from the Town boss. He said: 'Although I have decided to leave Russell Osman out of the side today I fully expect him to go on and play some great football for the club over the next 15 years. He has lost a little confidence recently and no matter how brief his absence may be it will go a long way to restoring him to the level he was at three months ago.' Robson spoke of the players' attitudes being spot-on by kick-off, and just six minutes into the game Ipswich were awarded a penalty that enabled them to make a dream start.

A promising build-up involving Colin Viljoen, Clive Woods and Burley ended with a through ball for Paul Mariner to chase, only for the England striker to be sent crashing to the deck under a challenge from Derrick Downing. Hartlepool were incensed by referee John Homewood's decision but he ignored their protests and Colin Viljoen stepped up to beat ex-Newcastle United goalkeeper Eddie Edgar with a clinical finish. Ipswich appeared fitter, faster and more skilful than the visitors, which was to be expected, and they extended their lead 21 minutes later. Once again Viljoen was prominent, this time forcing a save from Edgar, and when the ball ran loose Mariner was in the right place to take advantage and score on the rebound, taking his season's tally to 16.

Plucky Hartlepool hit back five minutes before the interval to reduce the deficit, Downing making amends for conceding the early penalty with a ferocious right-foot drive that flew past Paul Cooper for the game's most spectacular goal. But within four minutes of the restart Ipswich had restored their two-goal advantage when a slick-passing move ended with midfield man Brian Talbot sliding the ball past Edgar for his fourth goal of the campaign. Town threatened to run riot as they engulfed their opponents with a series of menacing raids, one of which saw Woods crash a shot against an upright. However, the visitors gallantly tried to hit back and on one occasion, with Cooper stranded, Ipswich needed Beattie to prevent Gibb from scoring. Any hopes Hartlepool may have had about forcing a replay were dashed for good, however, as Viljoen, who had failed to score in his 10 previous appearances of the season, claimed his second goal of the game. It came after 66 minutes when the South African-born England international linked up with Robin Turner, who was making his FA Cup debut, and waltzed round the 'keeper before finding the unguarded net.

Hartlepool were gracious in defeat and acknowledged that they had been outclassed by a slicker side, but they refused to accept that the referee had called it right with his early decision to award a penalty. Manager Billy Horner said he was proud of his players' performance, then added: 'It was a harsh decision and a real sickener. I felt that if Ipswich did not score in the first 20 minutes then they would have become worried. In the end we failed to take our chances but they tucked away the majority of theirs.' A clearly dejected Downing, no relation to current Boro and England winger Stewart, said: 'I wouldn't cheat. I slid in and knocked the ball back to the goalkeeper and Mariner fell over me.' To his credit, Robson admitted the penalty decision was 'suspect' but went on to add: 'However many chances they made, we were always going to make more. It was just the result we wanted.'

Robson's gamble in utilising two wingers, Mick Lambert and Woods, in a bold 4-2-4 formation paid off, as did his decision to play Beattie after an eight-week absence and just one practice match. The powerhouse defender turned in an impressive display and the Town boss smiled: 'Hartlepool may have thought Beattie was good – and he was – but that was only one third of him. It was almost a super-human effort for him to play again after three months on the sidelines and only five days' training behind him. His value to the club is immense – he can often be worth two players to us, and we need him at such a critical time.' It was clearly the case that Beattie's best, along with that of his teammates, was still to come, but for the time being the guarantee of a place in the competition's last 16 gave everyone at Portman Road a massive lift.

However welcome it may have been, Robson was not in the mood to dwell on the win over Hartlepool and warned: 'Now that we are safely through to the fifth round of the FA Cup we must put this competition to the back of our minds and concentrate on our next two vital League games.' Town were preparing to face Leeds at home and Liverpool away, a game that was subsequently postponed, and the manager added: 'Our League position has slipped drastically and we simply must improve. We don't want to be involved in a fight against relegation and we can only avoid it if we meet the challenge with confidence, spirit and determination.' Coincidentally, those were exactly the attributes the Ipswich players would be required to display in abundance in order to maintain their FA Cup interest.

DID YOU KNOW?

• Hartlepool have played at Portman Road on just two occasions – and John Wark is the only player who appeared in both games. The North East club were also paired with Ipswich in an FA Cup third-round tie in 1992 and, after a 1–1 draw Town won 2–0 in the replay.

Bristol Rovers vs Ipswich Town

18 February 1978 • FA Cup Fifth Round

Bristol Rovers: 2 (Williams 58, 64)	Ipswich Town: 2 (Turner 27, 86)
Thomas, Aitken, Bater, Day, Taylor, Prince, Barry, Pulis, Gould, Williams, Randall. Sub not used: Powell.	Cooper, Burley, Mills, Talbot, Hunter, Osman, Wark, Viljoen (Osborne 70 mins), Mariner, Turner, Woods.

Referee: Mr B. Daniels (Brentwood)
Attendance: 23,453

History will forever show that it was Roger Osborne who scored the all-important goal that won the FA Cup for Ipswich. But tucked away far less prominently in the record books will be the information to confirm that but for Robin Turner's two-goal contribution at Eastville, the club's interest in the competition would have ended, there and then, on a skating rink of a pitch. Arguments still rage as to whether the game should have been allowed to go ahead but the man with the final word was referee Brian Daniels and he decided, to the surprise of everyone present, to give the thumbs-up.

The memorable day had started with the pitch inspection and continued when Town physiotherapist Tommy Eggleston turned life-saver during a morning walk through the city streets. A player with Derby, Leicester and Watford, Eggleston, who had only joined the Portman Road staff earlier that season to replace Brian Simpson, had been an FA Cup winner in 1966 with Everton, where he was second in command to boss Harry Catterick. As Eggleston strolled the streets, an elderly man collapsed, apparently after suffering a heart attack. He was on the scene to give the kiss of life and stayed in charge of the situation until an ambulance and its crew arrived to take control and drive the victim to hospital. The man would be eternally grateful to Eggleston and his life-saving actions that morning but it was Ipswich who needed rescuing that afternoon. Manager Bobby Robson still grimaces at the memory of a see-saw game that almost resulted in his team exiting the competition they were destined to win, although no one was thinking that far ahead at the time. He recalled:

I went down to the Eastville ground at about eight o'clock in the morning for the pitch inspection and I felt sure it was just a formality. I just thought it was a question of turning up, the referee saying it couldn't go ahead and then returning to the hotel, getting on the bus and heading for home. Instead the referee made an awful decision. Never mind the snow, the pitch was actually ice-bound. It was rock-hard and you couldn't turn. I remember saying to him: 'I know it's difficult, but if you want my opinion it isn't playable.' He just ignored me.

What made the decision even harder to bear was that former military policeman Mr Daniels did not even don his football boots to carry out the inspection. Nor did he ask for a ball before delivering his verdict within the space of just three minutes. It took the Ipswich players more than half an hour before deciding what footwear to use, and skipper Mick Mills was particularly scathing about the official's entirely unexpected 'game on' decision.

Mills and the rest of the Ipswich squad had been tucked up in bed at the team's city-centre hotel and were stunned when manager Robson and other club officials arrived back from the fleeting pitch inspection to reveal that the game would go ahead as scheduled. The players had seen the snow start to fall at a steady pace since they had arrived in Bristol the previous evening and were convinced they would be heading back up the M4 after breakfast. Instead, Town knew they could be up against it, while the home side took the contrasting view that the referee's surprise ruling offered them a far better chance of pulling off a shock result.

On a pitch where Bristol-born figure skater and Olympic champion Robin Cousins would have been perfectly at home, it was instead another Robin – Turner of Ipswich – who came up trumps and stole the show with his first FA Cup goals. Town were 2–1 down and heading out of the competition when Turner, deputising for the injured Trevor Whymark, netted his second goal just four minutes from time. Strike partner Paul Mariner set off on a clever run, starting well outside the box, and showed quite incredible skill in the near-impossible conditions. After squeezing past two Rovers players, he beat two more inside the area before sending in a low cross aimed for his less experienced colleague. Turner made good contact with his first effort, only to see the ball cannon back off the foot of a post. but as it rebounded to him he quickly reacted and did just enough to poke it over the line and bring Ipswich level in the pantomime on ice. There was confusion at the time as to whether Turner or substitute Roger Osborne had supplied the vital touch, with many of those in the press box adamant that it should be credited to the latter. But Osborne cleared up the mystery afterwards when he admitted: 'It was definitely Robin's goal. I thought I might be offside and I was actually trying to get out of the way!' Later, of course, Osborne came clean to confess he had supplied the finishing touch, something he kept quiet about for 30 years.

In the circumstances, it was perhaps only right that both sides should live to fight another day, although Rovers looked to have a legitimate complaint as they protested they should have been 3–1 ahead and had that been the case, even with Turner's late intervention, they would still have managed to record a famous victory. The Second Division side were furious with referee Daniels when they had the ball in the net, only to have what they insisted was a perfectly good goal disallowed for offside.

While television pictures in those days were nowhere near as conclusive as they are in 21st-century high definition times, it must be said that the evidence seemed pretty conclusive. It could be seen that Bobby Gould, the man who 10 years later was in charge of Wimbledon when they defeated Liverpool at Wembley, was put in the clear by Allan Hunter's wayward back-pass and therefore could not have been offside before he slid the ball beyond Paul Cooper. That was a lucky break for Ipswich and they might even have celebrated a victory but for a magnificent save by home 'keeper Martin Thomas, who kept out a Mariner header with barely three minutes left to play. Nevertheless, the overall feeling within the Ipswich camp was one of huge relief that their FA Cup prospects remained intact on a day when it would have been a travesty had the tie been decided either way.

Town had overcome their reservations about the pitch to make a bright start. They were kitted out in a brand new rig-out of orange shirts and black shorts because it was felt that both their first and second-choice strips would have clashed with the blue and white quartered tops of their hosts. With 27 minutes on the clock their well-rehearsed throw-in routine on the left worked a treat as Brian Talbot fed the ball to Clive Woods and the tricky winger, in turn, crossed to Turner to stick the ball past Thomas from 10 yards.

Ipswich, aided by a strong wind, were in control of the first half and the home side were relieved that they went in at the break only trailing by that one goal. However, two second-half corners caused problems for Town. From the first, a vicious in-swinger taken by Gould, goalkeeper Cooper could only punch the ball into the air, and when it came down again it was David Williams who headed into the net. Part-timer Williams, a schoolteacher who later joined Norwich and became first-team coach at Carrow Road during Dave Stringer's spell as manager, later moving to Everton to assist ex-Canary boss Mike Walker, was only in the Rovers side because skipper Dave Staniforth had been ruled out with a hamstring injury. But he was a hero all over again when he headed a second goal just six minutes after his first. Russell Osman cleared Gould's corner and the ball was headed back into the crowded goalmouth by Mike Barry for Williams to divert it past Cooper with a deft twist of his neck.

The drama of Gould's disallowed goal followed before Ipswich levelled to force a replay, although the Town players' obvious relief did not prevent them speaking of their disbelief that the game had been allowed to take place. Mills echoed the views of his colleagues when he said: 'What's all this about the pitch being flat? It was like concrete and I don't see what being flat has to do with it. To play such an important match on a surface like that was diabolical.' Manager Robson further recalled the events of that extraordinary day:

I wasn't very happy with the decision to play the game, but when I look back I can actually see the funny side of it. We're 1–0 up and Bobby Campbell, the Bristol Rovers manager, is hollering at the top of his voice: 'This is a lottery.' I'm thinking: 'No it's not' but then they're 2–1 up and I'm shouting for it to be abandoned. But Bobby was looking quite content at that point. We looked well in command when Robin gave us the lead but on a pitch like that we knew that anything could, and probably would, happen. Rovers' two quick goals had us trailing and there was definitely a time when I thought we were going to be eliminated. We kept plugging away on a pitch that was getting steadily worse as the game progressed and Robin's equaliser five minutes from the end was no more than we deserved. Conditions were as difficult as they could have been and that was the case for both teams. Whether or not the game should have been played is of no importance now but I think it was only fair that neither side should suffer a Cup knockout on the day and instead live to fight again.

That was a sentiment with which everyone tended to agree, although it had been a narrow escape for Ipswich and they knew it. Rovers had eliminated Sunderland and Southampton in the third and fourth rounds and were an improving side under Campbell, so to journey home to Suffolk with their chances of FA Cup glory still intact was a great relief to the Town party and their thousands of followers who made the trip to the West Country.

On a day when most big-time football had fallen victim to the Arctic weather that swept the country, the Ipswich players had passed a stiff examination of their character and resolve. Initially unhappy at being asked to perform and risk serious injury on an unfit playing surface, they cast aside their disbelief and disappointment to gain a result that was pivotal to their eventual success. Not surprisingly, having survived such a nerve-racking experience, they were determined to make the most of their second chance by winning the replay and advancing into the last eight. The fact that the quarter-final draw had already been made, and paired the victors with Millwall, provided Town with an extra incentive to make the very most of what they considered a very welcome reprieve.

DID YOU KNOW?

• Bristol Rovers defender Phil Bater later became a football agent and acted on behalf of Bristol-born Marcus Stewart, who launched his career with Rovers. Stewart was transferred from Huddersfield to Ipswich in 2000 and his goals not only helped Town win promotion but also played a big part in them finishing fifth in the Premiership the following year.

Ipswich Town VS Bristol Rovers

28 February 1978 • FA Cup Fifth-Round Replay

Ipswich Town: 3 (Mills 27, Mariner 57, Woods 78)	Bristol Rovers: 0
Cooper, Burley, Mills, Talbot, Hunter, Osman, Wark, Viljoen, Mariner, Turner (Brazil 75 mins), Woods.	Thomas, Aitken, Bater, Day, Taylor, Prince, Barry, Pulis, Gould, Staniforth (Williams 36 mins), Randall.

Referee: Mr B. Daniels (Brentwood)

Attendance: 29,532

Talk of possible FA Cup glory was rife among Ipswich supporters ahead of the replay against Bristol Rovers. The fans' reasoning was simple and straightforward: Town were firm favourites to clinch a quarter-final place where they would meet Millwall, and the supporters were confident that that hurdle could also be cleared, leaving their team in the semi-finals and 90 minutes from Wembley. While manager Bobby Robson wanted nothing more than for his players to concentrate on the job in hand, he also had one eye on the situation towards the bottom end of the First Division. However, a win at Newcastle – Town's first away League success of the season at the 14th time of asking – just three days before the Cup-tie turned out to be the perfect tonic as Robson sought to keep things ticking over on both fronts.

Knowing they were more than a tad fortunate to still have an interest in the competition, having suffered a massive scare in the snow and ice at Eastville, the Ipswich players were determined to see off their Second Division opponents and earn the sixth-round trip to South London that awaited the victors. Robson was taking nothing for granted, of course, and despite the clear advantage of taking on the Bristol side on a perfect playing surface rather than a skating rink, he urged caution ahead of the kick-off. He said:

Rovers' recent results prove they are playing with confidence and that is an essential quality for a side with Cup ambitions. They have climbed the League since Bobby Campbell took over as manager and have already claimed the scalps of leading sides Sunderland and Southampton in the FA Cup. Because of this they deserve to be treated with the utmost respect. Like ourselves, they can see a victory taking them to within one game of the semi-finals where, as has been proved so often in the past, anything can happen.

While the continued absence of senior stars Kevin Beattie and Trevor Whymark meant Town were not at full strength, Robson said he was hopeful of successfully negotiating the replay without them and went on to deliver a fitness report on the duo. He added: 'Kevin has seen a specialist and has been advised to continue in light training. His knee has been very inflamed but a further check-up in the next couple of weeks will decide whether an exploratory operation is going to be required. Trevor has been out of action for about eight weeks now and needs to step up his training and play in a few reserve games before being ready for a first-team return.'

Ipswich fielded the same starting line-up as in the first game but there was a change on the bench that saw Roger Osborne make way for young Scottish striker Alan Brazil, who had made his League debut as a substitute in the previous month's 2–1 home defeat by Manchester United. Ahead of the game, skipper Mick Mills commented on the mood of expectation among supporters when he said:

Here we are facing a fifth-round FA Cup replay and yet for the past week or so most of the Town fans to whom I have spoken have Wembley on their minds. I'm sure a lot of supporters are seeing the twin towers in their dreams and I know a lot who have left May 6, the date of the Final, free in their diaries. The reason for their confidence is not hard to explain. Victory tonight takes us on to a sixth-round tie away to Millwall, where a win will earn us a semi-final place for the second time in four seasons – and only the second time in the club's history. On paper it looks fairly straightforward but I can assure every one of our supporters that we at the club don't see it that way. We can expect strong resistance from Bristol Rovers tonight and if we do get through we will get it just as tough at The Den.

Mills also pointed to the team's display in capturing both points at St James' Park three days previously, thanks to left-winger Clive Woods' second goal of the season, a rare header. He added: 'I was just as delighted with the way we achieved the win as I was at picking up two valuable points. I saw encouraging signs of the spirit returning, everyone helping each other and fighting for every ball. The spirit could hardly have picked a better time to return. Here's hoping it is still there tonight and for every game between now and the end of the season.'

Ipswich were actually slow starters in the replay and it was Rovers, no doubt lifted by the fact that they had come within five minutes of a shock knock-out at their place, who opened brightly as Ipswich seemed stuck in first gear. The visitors should have been ahead in the 26th minute when Bobby Gould sent Paul Randall racing clear of a square Town defence. Thankfully, as goalkeeper Paul Cooper sprinted off his line, the young striker sent a rather tame effort beyond the far post. The close call seemed to bring Ipswich to their senses and within seconds they were ahead as skipper Mills scored one of his eight goals that season, quite a contribution from someone whose primary role was to defend. Woods' corner on the left was diverted to the back post by Tony Pulis, who went on to become a manager at Gillingham, Portsmouth and Stoke, and Mills was ideally placed to head his fourth goal of the campaign.

Rovers had gambled on the fitness of their own captain, Dave Staniforth, who was absent from the first game with hamstring trouble, and his recall meant that their two-goal Eastville hero, David Williams, was relegated to the bench. However, when Staniforth suffered a recurrence of his injury in the 36th minute and was forced to limp off, that was the signal for Williams to come on and he was very nearly a hero all over again. He had a chance to pull his side level on the stroke of half-time when the Town defence failed to mark him from Randall's long throw. However, there was a collective sigh of relief that swept around the ground as he lashed his shot wildly over the top.

Allan Hunter, who had demonstrated his authority at the back as Town started the game in a surprisingly lethargic mood, launched the move from which Ipswich scored their second goal in the 57th minute. The big defender, who was blessed with far more skill on the deck than a lot of people realised, played the ball wide to Mills on the left and the skipper in turn sent Woods racing down the left wing. Woods wasted no time in looking up and picking out Paul Mariner with a super cross that enabled the England striker to maintain his goal-a-round record by heading number 17 for the season.

Cooper had to make his only genuine save of the game after 71 minutes to deny Peter Aitken, and Brazil was introduced for his FA Cup debut as Robin Turner made way four minutes later. John Wark, who had earlier missed a good chance to score when he hit teammate Turner, blasted a shot against the legs of goalkeeper Martin Thomas before Town wrapped up a comfortable victory with a magnificent third goal. It was a wonderful effort by Woods, and reminiscent of his memorable strike that decided the sixth-round marathon tie with Leeds three years earlier, as he cut in from the left before letting rip with a rising right-foot drive that flew into the roof of the net. Afterwards, manager Robson was at a loss to explain why his side had taken so long to stamp their authority on proceedings and break brave Rovers' resistance. He said:

I told the players at half-time that we had played in bigger matches than this. I expected us to settle a lot quicker. Once we went two ahead we could have hit them for five. The win was richly deserved and Rovers can have no complaints. They played their part in providing an entertaining evening of football and deserve praise for that. It was so typical of our skipper, Mick Mills, to pop up for the first goal. He has been a model of consistency this season and has done a good job, either at full-back or in midfield, and how pleased I am to see the fans backing him at all times. We had a great crowd, not far short of 30,000, and I would like to put on record my appreciation of the tremendous support the team received. The players talked about it as well so please keep it up!

Mills, meanwhile, needed no arm-twisting to discuss the goal that put Ipswich on their way to the sixth round and a trip to Millwall. He added:

Without giving too many secrets away, I can tell you it came as a direct result of a tactical move we had decided to use after what we had seen of Rovers in the first game. My job at corner kicks was to get between the ball and the goalkeeper. Being a lot shorter than some of the other lads, we felt there was a chance I wouldn't be taken too seriously because defenders would obviously be marking our taller lads more carefully. That's just the way it turned out, but I was only able to get the touch after a lucky deflection. Clive Woods actually aimed his corner for Paul Mariner at the near post but a Rovers defender got a touch to change the flight of the ball. Like the Rovers goalkeeper I made to move towards the near post but when I saw it had been deflected I stopped and managed to get back a couple of yards and get my head to the ball. Because he had moved so early, the 'keeper was stranded. It's not a tactic that will always work, perhaps, and it's not one that we will use all the time. But the fact that it produced a goal certainly made it worthwhile.

Mills explained why the team took so long to get into their stride:

Everything we did was too hurried, with players appearing over-anxious and not showing sufficient patience. I've never known us to take so long to settle into a proper pattern and it was only really after Paul Mariner scored our second goal that we began to play good, intelligent football and emphasise the difference in quality between the two sides.

Casting his mind back three years, to when Town's FA Cup hopes were dashed in a semi-final replay against West Ham, it was clear he was determined to go all the way. Mills added: 'We excited an awful lot of people without reaching Wembley in 1975. This time, quite frankly, I don't care if we fail to excite people just as long as we get there.'

DID YOU KNOW?

• Maybe Bristol Rovers defender Stuart Taylor was disappointed when his side's FA Cup run came to an end, but he still had good reason to be grateful to Ipswich that season. As the club's longest-serving player, with more than 500 appearances to his name, he was awarded a testimonial and invited Town to Eastville for his match, in November 1977, which ended goalless.

MILLWALL VS IPSWICH TOWN

11 March 1978 • FA Cup Sixth Round

MILLWALL: 1 (Mehmet 84)	IPSWICH TOWN: 6 (Burley 10, Mariner 52, 72, 89, Wark 87, Talbot 88)
Johns, Donaldson, Moore, Walker, Kitchener, Hazell, Pearson, Chambers, Hamilton, Lee, Cross (Mehmet 63 mins).	Cooper, Burley, Mills, Talbot, Hunter, Osman, Osborne (Lambert 73 mins), Wark, Mariner, Turner, Woods.

REFEREE: Mr W.J. Gow (Swansea)
ATTENDANCE: 23,082

The sickening sight of Ipswich fans, young and old, with blood pouring from head wounds, rather than the wonderful display their team provided, remains the abiding memory of an occasion still worthy of celebration but undeniably tarnished by the yob element among the home crowd. Prompted by their own side's shortcomings, although that was no excuse for such despicable behaviour, a section of The Den's largest attendance of the season decided to take matters into their own hands. Despite pleas to the contrary from the south London club, whose reputation suffered as a result, their hooligan followers seemed hell-bent on proving their notoriety and attempting to interrupt the flowing football provided by Bobby Robson's team. Sadly, they succeeded, to the extent that referee John Gow was forced to instruct both sets of players to leave the pitch and seek refuge in the dressing rooms for 18 minutes while police and stewards battled to restore order, following a pitch invasion. A hail of missiles into the section reserved for visiting supporters caused chaos and some fans suffered facial wounds that required treatment from St John Ambulance crews. Women and children were among those forced to flee for their own safety as the game was halted, and a number of offenders were arrested after a series of scuffles broke out.

When the draw paired the winners of the fifth-round replay between Ipswich and Bristol Rovers with Millwall, it was welcomed in both camps. It was Town, of course, who went through to the quarter-final stage and, prior to the trip to the capital, manager Bobby Robson said: 'We have to be honest and say we are pleased with the draw.' Ironically, in view of events on the day, Ipswich were cheered on by only a tiny fraction of the supporters who wanted to be there. Restrictions on the number of away followers who could be accommodated resulted in thousands of fans scrambling for only a few hundred tickets.

Those who did attend saw Town turn on the style, emphasising the gulf between the sides, although few could have anticipated it would turn into such a stroll. For example, on the eve of the game, skipper Mick Mills said: 'Anybody going there thinking it will be easy might as well stay at home.' By the end of the day, however, having led his side to victory by a winning margin not seen at that stage of the famous competition since 1926, when Manchester City trounced Clapton Orient in the capital, he was forced to concede: 'I couldn't believe how easy it turned out to be. It was a non-event as far as I was concerned. I didn't enjoy the match at all because it was so one-sided and, of course, because it was interrupted by a few mindless morons.' Strong stuff from the Ipswich captain? Maybe so, but perfectly understandable in the circumstances, and remarkably restrained when compared to the statement attributed to Bobby Robson on that evening's *Match of the Day* programme by host Jimmy Hill, his former Fulham teammate. The Town manager was at home with his wife, Elsie, and almost choked on his late-night cuppa as he heard Hill tell the nation about the crowd trouble at Millwall before adding: 'Bobby Robson said they should turn the flamethrowers on them.'

Robson did not deny having uttered the words but he had done so in private within a small company of friends after the dust had settled on a day tinged with both disappointment and delight. He had either been overheard or betrayed. He said later:

My after-match comments were not meant to be for public consumption but it has been obvious from the letters I have received that they summed up the feelings of all genuine football-lovers. I even received a telephone call from a policeman on duty at the game. He explained how difficult it had been to contain the hooligans and apologised for the fact that so many of our supporters were made to suffer. There have been apologetic letters from genuine Millwall fans ashamed of what happened and just as anxious as we are that the thugs are wiped off the face of football. In many respects, we feel sorry for those real supporters at The Den.

Robson's anger at the scenes he had witnessed, together with his fervent wish that they should never be repeated, even led him to suggest that a drastic measure like the birch be considered as a deterrent. He added:

I have never witnessed such horrifying scenes as I did at Millwall. Using whatever they could lay their hands on as weapons, the thugs mounted cowardly attacks on decent supporters who only wanted to enjoy a game of football. I feel that we as a club must apologise to all our supporters who made the trip to Millwall for the shabby treatment they received. Because of how strongly I felt about the situation, my quotes were broadcast nationally via television so no one should be in any doubt as to my feelings.

No matter how well they had performed, Robson's players fared second-best in the publicity stakes as national newspapers condemned the hooliganism and the powers that be searched for a remedy. Skipper Mills provided a player's perspective when he said:

While the game was going on I could sense there were problems in the area behind the goal we were attacking and I can't say I was surprised when the game had to be stopped. Even before the match, about 45 minutes prior to the kick-off, I was convinced there would be trouble. I had asked where our fans were going to be and was amazed when I was told they were not going to be in any certain area. My idea was to lead the team over to where the bulk of our fans were standing and give them a wave before the match. But when I heard that no segregation had been organised I scrapped the plan. Surely Millwall as a club should have made it a priority to keep rival fans apart at all times. They cannot exactly boast a trouble-free record at The Den so that should have emphasised the need for segregation. It made me sick to see so many good Ipswich fans being treated at the first-aid room near our dressing room and it made me worse when I saw the Millwall thugs who had inflicted the damage.

Mills pulled no punches as he added:

Their place is behind bars. Fines are no good. The punishment has to fit the crime and judging by the sentences dished out in court this is not the case. If one individual brutally attacks another in the street then there's a good chance the offender would go to jail. Why should there be any difference if the attack takes place at a football ground? It is not their money that has to be taken away but their freedom. Put them in prison for long spells so that they cannot spread the disease that could eventually kill our great game.

At least the hooligans were not able to affect the outcome, which was undoubtedly their intention, and Ipswich enjoyed a comfortable victory that was never in doubt from the 10th minute, when right-back George Burley opened the scoring with his first goal of an injury-plagued season. The Scot was 30 yards out when he raced on to Brian Talbot's precision pass and unleashed a magnificent 30-yard shot that Millwall's 'keeper Nicky Johns reached with his fingertips but was unable to prevent crashing into the roof of the net.

Seven minutes after the interval Paul Mariner made it 2–0 en route to a hat-trick, the second of three he bagged for the club. If his first shot seemed a tad casual and allowed Jonathan Moore to clear off the line, he emphatically banged in the rebound.

Town extended their lead in the 72nd minute, when Mariner combined with strike partner Robin Turner from Paul Cooper's long clearance to claim his second goal. Millwall earned themselves an apparent lifeline 12 minutes later when veteran defender Barry Kitchener's shot crashed back off Cooper's legs and young substitute David Mehmet followed up to net. But the miracle Millwall needed to earn a replay failed to materialise and instead it was Ipswich who embarked on an impressive late scoring spree to book their semi-final place. Within three minutes of the home side hitting back, Mills' free-kick was met by Mariner's header into the path of John Wark, who promptly claimed his first FA Cup goal for the club. Seconds later Mills crossed from the left, Turner tried and only narrowly failed to get his head to the ball and instead Talbot found the net with a superb first-time effort.

Ipswich made it three goals in as many minutes to complete the rout. Burley sent substitute Mick Lambert away on the right and his cross was headed home by the grateful Mariner, who was soon collecting the match ball as a memento of the occasion. The hat-trick hero was quick to lavish praise on sidekick Turner when he said: 'Robin helped me out tremendously by sharing the workload against two very uncompromising central defenders. I have to take more responsibility with Trevor Whymark out of the side through injury. Robin is only a little younger than me but I have had more first-team experience so I have to be more responsible.'

England manager Ron Greenwood was at the game and one of the players under scrutiny, midfield dynamo Brian Talbot, did his international chances no harm with a typical all-action display topped with a goal. Greenwood was also checking up on players like Mills and Mariner, key members of his squad, while another name worth noting was that of young defender Russell Osman, who was again impressive as he deputised for knee injury victim Kevin Beattie.

Talbot revealed Town's ploy to expose the left side of Millwall's defence and added: 'It seems the luck we have not been having in the League is with us in the FA Cup. Over a season it tends to even itself out.' But the last word belonged to Mariner who added, somewhat prophetically as it turned out: 'We have the feeling that someone up there is looking down on us and saying "Go on, boys, go all the way to Wembley".'

The crowd trouble aside, it had been a tremendous occasion as Ipswich went into the Lions' Den and tamed them with a mesmerising display of attacking football. By the time Ipswich had finished with them, Millwall's performance certainly matched their League status – a team sitting in 20th place in the Second Division and totally outclassed. Their manager, George Petchey, had no alternative but to confess: 'We were outplayed. We were very, very poor on the day.' The reality was that Town had dished out a footballing lesson and better sides than Millwall would also have suffered had they been on the receiving end.

The unexpectedly high winning margin made people sit up and take notice. Perhaps the club's League position was still of some concern but the fact that Town were in the last four of the FA Cup, for the second time in four seasons, was a huge consolation.

A bunch of people calling themselves supporters had done their best to bring about a postponement, thus forcing a replay, but instead their attempts proved futile as Ipswich secured a significant victory, not only for themselves but for the game of football as a whole.

DID YOU KNOW?

• When Ipswich played Millwall in a pre-season game and defeated them 6–1, no one expected that the teams would meet at the quarter-final stage of the FA Cup and that the score would be exactly the same. Millwall were captained by ex-Ipswich midfield star Bryan Hamilton, a close pal of Ipswich skipper Mick Mills. Three years earlier Hamilton had scored twice for Town in an FA Cup replay against West Ham at Stamford Bridge, only to have both 'goals' disallowed, enabling the Hammers to go on and beat Fulham at Wembley. In later years Hamilton returned to Portman Road twice to assist with coaching duties and also had spells in charge of his native Northern Ireland and Norwich.

WEST BROMWICH ALBION VS IPSWICH TOWN

8 April 1978 • FA Cup Semi-Final

WEST BROMWICH ALBION: 1 (T. Brown 76 pen)	IPSWICH TOWN: 3 (Talbot 8, Mills 20, Wark 89)
Godden, Mulligan, Statham, T. Brown, Wile (Cunningham 60 mins), Robertson, Martin, A. Brown, Regis, Trewick, Johnston.	Cooper, Burley, Mills, Talbot (Lambert 18 mins), Hunter, Beattie, Osborne, Wark, Mariner, Turner, Woods.

REFEREE: Mr C. Thomas (Treorchy)
ATTENDANCE: 50,922

Ipswich, by virtue of their lowly League position, were considered the underdogs going into their FA Cup semi-final showdown with West Bromwich Albion at Highbury. New boss Ron Atkinson's team were several points better off, riding high in the First Division in pursuit of a UEFA Cup qualifying place, while Bobby Robson led his troops into the game amidst fears of relegation from the top flight – hence the bookies' verdict.

Having clinched their semi-final spot, Ipswich went on to play six League games before going head to head with the Midlands men, for whom Robson had been a star inside-forward around 20 years earlier. Of the half-dozen, only one resulted in a win – the welcome 4–0 thrashing of Norwich at Portman Road – and from a possible 12 points they banked six, leaving their League fate far from decided; however, this simply had to be forgotten on the day, and nothing else mattered beyond the outcome of the game in North London.

The appointment of Welsh referee Clive Thomas was greeted with groans of disbelief by a large number of Town supporters; memories were still vivid in their minds of how his no-goal decisions in a semi-final replay three years earlier had proved so costly. However, Ipswich were not about to allow side issues to affect their concentration and wisely declined various media invitations to be drawn into any controversy, merely stating that they were happy with the decision and rated the Welshman as one of the country's leading referees.

As the big day approached, Robson was only too willing to announce: 'We are up for it and we are confident. Albion are a good side but while they may be favourites we have no fears about facing them. Some people may see us as country cousins but they could be in for a surprise.'

The teams had met only five weeks earlier at Portman Road, when they shared four goals, but that was deemed of little significance as the various pundits seemed to favour the Black Country outfit. Albion's veteran defender Paddy Mulligan was equally confident about his side's chances, even predicting a 3–1 win and adding: 'That is based on what I believe to be true – that we are a better team than Ipswich the way we are playing right now.' Mulligan had been to Wembley once before, with Chelsea in the League Cup Final six years earlier, and went on:

I know that on the day Clive Woods could take me to the cleaners. But I also know I'm good enough to wrap him up and stop him playing. It's just a question of how it turns out on the day. At the moment I would say our own Willie Johnston is the best left-winger in the country. He's playing well but I must admit I've also got great respect for Woodsy. Actually, I call Clive 'Harpo' because I think he looks like the Marx brother with all the blond curly hair. And tell him I know he's not far off being as old as I am!

Republic of Ireland international Mulligan was asked how the arrival of Atkinson from Cambridge United had changed things at the Hawthorns, and he laughed:

We're running two miles a day instead of one and I'm feeling it more than most. To be honest, he's done a great job as our results have proved. I still have nightmares about that 7–0 defeat at Portman Road last season but since then we've had a good run. That game still rankles a bit. On the day, Ipswich had nine shots, scored with seven, and the other two hit the bar. You could say it was their day – on April 8 it might be our turn.

Nice guy Mulligan was entitled to his opinion but Ipswich were every bit as upbeat about their chances and, as the big day approached, manager Robson directed his comments to the supporters who had been lucky enough to bag a ticket:

Take it as read that the team will do all they can in terms of their footballing ability and their passion for the game because appearing at Wembley in a Cup Final is a lifelong ambition for all of them. They say Suffolk people don't know how to sing and cheer but your support in the FA Cup three years ago, particularly on that memorable night at Leicester when we finally eliminated Leeds United, proved them wrong. Give us a repeat performance this year and roar us on in style.

The match will be broadcast nationally on television and it gives Town fans the chance to show the entire country that they know how to support their team. Your vocal encouragement would be a tremendous spur to the players as they are poised to take the club to Wembley for the first time in its history. I cannot stress how vital it is that our fans make themselves heard. The players will try not to let you down on the day. They know it is probably the most important game of their careers to date. This is our chance to show the rest of the country that we are a force to be reckoned with – on and off the field.

Robson's rallying call served its purpose, with the Blue Army in magnificent voice at Highbury before the kick-off, and within just eight minutes of the game starting they turned the volume up even higher to celebrate the game's first goal. Mick Mills dashed down the left, took a pass from Woods in his stride and crossed for Brian Talbot to dive and power home with his head. However, while his teammates went wild with delight, the industrious midfielder lay dazed on the turf. It transpired that Talbot had clashed heads with Albion skipper John Wile, who made a vain bid to clear, and they were both clearly struggling as they were helped off. Wile managed to continue with a huge bandage wrapped round his head, although it was obvious that blood was still pumping out of the wound. As for Talbot, he was groggy and seeing double as his right eye puffed up.

Ipswich battled on with 10 men for a further 10 minutes, but it was clear that Talbot was in no shape to continue. Despite his pleas to go back on, it was decided the risk was not worth taking and Mick Lambert came on to trigger a reshuffle in the ranks. Amazingly, within two minutes the new-look Town side were celebrating again as they doubled their advantage thanks to Mills, who was playing a real stormer. From Lambert's corner, the skipper fired a low shot past Tony Godden in the Albion goal from eight yards.

Although Talbot's penetrative runs were missed, Ipswich had no real anxious moments and looked to be capable of seeing the game out until, that is, the 76th minute when Allan Hunter inexplicably stuck up an arm to meet Mick Martin's cross as he was challenged by Cyrille Regis. Referee Thomas rightly awarded a penalty and it looked like being an anxious last 14 minutes or so after Tony Brown converted from the spot, bringing the Albion fans to life and stirring the players to make the most of their unexpected lifeline. By that time Wile had been forced to call it a day, albeit reluctantly, and the situation had Ipswich supporters recalling how Albion had snatched a last-gasp equaliser in the 2-2 League draw between the sides at Portman Road the previous month. Was history about to repeat itself?

What threatened to be a nail-biting wait was cut short, however, when John Wark headed an 89th-minute third goal. Lambert won a corner, Woods floated the ball over and the young Scot rose to power the ball into the net. The timing of the goal, together with their two-goal advantage, could mean only one thing – Ipswich were going to Wembley, and confirmation, in the shape of the final whistle, was greeted in predictable fashion.

Most of Town's 26,000 fans were packed in behind the goal at Highbury's Clock End and as they headed off to celebrate, either in London's West End or back home in Suffolk, the champagne flowed in the victorious team's dressing room. The noise was deafening as the players let rip and goalscorer Talbot, gutted not to have lasted beyond the eighth minute but delighted that his teammates won through, explained his early withdrawal. 'I just couldn't see,' he revealed. 'To give you an idea of how bad it was, I was certain it was Robin Turner and not John Wark who scored the third goal.' Kevin Beattie, who survived the 90 minutes despite fears about his knee injury, said:

This will be my fourth game at Wembley. I've already played there three times for England but this is the one I've always wanted. I still can't believe we have finally made it. I called Big Al a few names when he gave away that penalty but when Warky put his header away we all knew it was over. It was a great feeling just playing out the last minute or so knowing there was nothing that anyone could do to stop us.

Roger Osborne sipped bubbly as he took a bath and said: 'I feel fantastic now but strangely enough I did not enjoy the game that much. I didn't get much chance to attack because I was too busy marking Tony Brown. But it's been a tremendous day.'

The victory was all the sweeter for those players who had been reduced to tears three years earlier at Stamford Bridge when they lost out to West Ham in a semi-final replay. Among them, of course, was skipper Mills and, although delighted for himself, it was typical of the man that he should have thoughts for the Albion players forced to accept defeat and whose dressing room was almost funereal by comparison. Mills said: 'I felt for them because I knew just what they were going through. I have friends among them and I sympathised. Football can be so cruel at times.' Kind words from one of the game's true gentlemen and scorer of his side's second goal, and he reflected on the strength-sapping 90 minutes as he added: 'I felt real relief when we scored our third. The moment of joy hit home then. This is the greatest day of my career.'

Having heard the news that Arsenal had defeated Orient in the other semi-final across London at Stamford Bridge, Mills could not resist looking forward to Wembley and went on: 'It will be a bloody hard game for them, believe me. We have a lot of very determined, very willing people. Arsenal will have to fight very, very hard, and to the very end, to beat us. If we lose at Wembley we will have had a good day out but achieved nothing. That's why it is very important to us to win.'

Robson was joined in the dressing room by brothers John and Patrick Cobbold, chairmen past and present, who were also close to tears as they savoured the moment. 'We had to reshuffle after the first goal,' reflected the Town boss, 'but then Millsy got a second and it was looking good. But I saw Hunter stick a hand up and I thought "What's he doing?" They score from the penalty and suddenly it's game on. It's on a see-saw. But we battled it out. Our old habits – tucking in, filling space – got us through.' He concluded: 'Everybody worked hard and we were disciplined and organised. Warky got that late header. We were there. The feeling was incredible.'

DID YOU KNOW?

• West Brom's late challenge to at least force a replay – which would have taken place at White Hart Lane – was not helped by the dismissal of Republic of Ireland international midfielder Mick Martin, who happens to be the uncle of current Ipswich star Owen Garvan.

ARSENAL VS IPSWICH TOWN

6 May 1978 • FA Cup Final

ARSENAL: 0	IPSWICH TOWN: 1 (Osborne 77)
Jennings, Rice, Nelson, Price, O'Leary, Young, Brady (Rix 66 mins), Sunderland, Macdonald, Stapleton, Hudson.	Cooper, Burley, Mills, Talbot, Hunter, Beattie, Osborne (Lambert 78 mins), Wark, Mariner, Geddis, Woods.

REFEREE: Mr D. Nippard (Bournemouth)

ATTENDANCE: 100,000

To the vast majority of people, the most surprising thing about the FA Cup Final of 1978 was the outcome, since underdogs Ipswich saw off red-hot favourites Arsenal in far more convincing fashion than the scoreline might suggest. But they would have been even more amazed had the game not been played at all, which was a very real possibility when referee Derek Nippard arrived at Wembley three and a half hours before the scheduled 3pm start.

The veteran official, for whom his first Final also brought down the curtain on an illustrious career, recalled: 'I got to the stadium at 11.30am and the first thing I saw was members of the ground staff pumping water off the pitch. I must admit it immediately crossed my mind that I might be the first referee to postpone an FA Cup Final.' Fortunately there was no need for such drastic action, although a combination of the soggy pitch and the afternoon sun, that beat down, made for strength-sapping conditions that took their toll on both sets of players long before the final whistle.

The four-week period between the team's famous semi-final victory at Highbury and the historic first trip to Wembley had been something of a rollercoaster ride. They encountered the high of preserving First Division status, courtesy of a home win over Bristol City, that meant there was no danger of Ipswich being dragged into the relegation scrap. They also experienced a potentially morale-busting League defeat when they were thrashed 6–1 at Aston Villa just a week before they were due to face Arsenal in the biggest game in the club's history.

Manager Bobby Robson was forced to make a number of changes to his starting line up at Villa Park. Injuries ruled out three eventual Wembley heroes in goalkeeper Paul Cooper, central defender Kevin Beattie and striker Paul Mariner. Young 'keeper Paul Overton, just 17, was called up for his debut and what proved to be his only senior outing for the club, and Russell Osman again deputised for Beattie, while the absence of Mariner gave Trevor Whymark a chance to stake his claim for a place in the Final. Whymark, who had managed just one previous start since being stretchered off during the Boxing Day defeat at Norwich, scored Town's only goal on an otherwise forgettable day but was unable to prove himself 100 per cent fit for the Final. Most intriguingly of all, however, was the inclusion of Colin Viljoen, as Robson looked to give the midfield man an opportunity to show he was ready to start at Wembley seven days later – a bold decision that saw Roger Osborne drop to the bench.

The gamble of including Viljoen backfired spectacularly as Town suffered their heaviest defeat of the season and Viljoen failed to make the sort of impact that would have given Robson a selection headache the following week. Most worrying of all, however, was the suggestion that the rest of the Ipswich side had rebelled against Viljoen's inclusion to the point where they wanted to fail in order to convince the manager that his plan to include Viljoen at Wembley was ill-advised. The in-phrase at the time was player power and the tabloids feasted on the fact that an FA Cup Final camp appeared to be in a state of chaos in the countdown to the big game. Years later Robson said:

Yes, the press called it player power, but that was a load of rubbish. But a 6–1 defeat has to be the worst defeat any team has ever suffered going into an FA Cup Final. And if I'm honest, it could have been 12. I felt I had to look at Viljoen. He was a great player and we all knew he was a better player, technically, than Osborne. I felt he should have a go to see if he was fit. The team let him down. They played badly on the day but I don't believe for one minute that they played badly on purpose. I was angry at the end. Our best player was a 17-year-old kid making his debut in goal. How could that be? I asked the rest of the team and all I got was blank faces. They had disgraced the club and I let them know. Okay, they might not have wanted to get injured but that was no excuse for the display they turned in.

The huge negative of Villa Park, as the clock ticked towards Wembley, turned out to be a massive positive. Robson added: 'I think it galvanised things. It brought the players closer together in the days before the Final. I could sense they wanted to make amends.'

Viljoen, his chances of appearing beneath the Twin Towers clearly wrecked, refused to travel with the squad to their hotel base at St Albans on the Wednesday of Wembley week.

He effectively dropped himself, and Robson said: 'I could understand it.' The official party stopped off in Colchester to collect their FA Cup Final outfits of light-blue blazers and black trousers, although even that was far from plain sailing. Some of the female workers at the clothing factory decided to play a series of pranks on the players – switching the trousers of Eric Gates and Paul Mariner, for example – which caused much hilarity as they tried them on.

The Town party checked in to the Sopwell House Hotel at St Albans, a popular base for Wembley teams, and the light-hearted mood continued over the next few days. After arriving in Hertfordshire, manager Bobby Robson and his players met the media for interviews and pictures, and seasoned national newspaper journalists remarked that the squad seemed far more relaxed than others they had met over the years.

Thursday saw Football Association secretary Ted Croker visit the hotel to discuss Wembley protocol and it was at this point that Robson and his players first became aware of the fact that the Final was in doubt because of unprecedented rainfall. In his briefing, Croker paid particular attention to the Royal guest, HRH Princess Alexandra, and, looking Kevin Beattie in the eye, said it was important that no player should shake her gloved hand too tightly. Other details, such as which club personnel would occupy the seats on the bench alongside Robson, his coaching staff, physiotherapist and substitute, were ironed out before Croker returned to his office at Lancaster Gate.

On the morning of the match, it was confirmed that Allan Hunter had passed a fitness test held on the hotel lawn before breakfast. The big defender had hardly slept and was so anxious to know his fate that he was ready almost four hours ahead of the scheduled test at 11am. Robson and his staff, who had been asleep, were alerted to the fact that Hunter was refusing to wait any longer. They looked on as the experienced Irishman, who had been ever present in the previous rounds, went through a routine to confirm his knee would at least enable him to start the game. It was good news for Hunter, but there was sympathy from him for youngster Russell Osman, who had been placed on stand-by and was to suffer further disappointment later that morning when Robson confirmed the number 12 shirt would be worn by Mick Lambert.

The upbeat atmosphere that had prevailed since the team bus pulled out of the Portman Road gates three days earlier was still much in evidence, to the point where the players convinced themselves that victory over Arsenal would be theirs and the FA Cup would be heading back to Suffolk for the very first time. Robson confirmed:

Our build-up was relaxed, I remember that. John Motson came to the hotel on the morning of the game to do live interviews with the players and the atmosphere was very calm. We saw the Arsenal lads being interviewed and they looked a bit subdued; that didn't do us any harm. When we were having lunch, Mick Lambert was gathering money to put a bet on. I gave him £20. We were 5-2, ridiculous odds, and I thought it would show my confidence in the team. I couldn't see us losing.

After a light meal, the players returned to their rooms to pack their bags and board the team bus for the journey to Wembley. ITV commentator Gerry Harrison was onboard with a crew to broadcast live links as armchair fans all over the world tuned in to enjoy the build-up. A police escort ensured the journey was without hitches and the bus was directed in through the giant double gates to park in the famous tunnel, where the players disembarked and made their way to the south – or home – dressing room. This was due to a long-standing FA rule, that the dressing rooms be allocated alphabetically starting with the north one. The two clubs reached agreement themselves on kit – Ipswich wearing their first choice blue and white colours while Arsenal switched to an alternative rig-out of yellow shirts and blue shorts.

Before the game, the players read a host of good luck messages and telegrams that had been sent by family, friends and fans before appearing on the pitch for the traditional walkabout, at which point reporters from both the BBC and ITV grabbed the opportunity to have a quick chat.

The Ipswich players were delighted that their fans had been allocated the terracing at the tunnel end, which enabled them to stand and admire the many special banners that had been prepared – one spelling out the message 'Woods Fries Rice' particularly caught the eye – without having to walk the length of the pitch, as their Arsenal counterparts were required to do. Among the capacity crowd was ex-Town striker David Johnson, by then a Liverpool player and with his leg in plaster after he suffered a broken ankle. However, he was not going to let injury prevent him joining his former teammates and potentially celebrating with them. Interestingly, despite a trophy-laden few years at Anfield, one major honour eluded the man they called Jonty – the FA Cup – and now his former team were fighting for it. Nevertheless, it was on with the show, and rival managers Robson and Terry Neill led their teams out of the tunnel to a tumultuous reception from the 100,000 crowd.

Players from both sides looked for loved ones in the crowd either side of the Royal Box and after being presented to HRH Princess Alexandra, followed by the national anthem, they warmed up as the big kick-off loomed. Soon after the start, any doubts surrounding Hunter's fitness were quickly dispelled as he slid in with crunching challenges on Arsenal strikers Frank Stapleton and Malcolm Macdonald. That set the tone, with Hunter and defensive partner Beattie firmly in charge as their midfield and forward colleagues took the game to the Gunners and carved out a series of chances. Although Town took until near the end to score the all-important goal, Paul Mariner had struck the crossbar after just 11 minutes and then John Wark proceeded to smash near-identical shots against the same post. Arsenal goalkeeper Pat Jennings also made a truly world-class save from George Burley and it seemed the breakthrough would never come. When it finally did, it reflected brilliantly on Robson's decision to name David Geddis in his starting line-up because, although the youngster from Carlisle wore the number 10 shirt that had been earmarked for Whymark, he occupied an unfamiliar role on the right side.

Coach Bobby Ferguson watched Arsenal closely in the run-up to the Final and quickly sussed that they were most dangerous down their left side and, more often than not, attacks started with Jennings rolling the ball to full-back Sammy Nelson. Geddis was asked to cut the supply line, which he did brilliantly, and when he received the ball wide on the right in the 77th minute he had only one thing on his mind – to race beyond Nelson and fire low into the box. Willie Young could only half clear and when the ball landed at Roger Osborne's feet, he let fly with a low, left-foot shot that whizzed past Jennings and sent one half of the national stadium wild with delight. But in one of the oddest-ever Wembley episodes, goalscorer Osborne emerged from the celebrations in no fit state to continue and had to be substituted as a mix of excitement, emotion and exhaustion brought him to a standstill. He sat on the bench for what seemed like an eternity before the final whistle sounded and the celebrations, for players and fans alike, began in earnest. Robson stated:

In the dressing room before the game I told them: 'We only have one chance and we don't want to come back in here with any regrets about what we didn't do.' I told them to make it a performance to remember. They had nothing to be afraid of. We were better than our League position, we all knew that, and I reminded them that they had a better semi-final result than Arsenal. Our tactics worked a treat. David Geddis had never played wide on the right before but he played the game of his life. We could do that because we had Paul Mariner, who was good

The front cover of the FA Cup Final programme.

enough to play on his own up front. The three midfield players took it in turns to get through. John Wark hit the post twice and Roger Osborne got the goal when we wondered if we were ever going to score. It was all too much for the lad. A hot, humid day and he was overcome with exhaustion. He almost passed out when the rest of the team jumped on him. Cyril Lea came over and said: 'His legs have gone, he'll need to come off.' We sent Mick Lambert on and he played at right-half for the first time in his career. Then, eventually, the final whistle went and the Cup was ours. It was a dream day.

Winger Clive Woods, whose trickery gave Arsenal skipper Pat Rice a torrid time throughout, was named Man of the Match, but it was a day when all the Town players were superior to their immediate opponents and, although the scoreline suggested a narrow victory, in reality it was a crushing 1–0 success.

Robson's good friend Don Howe, the assistant manager of Arsenal and a former teammate with both West Bromwich Albion and England, was quick to congratulate him and Mariner was seen to take time out to commiserate with Arsenal's young defender, David O'Leary, who had slumped to the deck in utter despair.

Soon it was time for Mick Mills to lead his team up the 39 steps and receive the trophy from HRH Princess Alexandra, and as they descended again they set off on a lap of honour, the trophy being passed around as photographers seized their chance to take pictures galore. The players were understandably reluctant to return to the dressing room, preferring instead to milk the moment. However, eventually they made their way back down the tunnel, and one of the first visitors to the Ipswich dressing room afterwards was Southampton manager Lawrie McMenemy, whose team also struck a blow for the underdogs two years earlier when they defeated Manchester United, also by the only goal, in an even bigger Final upset. After sipping champagne from the famous trophy, then showering and changing, the team bus left Wembley for the journey to the Royal Garden Hotel alongside Hyde Park in London's Kensington High Street, where the club's official banquet was to take place.

EAST ANGLIAN
DAILY TIMES

Ipswich, Monday, May 8, 1978

No. 34,098   Price 8p

In our Blue Heaven

Suffolk heroes bringing Cup to Ipswich

A HEROES' welcome for Ipswich Town.

This was the moment yesterday when Bobby Robson and his team arrived in the Cornhill . . . with the FA cup.

The team which confounded the soccer pundits by beating favourites Arsenal with ease received a rapturous welcome from a crowd of 100,000.

Many had been waiting for more than four hours

All in their Blue Heaven.

Inside: Four pages of action pictures.

Today's Anglian

Page
Sport .... 2 and 3
Business Scene 4
Crossword 6
Letters to the Editor 6
Edmund Orwell 6
Ann Meadows 6
Weather Forecast 6
Radio Music 6

CLASSIFIED MARKET
ON PAGES 8 TO 11

Ipswich goes wild as 100,000 greet the winners

Robson and his aces arrive on the Cornhill

By DAVE VINCENT, SAM BROWN and ERIC JOHNSTONE

YES, the FA Cup is ours!

The most glittering prize in English football came to Suffolk for the first time yesterday, brought back by the Super Blues of Ipswich Town.

Ipswich was a Blue Heaven as an estimated 100,000 people turned out to see their heroes parade the trophy through the town in an open-top bus.

Not only Suffolk acclaimed the 1—0 win over Arsenal. It was a triumph heralded by the nation, so convincing was it.

And if the players captured the imagination of millions, the fans can hold their heads high, too.

The 25,000 Town supporters who travelled to Wembley — providing an ocean of blue and white at the tunnel end — put home to a tumultuous reception — and more than a few tears were shed.

They sang "Abide With Me", the traditional Cup Final hymn, with gusto. And the National Anthem was given the proper treatment.

One of the nicest touches was the number of blue and white balloons set off by the fans just before kick off.

The Wembley wonders came home to a tumultuous reception — and more than a few tears were shed.

Fans climbed roofs, chimneys, ledges, lamp-posts and even a 150-foot crane to get a glimpse of their heroes outside the Town Hall.

Many of the crowd had difficulty seeing manager Bobby Robson and his players and staff when they were received by Ipswich Mayor, Mr. David Myer, on the Town Hall steps.

The fans called and chanted for the players to go up on the balcony.

The official business over, the

Wembley heroes did just that, thanking the supporters and holding the Cup aloft. Kevin Beattie and David Geddis sang "You'll Never Walk Alone".

Pandemonium greeted Town as they arrived at the Cornhill, the open area in front of the Town Hall.

Several children had to be helped away by St. John Ambulance after being hurt in the crush.

Thousands had attempted to cram into the area for the end of the victory tour.

The Mayor said the Cup triumph was of "immeasurable benefit to the morale of the local community, its commerce and industry as well as the football club itself."

He paid tribute to the club's tremendous achievement in getting to Wembley and the way in which they had won the Cup.

"We have waited a long time for this Cup and you have brought it to us in the grand manner," he said.

Manager Robson introduced his players, his directors — "the best board in the country" — and the club's president, 80-year-old Lady Blanche Cobbold.

Players danced jigs as the crowd chanted their names.

Inside, the champagne flowed and individual players went on the balcony to do their party pieces.

Paul Cooper, nicknamed "Tommy", said they won the Cup "Just Like That."

Bobby Robson, greeted by a wave after wave of cheers, said: "Not only do we have the best team, but we have the best supporters."

The crowd answered with "We'll Support You Evermore", "We've Never Lost at Wembley" and "Forest, Forest here we come." (Town's opponents in the Charity Shield match next August).

So happy were the fans that they forgave Leader of the Opposition, Mrs. Margaret Thatcher, for her radio comment after the game singling out Trevor Whymark as her man of the match.

Whymark, and not David Geddis, was listed in the official programme which unfortunately had not been pointed out to the Conservative leader.

But the fans will find it difficult to exonerate the Sunday newspaper which, "Bee By Gum", associated goal hero Roger Osborne with Yorkshire.

Osborne comes from Otley, Suffolk, not Otley, Yorkshire. The homecoming was triumphant from the minute the team left their London hotel.

Continued on Page 7

The headline says it all as a local newspaper covers the Ipswich players' open-top bus ride through the packed streets of the town prior to a Civic Reception.

co-operative household removals & storage
FULL DIVIDEND
Derby Rd Ipswich
Tel 7010

Ipswich Monday, May 8, 1978, No. 28,302 Price 7p

Evening Star

MAIN TOWN

THE GREATEST . . .

● Town players in jubilant mood as they travelled through Ipswich to a Civic reception.

Exclusive new Cup pictures in tonight's souvenir pull-out

Ipswich buses hit again

THOUSANDS HAIL THE CONQUERING HEROES

By SAM BROWN, DAVE VINCENT and ERIC JOHNSTONE

THAT blue and white magic was still casting its spell over Ipswich today — 48 hours after Bobby Robson's heroes collected soccer's premier prize.

But if that Wembley win wasn't enough, no one will forget the delirious welcome home the Super Blues received from the town yesterday when an open-top bus carrying the team and trophy seemed to float along on a living sea of blue and white to a civic reception at the Town Hall.

IPSWICH busmen stage another lightning stoppage today again hitting commuters and some school traffic with a two hours cut in service between 7.30 and 9.30 a.m.

The busmen are not due to meet again to consider further action until late this evening but the authorities have not ruled out the possibility of a second stoppage today.

There were two service cuts on Saturday between 11.30 a.m. and 1.30 p.m. and again between 9.30 p.m. and 11.30 p.m.

In a new statement today, Mr. David Cox, branch chairman of the men's union, the Transport and General Workers, said the men were still prepared to meet and talk with council representatives and that industrial action would cease as soon as they sat down at the talks table.

The council has said it will not agree to talks unless the men follow a disputes procedure and stop their action before the meeting.

The union statement went on: "Due to the fact that no firm commitment has been received by this branch regarding constructive moves towards a settlement, we regret our industrial action will continue.

"We have again today informed the council of our willingness to call it off immediately there is a meeting with the Public Transport sub committee to discuss, along constructive lines, the re-employment of staff.

"However, we are informed that the sub committee is not prepared to call a meeting under these conditions.

"The reason is that in the past, action has been called off only to find that a meeting could not be arranged within a reasonable period of time and even then the meeting was found to be a waste of time."

Fans climbed roofs, chimneys, ledges, lamp-posts and even a 150 foot crane to get a glimpse of their heroes outside the Town Hall.

Many of the crowd had difficulty seeing manager Bobby Robson and his players and staff when they were received by Ipswich Mayor, Mr. David Myer, on the Town Hall steps.

The fans called and chanted for the players to go up on the balcony.

The official heroes over, the Wembley heroes did just that, chanting the supporters and holding the Cup aloft. Kevin Beattie and David Geddis sang "You'll Never Walk Alone".

Pandemonium greeted Town as they arrived at the Cornhill, the open area in front of the Town Hall.

Several children had to be helped away by St. John Ambulance after being hurt in the crush.

Thousands had attempted to cram into the area for the end of the victory tour.

Not only Suffolk acclaimed the 1—0 win over Arsenal. It was a triumph heralded by the nation, so convincing was it.

And if the players captured the imagination of millions, the fans can hold their heads high, too.

The 25,000 Town supporters who travelled to Wembley — providing an ocean of blue and white at the tunnel end — put sportsmanship back into the Cup Final.

The Wembley wonders came home to a tumultuous reception — and more than a few tears were shed.

Victory peal

THE BELL-RINGERS of St. Mary le Tower Church, Ipswich who rang a special peal yesterday to celebrate Ipswich Town's victory will ring again tomorrow during the Town's final league match of the season. The bell-ringers will begin their three-hour peal at about 6.15 p.m. The title of the peal? Wembley Surprise Major.

More than 50 faintings

THREE people were taken to hospital and more than 50 people fainted during yesterday's FA Cup celebrations. St. John Ambulance personnel manned a mobile first aid unit in Princes Street

throughout the afternoon. A spokesman for Ipswich police said, "We had no problems at all. It was a family day out." In fact, the police were full of praise for the Ipswich fans.

The Mayor said the Cup triumph was of "immeasurable benefit to the morale of the local community, its commerce and industry, as well as the football club itself."

He paid tribute to the club's tremendous achievement in getting to Wembley and the way in which they had won the Cup.

"We have waited a long time for this Cup and you have brought it to us in the grand manner," he said.

Manager Robson introduced his players, his directors — "the best board in the country" — and the club's president, 80-year-old Lady Blanche Cobbold.

Players danced jigs as the

crowd chanted their names.

Inside, the champagne flowed and individual players went on the balcony to do their party pieces.

Paul Cooper, nicknamed "Tammy", said they were the best Cup "Just Like That."

Bobby Robson, greeted by wave after wave of cheers, said, "Not only do we have the best team, but we have the best supporters."

The crowd answered with "We'll Support You Ever more", "We've Never Lost at Wembley" and "Forest, Forest here we come." (Town's opponents in the Charity Shield match next August).

So happy were the fans that they forgave Leader of the Opposition, Mrs. Margaret Thatcher, for her radio comment

● **Turn to Page 7**

THE WEATHER	FT INDEX
CLOUDY See Page 6	481.7 Up 0.2

LETTER

Well done, Super Star . . .

YOU boys at the Evening Star certainly pulled out all the stops in producing the Cup Final edition on Saturday.

I removed my copy from the letter-box scarcely an hour after television coverage had ended, expecting to read the customary three lines in the Stop Press to the effect that there was no score at half-time — but what did I find?

Lo and behold! There was a colourful souvenir edition with the final score in banner headlines, two separate reports of the entire match (with no more typographical errors than usual), and action pictures galore, including one which was obviously taken several minutes after presentation of the Cup.

Our soccer team thoroughly deserve all the congratulations which are being showered on them, but I feel that your team also merit the highest praise for this very efficient demonstration of journalistic skill.

Yours in admiration
RONALD F. TURNER, 13 Bromhall Close, Ipswich.

Friends and neighbours

● It looks like Christmas at the Osborne household in Ipswich today thanks to the efforts of his proud neighbours. And a better Christmas present than an FA Cup goal is unthinkable. Certainly the celebrations will last well into December!

☐ How Mrs. Osborne took the biscuit—Page 7

INSIDE

☐ TV, Television 2
☐ Specially for Women 3
☐ Diary 6
☐ Letters 6
☐ Crossword 6
☐ Starscope 6
☐ Ipswich plan 7
☐ Star Turn 7
☐ Classified Market ... 8-11
☐ Sport .... 4 and 12

The front page of a local newspaper on Monday 8 May 1978, reporting the Ipswich team's victory parade through the town.

190

Fenced in but happy — a section of the Ipswich supporters who enjoyed their day out at Wembley.

The joy.. .and the sorrow

● It's ours, all ours . . . Jubilant Town players gather round the coveted cup in the dressing room after the match. Paul Mariner (right) toasts the cup with a refreshing pint of milk but of course there were stronger celebratory liquids also floating around.

● "WILL I get another chance?" could be what Gunners ace striker. Malcolm – alias Supermac – Macdonald is pondering as he trundles dejectedly away from the arena.

● ALLAN Hunter (left) and Kevin Beattie, the pair publicly tagged "bacon and eggs" by Town boss Bobby Robson at the civic reception share one of their many moments of glory at Wembley with one of the great driving forces behind their success — Ipswich coach Cyril Lea.

Newspaper cuttings show the scene inside the Ipswich dressing room and emphasise the difference between winning and losing as the Ipswich trio of Allan Hunter, coach Cyril Lea and Kevin Beattie celebrate, while Arsenal striker Malcolm Macdonald looks disconsolate in defeat.

The two teams emerge from the Wembley tunnel prior to kick-off with the Ipswich fans in the background.

The Town players with the FA Cup at Portman Road for the first time.

(Photograph courtesy of Owen Hines)

The winning team with the FA Cup. Back row, left to right: Allan Hunter, Mick Lambert, John Wark, Paul Cooper, Kevin Beattie, Roger Osborne and David Geddis. Front row: Bobby Robson (manager), Paul Mariner, Clive Woods, Mick Mills, George Burley, Brian Talbot and Cyril Lea (coach).

(Photograph courtesy of Owen Hines)

Ipswich have their hands on the FA Cup at Wembley as some players take a close look at their medals.

That wonderful Wembley winning feeling kicks in as the Ipswich players display the famous trophy.

Brothers John and Patrick Cobbold, chairmen past and present, get their hands on the FA Cup.

Ipswich Town FA Cup Appearances

1936–2008

	Player	Era	Apps	Subs	Total
1.	Mills, Mick	1967–1982	57		57
2.	Wark, John	1975–1996	55	1	56
3.	Cooper, Paul	1976–1987	45		45
4.	Burley, George	1974–1985	43		43
5.	Parker, Tommy	1945–1955	37		37
6.	Mariner, Paul	1977–1984	31		31
7.	Osman, Russell	1978–1985	30	2	32
8.	Rees, Doug	1950–1958	29		29
9.	Butcher, Terry	1979–1986	28		28
10.	Viljoen, Colin	1968–1978	28	1	29
11.	Stockwell, Mick	1986–1999	28	3	31
12.	Elsworthy, John	1952–1963	27		27
13.	Hunter, Allan	1972–1982	26		26
14.	Garneys, Tom	1951–1958	25		25
15.	Beattie, Kevin	1973–1981	24	2	26
16.	Woods, Clive	1971–1980	24	3	27
17.	Baxter, Billy	1962–1971	23		23
18.	Talbot, Brian	1974–1978	23		23
19.	McCall, Steve	1981–1987	23	1	24
20.	Gates, Eric	1976–1985	23	3	26
21.	Little, Jackie	1936–1950	22		22
22.	Myles, Neil	1952–1958	22		22
23.	Dozzell, Jason	1985–1993	22		22
24.	Whymark, Trevor	1973–1979	21		21
25.	Bailey, Roy	1956–1964	19		19
26.	Leadbetter, Jimmy	1956–1965	19		19
27.	Muhren, Arnold	1979–1982	19		19
28.	Sivell, Laurie	1971–1984	19		19
29.	Crawford, Ray	1959–1969	18		18

	PLAYER	ERA	APPS	SUBS	TOTAL
30.	Feeney, Jim	1950–1955	18		18
31.	Linighan, David	1989–1995	18		18
32.	Parry, Ossie	1936–1948	18		18
33.	Williams, Geraint	1993–1998	18		18
34.	Brazil, Alan	1978–1983	18	2	20
35.	Thompson, Neil	1990–1994	17		17
36.	Bell, Dave	1938–1949	16		16
37.	McLuckie, Jimmy	1936–1945	16		16
38.	McNeil, Mick	1965–1972	16		16
39.	Lambert, Mick	1971–1978	16	5	21
40.	Acres, Basil	1952–1958	15		15
41.	Carberry, Larry	1956–1963	15		15
42.	Morris, Peter	1969–1974	15		15
43.	Parry, Jack	1951–1955	15		15
44.	Thijssen, Frans	1979–1983	15		15
45.	Johnson, David	1973–1976	15		15
46.	Yallop, Frank	1985–1996	15	3	18
47.	Forrest, Craig	1990–1996	14		14
48.	Perrett, George	1936–1948	14		14
49.	Reed, Billy	1953–1958	14		14
50.	Kiwomya, Chris	1989–1995	14		14
51.	Wilnis, Fabian	1999–2008	14		14
52.	Malcolm, Ken	1955–1961	13		13
53.	Phillips, Ted	1955–1963	13		13
54.	Wright, Richard	1996–2001	13		13
55.	Holland, Matt	1998–2003	12		12
56.	Milton, Simon	1990–1996	12		12
57.	Brennan, Mark	1985–1988	12		12
58.	Johnson, Gavin	1992–1995	12	1	13
59.	Baird, Harry	1946–1950	11		11
60.	Brown, Thomas	1952–1954	11		11
61.	Burns, Mick	1938–1952	11		11
62.	Hegan, Danny	1964–1969	11		11

	PLAYER	ERA	APPS	SUBS	TOTAL
63.	McLuckie, George	1953–1958	11		11
64.	Nelson, Andy	1960–1964	11		11
65.	Cranson, Ian	1985–1988	11	1	12
66.	Hamilton, Bryan	1973–1975	11	1	12
67.	Zondervan, Romeo	1985–1992	11	2	13
68.	Compton, John	1962–1964	10		10
69.	Houldsworth, Fred	1936–1937	10		10
70.	Millward, Doug	1956–1961	10		10
71.	Wilson, Kevin	1985–1987	10		10
72.	Brogan, Frank	1965–1970	10	1	11
73.	Baker, Gerry	1964–1967	9		9
74.	Deacon, David	1952–1953	9		9
75.	Mowbray, Tony	1996–1999	9		9
76.	Hill, Mick	1970–1972	9		9
77.	Marshall, Ian	1994–1996	9		9
78.	Putney, Trevor	1983–1986	9		9
79.	Scowcroft, James	1996–2001	9	1	10
80.	D'Avray, Mich	1982–1988	9	2	11
81.	Broadfoot, Joe	1964–1967	8		8
82.	Bruce, Bobby	1936–1937	8		8
83.	Carter, Jock	1936	8		8
84.	Cowie, Charlie	1936–1937	8		8
85.	Lea, Cyril	1965–1967	8		8
86.	Parker, Stan	1946–1950	8		8
87.	Roberts, Jimmy	1950–1952	8		8
88.	Robertson, Jimmy	1971–1972	8		8
89.	Stephenson, Roy	1961–1963	8		8
90.	Taricco, Mauricio	1996–1998	8		8
91.	Thomson, Bob	1936	8		8
92.	Wright, Jermaine	1999–2004	8	1	9
93.	Whitton, Steve	1992–1994	8	1	9
94.	Palmer, Steve	1991–1994	8	3	11
95.	Osborne, Roger	1975–1978	8	4	12

	Player	Era	Apps	Subs	Total
96.	Naylor, Richard	1997–2008	8	6	14
97.	Best, David	1969–1974	7		7
98.	Blackwell, Jack	1936	7		7
99.	Davin, Joe	1964–1966	7		7
100.	Driver, Allenby	1950–1952	7		7
101.	Fletcher, Charlie	1938–1945	7		7
102.	Hancock, Ken	1966–1968	7		7
103.	Moran, Doug	1962–1964	7		7
104.	Williams, Jackie	1936	7		7
105.	Johnson, David	1998–1999	7		7
106.	Magilton, Jim	1999–2006	7	2	9
107.	Ball, Joe	1952–1953	6		6
108.	Clarke, Frank	1971	6		6
109.	Hammond, Geoff	1971	6		6
110.	Jefferson, Derek	1967–1972	6		6
111.	Jennings, Bill	1947–1950	6		6
112.	Murchison, Ron	1951–1952	6		6
113.	Newman, Eric	1945–1952	6		6
114.	O'Mahoney, Matt	1945–1946	6		6
115.	Tibbott, Les	1976–1979	6		6
116.	Harper, Dave	1966–1967	6		6
117.	Hreidarsson, Hermann	2001–2003	6		6
118.	Slater, Stuart	1994–1995	6		6
119.	Guentchev, Bontcho	1993–1994	6	2	8
120.	Richards, Matt	2003–2007	6	2	8
121.	Baker, Clive	1993–1995	5		5
122.	Blackwood, Bobby	1963–1964	5		5
123.	Brown, Jackie	1948–1950	5		5
124.	Brown, Tom	1948–1950	5		5
125.	Crowe, Alex	1953–1955	5		5
126.	Gaynor, James	1952	5		5
127.	Harper, Colin	1970–1973	5		5
128.	Houghton, Billy	1967–1969	5		5

	PLAYER	ERA	APPS	SUBS	TOTAL
129.	McCrory, Sam	1950–1951	5		5
130.	McGreal, John	1999–2004	5		5
131.	Mulraney, Ambrose	1937–1939	5		5
132.	Rees, Derek	1958–1959	5		5
133.	Rumbold, George	1946–1950	5		5
134.	Sedgley, Steve	1995–1996	5		5
135.	Thomsen, Claus	1995–1997	5		5
136.	Tyler, Len	1950–1951	5		5
137.	Dyer, Kieron	1997–1999	5		5
138.	Turner, Robin	1978–1983	5	1	6
139.	Youds, Eddie	1993–1994	5	1	6
140.	Collard, Ian	1971–1975	5	1	6
141.	Petta, Bobby	1998-1999	5	1	6
142.	Tanner, Adam	1995–1999	5	2	7
143.	Counago, Pablo	2002–2008	5	2	7
144.	O'Callaghan, Kevin	1981–1984	5	5	10
145.	Bolton, Jack	1964–1966	4		4
146.	Chadwick, Fred	1938–1939	4		4
147.	Cundy, Jason	1997–1998	4		4
148.	Dale, Billy	1938–1939	4		4
149.	Dobson, George	1936	4		4
150.	Harding, Dan	2007	4		4
151.	Humes, Tony	1987–1990	4		4
152.	Marshall, Andy	2002–2003	4		4
153.	Mitchell, Alex	1949–1950	4		4
154.	O'Brien, Joe	1949–1950	4		4
155.	Pickett, Reg	1958–1961	4		4
156.	Price, George	1945	4		4
157.	Roberts, Dale	1977–1979	4		4
158.	Roberts, Gary	2007	4		4
159.	Bell, Bobby	1971	4		4
160.	Bent, Marcus	2002–2003	4		4
161.	Bruce, Alex	2007–2008	4		4

	PLAYER	ERA	APPS	SUBS	TOTAL
162.	Legwinski, Sylvain	2007	4		4
163.	Venus, Mark	1998–2001	4		4
164.	Stewart, Marcus	2001–2002	4		4
165.	Gernon, Irvin	1983–1984	4	1	5
166.	Bramble, Titus	1999–2002	4	1	5
167.	Williams, Gavin	2006–2008	4	1	5
168.	Haynes, Danny	2006–2008	4	2	6
169.	Reuser, Martijn	2001–2004	4	2	6
170.	Uhlenbeek, Gus	1996–1998	4	3	7
171.	Clapham, Jamie	1999–2003	4	3	7
172.	Mason, Paul	1994–1996	4	3	7
173.	Berry, Peter	1959	3		3
174.	Clarke, George	1949–1950	3		3
175.	Davies, Bryn	1938–1939	3		3
176.	Davis, Kelvin	2004–2005	3		3
177.	De Vos, Jason	2005–2007	3		3
178.	Dobson, Peter	1951–1952	3		3
179.	Edwards, Dave	1945	3		3
180.	Grant, Wilf	1955	3		3
181.	Jobson, Tom	1936	3		3
182.	Johnstone, Bobby	1959	3		3
183.	Jones, Willie	1951–1953	3		3
184.	Lowe, David	1988–1991	3		3
185.	Owen, Aled	1960–1962	3		3
186.	Peddelty, John	1973–1976	3		3
187.	Price, Lewis	2007	3		3
188.	Saphin, Reg	1945	3		3
189.	Shufflebottom, Frank	1936–1937	3		3
190.	Snell, Vic	1959	3		3
191.	Steggles, Kevin	1982–1983	3		3
192.	Wardlaw, John	1945	3		3
193.	Westlake, Ian	2004–2006	3		3
194.	Lee, Alan	2007–2008	3	1	4

	PLAYER	ERA	APPS	SUBS	TOTAL
195.	Whelan, Phil	1993–1995	3	1	4
196.	Gleghorn, Nigel	1986–1988	3	1	4
197.	Peters, Jaime	2007–2008	3	1	4
198.	Miller, Tommy	2002–2005	3	2	5
199.	Clarke, Billy	2007–2008	3	2	5
200.	Alsop, Gilbert	1937	2		2
201.	Astill, Len	1937	2		2
202.	Atkins, Ian	1987–1988	2		2
203.	Belcher, Jim	1959	2		2
204.	Belfitt, Rod	1972	2		2
205.	Bevis, Dave	1965	2		2
206.	Brown, Wayne	1999–2002	2		2
207.	Carroll, Tommy	1968–1970	2		2
208.	Donowa, Louie	1990	2		2
209.	Fillingham, Tom	1938	2		2
210.	Fox, Geoff	1945	2		2
211.	Gibbons, John	1949	2		2
212.	Green, Don	1947–1952	2		2
213.	Hutcheson, Jock	1939	2		2
214.	Jones, Fred	1938–1939	2		2
215.	Kellard, Bobby	1966	2		2
216.	Mackay, Angus	1946	2		2
217.	Makin, Chris	2002–2003	2		2
218.	Redford, Ian	1989–1991	2		2
219.	Rodger, Bob	1937	2		2
220.	Roy, John	1946	2		2
221.	Smith, Jack	1946	2		2
222.	Smythe, Bert	1945	2		2
223.	Sowerby, Jock	1936	2		2
224.	Supple, Shane	2006–2007	2		2
225.	Thrower, Dennis	1965	2		2
226.	Vaughan, Tony	1995–1996	2		2
227.	Wookey, Ken	1950	2		2

	PLAYER	ERA	APPS	SUBS	TOTAL
228.	Wright, David	2007–2008	2		2
229.	Currie, Darren	2005–2006	2		2
230.	Harbey, Graham	1988–1989	2		2
231.	Peralta, Sixto	2002	2		2
232.	Thetis, Manuel	1999	2		2
233.	Kuqi, Shefki	2004–2005	2	1	3
234.	Parkin, Tommy	1978–1984	2	1	3
235.	Sunderland, Alan	1985	2	1	3
236.	Armstrong, Alun	2001–2002	2	1	3
237.	Geddis, David	1978–1979	2	1	3
238.	Sito, Castro	2006–2008	2	1	3
239.	Garvan, Owen	2006–2008	2	2	4
240.	Mathie, Alex	1996–1998	2	2	4
241.	Bent, Darren	2003–2005	2	2	4
242.	Alexander, Neil	2008	1		1
243.	Barnard, Chris	1967	1		1
244.	Barron, Scott	2006	1		1
245.	Blackman, Ron	1955	1		1
246.	Callaghan, Willie	1955	1		1
247.	Clements, Herbert	1936	1		1
248.	Croft, Gary	2001	1		1
249.	Curran, Pat	1938	1		1
250.	Deehan, John	1987	1		1
251.	Dempsey, John	1948	1		1
252.	Dougan, George	1964	1		1
253.	Fearon, Ron	1989	1		1
254.	Fletcher, Len	1955	1		1
255.	Gaardsoe, Thomas	2003	1		1
256.	Graham, Tom	1948	1		1
257.	Grew, Mark	1985	1		1
258.	Hall, Wilf	1962	1		1
259.	Hallworth, Jon	1988	1		1
260.	Hill, David	1989	1		1

	PLAYER	ERA	APPS	SUBS	TOTAL
261.	Horlock, Kevin	2005	1		1
262.	Hunt, Bobby	1968	1		1
263.	Kennedy, John	1999	1		1
264.	McMillan, George	1955	1		1
265.	Mitchell, Scott	2005	1		1
266.	O'Callaghan, George	2007	1		1
267.	O'Rourke, John	1969	1		1
268.	Pole, Ted	1947	1		1
269.	Smith, George	1949	1		1
270.	Spearritt, Eddie	1968	1		1
271.	Thompson, Ken	1966	1		1
272.	Treacy, Frank	1965	1		1
273.	Walsh, Roy	1966	1		1
274.	Wigg, Ron	1970	1		1
275.	Williams, George	1945	1		1
276.	Bart-Williams, Chris	2004	1		1
277.	Gregory, David	1990	1		1
278.	Karbassiyoon, Daniel	2005	1		1
279.	Kinsella, Tony	1984	1		1
280.	Ambrose, Darren	2003	1	1	2
281.	Austin, Terry	1976	1	1	2
282.	Miller, John	1972	1	1	2
283.	Sonner, Danny	1997–1998	1	1	2
284.	Trotter, Liam	2007–2008	1	1	2
285.	Woods, Charlie	1968–1970	1	1	2
286.	Casement, Chris	2007	1	2	3
287.	Goddard, Paul	1992–1993	1	2	3
288.	Abidallah, Nabil	2003		1	1
289.	Axeldal, Jonas	1999		1	1
290.	Bolton, Ron	1967		1	1
291.	Bowditch, Dean	2004		1	1

PLAYER	ERA	APPS	SUBS	TOTAL
292. Bozinoski, Vlado	1993		1	1
293. Cheetham, Michael	1989		1	1
294. Gayle, Brian	1990		1	1
295. Gregory, Neil	1996		1	1
296. Holster, Marco	1999		1	1
297. Juan, Jimmy	2006		1	1
298. Le Pen, Ulrich	2002		1	1
299. Logan, Richard	2001		1	1
300. O'Donnell, Chris	1989		1	1
301. Paz, Adrian	1995		1	1
302. Cole, Michael	1986–1987		2	2
303. Pennyfather, Glenn	1991–1992		2	2

303 players used in 199 games

Ipswich Town FA Cup Goalscorers

1936–2008

1.	Garneys, Tom	20
2.	Mariner, Paul	19
3.	Dozzell, Jason	12
4.	Wark, John	12
5.	Phillips, Ted	9
6.	Carter, Jock	8
7.	Gates, Eric	8
8.	Blackwell, Jack	7
9.	Bruce, Bobby	7
10.	Elsworthy, John	7
11.	Parker, Tommy	7
12.	Brazil, Alan	6
13.	Viljoen, Colin	6
14.	Own-goals	6
15.	Beattie, Kevin	5
16.	Brogan, Frank	5
17.	Chadwick, Fred	5
18.	Crawford, Ray	5
19.	Dobson, George	5
20.	Guentchev, Bontcho	5
21.	Hamilton, Bryan	5
22.	Leadbetter, Jimmy	5
23.	Little, Jackie	5
24.	Mills, Mick	5
25.	Baker, Gerry	4
26.	Brown, Thomas	4

27.	Burley, George	4
28.	Johnson, David (1970s)	4
29.	Parker, Stan	4
30.	Perrett, George	4
31.	Williams, Jackie	4
32.	Bent, Darren	3
33.	Brennan, Mark	3
34.	Dobson, Peter	3
35.	Hegan, Danny	3
36.	Lambert, Mick	3
37.	Marshall, Ian	3
38.	Mason, Paul	3
39.	Miller, Tommy	3
40.	Muhren, Arnold	3
41.	Myles, Neil	3
42.	Reed, Billy	3
43.	Rees, Derek	3
44.	Talbot, Brian	3
45.	Wilson, Kevin	3
46.	Brown, Jackie	2
47.	Clarke, Frank	2
48.	Crowe, Alex	2
49.	D'Avray, Mich	2
50.	Davies, Bryn	2
51.	Fletcher, Charlie	2
52.	Hill, Mick	2
53.	Johnson, David	2
54.	Johnson, Gavin	2
55.	Jones, Fred	2
56.	Kiwomya, Chris	2
57.	McLuckie, Jimmy	2

58.	Mulraney, Ambrose	2
59.	Peralta, Sixto	2
60.	Price, George	2
61.	Roberts, Jimmy	2
62.	Stephenson, Roy	2
63.	Stewart, Marcus	2
64.	Stockwell, Mick	2
65.	Thijssen, Frans	2
66.	Thompson, Neil	2
67.	Turner, Robin	2
68.	Whitton, Steve	2
69.	Whymark, Trevor	2
70.	Woods, Clive	2
71.	Zondervan, Romeo	2
72.	Alsop, Gilbert	1
73.	Ambrose, Darren	1
74.	Armstrong, Alun	1
75.	Astill, Len	1
76.	Baird, Harry	1
77.	Baxter, Billy	1
78.	Bent, Marcus	1
79.	Blackwood, Bobby	1
80.	Broadfoot, Joe	1
81.	Clapham, Jamie	1
82.	Clements, Herbert	1
83.	Driver, Allenby	1
84.	Gaardsoe, Thomas	1
85.	Gaynor, James	1
86.	Geddis, David	1
87.	Harper, Colin	1
88.	Harper, Dave	1

89.	Humes, Tony	1
90.	Hutcheson, Jock	1
91.	Jennings, Bill	1
92.	Kuqi, Shefki	1
93.	Lee, Alan	1
94.	Linighan, David	1
95.	Magilton, Jim	1
96.	McCall, Steve	1
97.	McCrory, Sam	1
98.	McLuckie, George	1
99.	Millward, Doug	1
100.	Milton, Simon	1
101.	Moran, Doug	1
102.	Naylor, Richard	1
103.	O'Rourke, John	1
104.	Osborne, Roger	1
105.	Osman, Russell	1
106.	Palmer, Steve	1
107.	Reuser, Martijn	1
108.	Richards, Matt	1
109.	Robertson, Jimmy	1
110.	Sunderland, Alan	1
111.	Wright, Jermaine	1
TOTAL: 346		

Statistics courtesy of prideofanglia.com